PROBLEMS OF MORAL PHILOSOPHY

Theodor W. Adorno

Edited by Thomas Schröder

Translated by Rodney Livingstone

Polity Press

Copyright © this translation Polity Press 2000

First published in Germany as *Probleme der Moralphilosophie* ©
Suhrkamp Verlag, 1996.

First published in 2000 by Polity Press in association with Blackwell
Publishers Ltd.

Published with the assistance of Inter Nationes, Bonn.

Editorial office:
Polity Press
65 Bridge Street
Cambridge CB2 1UR, UK

Marketing and production:
Blackwell Publishers Ltd
108 Cowley Road
Oxford OX4 1JF, UK

ISBN 0-7456-1941-X

A catalogue record for this book is available from the British Library.

Typeset in 10$\frac{1}{2}$ on 12 pt Sabon
by Best-set Typesetter Ltd, Hong Kong
Printed in Great Britain by MPG Books, Bodmin, Cornwall

This book is printed on acid-free paper.

PROBLEMS OF MORAL
PHILOSOPHY

Adorno's writings published by Polity Press

The posthumous works

Beethoven: The Philosophy of Music
Introduction to Sociology
Problems of Moral Philosophy

Other works by Adorno

Theodor W. Adorno and Walter Benjamin, *The Complete Correspondence 1928–1940*

CONTENTS

LECTURE ONE   1

Moral philosophy as a theoretical discipline • The concept of practice • Theory as resistance and a 'testing of reality'; against practicism • Naivety and reflection • On the tension between theory and practice • Spontaneity and resistance • The irrational • Hostility to moralities confined to particulars • Ethics as bad conscience; on behalf of a morality bluntly incompatible with our experience

LECTURE TWO   12

'Morality and its Discontents' • The problem of ethos and personality • The ethical is no natural category • Morality and social crisis • The sociology of the repressive character • The general and the particular • Plan of the lecture course • Texts to be studied

LECTURE THREE   22

Arguments *ad homines* • Lectures: attempts at critical models • The dual nature of reason in Kant: theory and practice, epistemology and metaphysics • The problem of freedom • On the theory of antinomies • Dialectics • The distinction between scepticism and 'the sceptical method'

LECTURE FOUR   33

The nature of the antinomies • Causality and freedom; spontaneity • The thesis of the third antinomy • The proof of the thesis • The motif of a causality born of freedom • The antithesis

LECTURE FIVE   44

The principle of causality and the necessity of the antinomies •
Dialectics in Kant and Hegel • Problem of the *prima
philosophia*: the first cause • Causality, law and freedom •
External nature of the concept of causality • Freedom as a given
• Summary: causality born of freedom

LECTURE SIX   55

The dual character of Kantian philosophy; the one and the
many • Once again: theory and practice • On the Doctrine of
Method: 1. The nature of reason • 2. Speculation • 3. Freedom
and the domination of nature • 4. The disappointing of
metaphysical expectations • 5. The rejection of philosophical
indifference • 6. The idea of God and the rights of criticism
• 7. The priority of practice

LECTURE SEVEN   67

Theory and practice of the 'Doctrine of Method' • Form and
content in practical philosophy • Practice as the exclusion of
experience; freedom as reason • What is primary and what is
secondary? The moral law as a given • Can social contradictions
be resolved? Bourgeois optimism • Can the moral law be learnt
through experience?

LECTURE EIGHT   78

Difficulty of distinguishing between *a priori* knowledge and
knowledge from experience • Necessity and universality; a
'second-order given' • The coercive character of empirically
given morality • Psychoanalytical objection • The ethics of
conviction • The return of teleology; the element of heteronomy

LECTURE NINE   89

The laws of freedom • The principle of exegesis; the 'extinction
of intention' • The dual character of nature • Kant 'breaks off'
the argument; Resistance to and acceptance of heteronomy •
The element of the Absurd • The historical dialectics of
morality; the 'growing old of morality'

LECTURE TEN   100

The intolerable dualism of freedom and law; The Protestant
tradition • The experience of spirit and nature as opposed to
domination • Methodological excursus: literal interpretation
versus the history of ideas • Kantian ethics is the moral
philosophy *par excellence* • Formalism and rigorism

LECTURE ELEVEN   110

The grounding of morality in reason: Against 'the education of
the heart' • Prince Hamlet • The element of non-identity;
coercion by a third party • Reason as practice • The restricted
nature of Kantian ethics; bourgeois calculus and bureaucratic
virtue • The ambivalence of the unmediated good • Autonomy
and heteronomy

LECTURE TWELVE   121

Self-determination • No cult of values • The absence of balance
between freedom and law • Formalism and social context •
Kant's writings on moral philosophy • The *Groundwork of the
Metaphysic of Morals*

LECTURE THIRTEEN   126

Excursus on phenomenology • The concept of the will •
Psychological aspect: Good will and ill will • Duty and
reverence • The element of repression • The disappearance of
freedom • Transition to the problem of an ethics of
responsibility and conviction

LECTURE FOURTEEN   136

The suppression of instinct as the general philosophical attitude
• Self-preservation and compensation • The fetishization of
renunciation • The idea of humanity: a hypothesis • The
totalitarianism of ends • Reason as an end in itself

LECTURE FIFTEEN   146

Kant's ethics of conviction [*Gesinnung*] • War on two fronts:
against empiricism and theology • Difference from Plato: the
idealism of reason • Early bourgeois pathos and Rousseauism •
Interiority and the German *misère*

LECTURE SIXTEEN

157

The dialectical element of morality • Excursus: Ibsen's *The Wild Duck* • Conscience: 'can be very hard' • Explication: entanglement in existing reality • The critique of Hegel's sublation [*Aufhebung*] of morality

LECTURE SEVENTEEN

167

Resistance to a false life • Fallibility in the face of the masks of evil • *Contra* Nietzsche's critique of morality • The limits of morality as the crisis of individualism; transition from critique to political consciousness

Editor's notes   177

Editor's afterword   214

Acknowledgements   217

Index   218

LECTURE ONE

7 May 1963

Ladies and Gentlemen,

You have come in such large numbers to a course of lectures whose subject cannot be expected to exert an immediate attraction for young people that I have the feeling that I owe you something of an explanation and even an apology, and that I should warn you against excessive expectations. When you attend a course of lectures given by someone who has written a book on the good – or rather the bad – life,[1] it is reasonable to assume that you – or many of you, at least – have come in the hope that these lectures will teach you something about the good life [*das richtige Leben*]. And that you will be able to learn something from these lectures that will be of direct benefit to you in your own lives, whether in private, or in public, in other words, in your existence as political beings. The question of the moral[2] life is one that will be put, or so I hope, in the course of these lectures. The form it will take will be to enquire whether the good life is a genuine possibility in the present, or whether we shall have to make do with the claim I made in that book that 'there can be no good life within the bad one.'[3] An assertion, incidentally, that – as I discovered later – comes very close to one made by Nietzsche.[4] But in these lectures I shall not be able to offer you anything resembling a practical guide to the good life. And you for your part would be wrong to expect anything like direct, immediate help for your own immediate problems, whether private or political – and the realm of politics is very closely connected to the sphere of morality. Moral philosophy is a theoretical discipline and as such must always be distinguished from the burning questions of the moral life. Kant, for example, insisted that it was not essential to have studied moral philosophy in order to be a decent or a good or a just human being.[5] Or I may cite a more recent statement that occurs to me. I am thinking of Max Scheler's book on ethics, *Der Formalismus in der Ethik und die materiale Wertethik* – a book diametrically opposed to that of Kant – where he distinguishes between ethics as an immediate – or what he terms a 'lived' – world view, of the kind expressed in epigrams, maxims and proverbs, and moral philosophy which has no direct connection with a lived reality.[6] The problems I shall be discussing here and which belong in the general horizon of your philosophical education are quite definitely those of moral philosophy as a theoretical discipline. So if I am going to throw stones at your heads, if you will allow the expression, it will be better if I say so at the outset than for me to leave you under the illusion that I am distributing bread. And if the bread that you hope to receive fails to materialize, this may mean that the stones I have thrown will miss, or – and this is my real hope – they will not turn out to be too terribly hard. For the theorems that I shall lay before you will not be too rigorously scholastic.

When I say that I hope that the stones will miss you or that they will not prove to be too terribly hard, I have something particular in mind that may in a certain sense help to re-establish that link with your own living interest. For even though I am quite clear in my mind that a course of lectures on moral philosophy can be of no direct assistance in your lives, I am no less convinced that you are justified in your desire to learn about the good life. The only problem here is that I do not in any sense feel authorized to hold forth to you about that. And precisely because I am aware that very many of you have great confidence in me, I would be extremely reluctant to abuse that confidence by presuming to slip into – even if it were only through my lecturing style – the false persona of a guru, a sage. I should wish to spare you that, but I should also wish above all to spare myself the dishonesty of such a pose. Nevertheless, when I say that there will be a link to you and your vital interests, I would like to indicate what it will *not* consist in. For however justifiable your interest in gaining useful knowledge from a course of lectures on moral philosophy, there is nowadays a great danger of what might be termed an illicit shortcut to practical action. And we must make clear from the outset that moral philosophy has a necessary connection with practical action. In the various divisions of philosophy moral philosophy is customarily defined as practical philosophy, and Kant's chief work, one that is devoted to moral philosophy, bears the title of a *Critique of Practical Reason*. I must mention here *en passant* that the concept of 'the practical' should not be confused with the degenerate concept that has become current nowadays and can be seen in the way people refer to a practical person as someone who knows how to tackle problems and cope with the problems of life in a clever way. 'Practicality' here goes back to its philosophical origins in πρᾶξις and πράττειν and to the Greek meanings of doing, acting. In the same way, the themes of Kant's practical philosophy – in the second part of the *Critique of Pure Reason*, the section dealing with the 'Transcendental Doctrine of Method' – are formulated in the celebrated question that is undoubtedly familiar to you all: 'What shall we do?'[7] According to Kant, who is, God knows, not the worst guide to the conceptualization of such problems, this question 'What shall we do?' is the crucial question of moral philosophy. And I would like to add that it is the crucial question of philosophy in general. For in Kant practical reason takes an unambiguous priority over theoretical reason,[8] and in this respect Fichte was less of an innovator when compared to Kant than he imagined.[9] Today, this question has undergone a strange modification. I have found again and again that when carrying out theoretical analyses – and theoretical analyses are essentially critical in nature – that I have been met by the question: 'Yes, but what shall we do?', and this question has been conveyed with a certain undertone of impatience, an undertone that proclaims: 'All right, what is the point of all this theory? It goes on far too long, we do not know how we should behave in the real world, and the fact is that we have to act right away!' I am not blind to the motives behind this protest, particularly in the light of the atrocities perpetrated under the Nazis, and also of the difficulties of direct and effective political action in our own day, difficulties that lead people obsessively to put such questions as: 'Very well, if there are barriers everywhere and every attempt to create a better world is blocked off, what exactly are we supposed to do?' But the reality is that the more uncertain practical action has become, the less we actually know what we should do, and the less we find the good life guaranteed to us – if indeed it was ever guaranteed to anyone – then the greater our haste in snatching at it. This impatience can very easily become linked with a certain resentment towards thinking in general, with a tendency to denounce theory as such. And from there it is not very long before people start to denounce intellectuals. Golo Mann, for example, has attacked theoreticians and intellectuals in a whole series of publications – including one that is aimed at me personally, and especially my *Theory of Half-Education*,[10] the question of what 'half-education' is – and has argued in particular that you cannot really 'do' anything with theory.[11] This reproach about the uselessness of theory, this impatient need to hurl oneself into action without delay spells the end of any kind of theoretical work and contains within itself, teleologically, as if it had been assumed from the outset, a relationship to a false, in other words, an oppressive, blind and violent form of practice.

Ladies and Gentlemen, I urge you therefore to exercise a certain patience with respect to the relations between theory and practice. Such a request may be justified because in a situation like the present – one about which I do not entertain the slightest illusion, and nor would I wish to encourage any illusions in you – whether it will be possible ever again to achieve a valid form of practice may well depend on not demanding that every idea should immediately produce its own legitimating document explaining its own practical use. The situation may well demand instead that we resist the call of practicality with all our might in order ruthlessly to follow through an idea and its logical implications so as to see where it may lead. I would even say that this ruthlessness, the power of resistance that is inherent in the idea itself and that prevents it from letting itself be directly manipulated for any instrumental purposes whatsoever, this theoretical ruthlessness contains – if you will allow me this paradox – a practical element within itself. Today, practice – and I do not hesitate to express this in an extreme way – has made great inroads into theory, in other words, into the realm of new thought in which right behaviour can be reformulated. This idea is not as paradoxical and irritating as it may sound, for in the final analysis thinking is itself a form of behaviour. In its origins thinking is no more than the form in which we have attempted to master our environment and come to terms with it – testing reality is the name given by analytical psychology to this function of the ego and of thought – and it is perfectly possible that in certain situations practice will be referred back to theory far more frequently than at other times and in other situations. At any rate, it does no harm to air this question. It is no accident that the celebrated unity of theory and practice implied by Marxian theory and then developed above all by Lenin should have finally degenerated in [Stalinist] dialectical materialism to a kind of blind dogma whose sole function is to eliminate theoretical thinking altogether. This provides an object lesson in the transformation of practicism into irrationalism, and hence, too, for the transformation of this practicism into a repressive and oppressive practice. That alone might well be a sufficient reason to give us pause and not to be in such haste to rely on the famous unity of theory and practice in the belief that it is guaranteed and that it holds good for every time and place.

For otherwise you will find yourself in the position of what Americans call a joiner,[12] that is to say, a man who always has to join in, who has to have a cause for which he can fight. Such a person is driven by his sheer enthusiasm for the idea that something or other must be done and some movement has to be joined about which he is deluded enough to believe that it will bring about significant changes. And ultimately, this enthusiasm drives him into a kind of hostility towards mind that necessarily negates a genuine unity of theory and practice.

Ladies and Gentlemen, what is at stake here is that you should be aware that Fichte's famous assertion that 'morality is self-evident' cannot be upheld, at least not in the way that Fichte intended at the time, even though the statement undoubtedly contains a grain of truth.[13] To be more specific, we may say that a particular historical conjuncture plays a role here. What I mean by this is that morality may very well appear to be self-evident in a world in which people feel themselves to be the exponents of a class in the ascendant, together with all the concrete ideals it wishes to make real, as was the case with the great bourgeois thinkers around the turn of the nineteenth century. The situation is quite different when every important practice whose theory one tries to grasp has the unfortunate and even fatal tendency to compel us to think in a way that conflicts with our own real and immediate interests. So in these lectures what is at issue is that we should reflect on the problems of moral philosophy – and not that I should present you with any specific norms or values or whatever other ghastly terms may offer themselves. To put it in another way, the subject of moral philosophy today requires that we do not naively respond to such questions about how to lay down absolute rules about behaviour, about the relation between the general and the particular in reference to behaviour, and about the immediate creation of a moral good. Such questions cannot simply be accepted at face value, or as they appear to so-called feeling, which often may turn out to be a poor guide. Instead they must be raised to the level of conscious reflection, so far as that is possible. Moral philosophy in this sense means making a sustained effort – without anxieties or reservations – to achieve a true, conscious understanding of the categories of morality and of the questions that relate to the good life and practice in that higher sense, instead of continuing to imagine that this entire complex of issues must be excluded from the realm of theory on the grounds that it is practical. For when people take this latter view what it usually amounts to is that practice, which is commonly claimed to be superior to theory, and purer than it, is then taken over ready-made from some authoritarian source, whether it be the traditions of one's own nation or another prescribed ideology. And in consequence they never reach the point that in Kant's eyes constitutes the locus of right action, namely the moment of freedom in the absence of which the good life cannot even be properly conceived. Such a formulation of the task of reflecting on moral philosophy of the kind I have just given you, however fragmentary, would moreover be in tune with the present stage of advanced psychological knowledge – that is to say, of psychoanalysis. For the essence of the latter is that 'where the id is', in other words, where the unconscious, where darkness rules, there 'ego shall be', in other words, there shall be consciousness.[14] Put differently, something like a true practice is only possible when you have passed through theory.

Ladies and Gentlemen, I should like to show you at this point, or rather I should like to express something that may well have occurred to you in a more or less well articulated form. This is the awareness that we cannot simply assert that all you need to arrive at correct practice is a correct theory. And those among you who have been kind enough to listen to me attentively will have observed that I did not in fact make any such claim. Instead, all I claimed was that there was a greater and more urgent need of theoretical intervention at the present time. On the other hand, it is no less true – and I believe that this must be asserted no less bluntly than the need for theory – that theory and practice do not slot into each other neatly, that they are not simply one and the same thing, but that – if you will forgive the hackneyed image – a kind of tension obtains between the two. Theory that bears no relation to any conceivable practice either degenerates into an empty, complacent and irrelevant game, or, what is even worse, it becomes a mere component of culture, in other words, a piece of dead scholarship, a matter of complete indifference to us as living minds and active, living human beings. This even holds good for art for, however mediated, however indirect or concealed it may be, such a link must nevertheless exist. Conversely – as I have already pointed out – a practice that simply frees itself from the shackles of theory and rejects thought as such on the grounds of its own supposed superiority will sink to the level of activity for its own sake. Such a practice remains stuck fast within the given reality. It leads to the production of people who like organizing things and who imagine that once you have organized something, once you have arranged for some rally or other, you have achieved something of importance, without pondering for a moment whether such activities have any chance at all of effectively impinging on reality.[15] This brings me to a fundamental theme of moral philosophy, namely the distinction between norms that simply relate to the pure will, as Kant taught, and norms that in the course of reflecting on moral questions also include the objective possibility of being made real in practice, as Hegel maintained in opposition to Kant. This problem has been formulated as the distinction between an ethics of conviction [*Gesinnungsethik*] and an ethics of responsibility [*Verantwortungsethik*], and we shall have something to say on this subject at a later date.[16]

However that may be, and however inseparable these two distinct disciplines – theory and practice – may be, since after all they both have their source in life itself, there is one further factor necessary for practice that is not fully explicable by theory and that is very hard to isolate. And I should like to emphasize it because I regard it as fundamental to a definition of the moral. We may perhaps best define it with the term spontaneity, the immediate, active reaction to particular situations. Where this factor is missing, or we might also say, where theory does not wish in the last analysis to achieve anything, something like a valid practice is not possible. Moreover, one task of the theory of the moral is to set limits to the scope of theory itself, in other words, to show that the sphere of moral action includes something that cannot fully be described in intellectual terms, but also that should not be turned into an absolute. What I have in mind is something that should not be treated as if it were an absolute, but that must in fact stand in a definite relationship to theory if it is not to degenerate into mere folly. Ladies and Gentlemen, I find it extraordinarily difficult to find words to describe this factor, and this is no accident, since we are attempting to describe in theoretical terms an element of morality that is actually foreign to theory – and so to describe it in theoretical terms is not without an element of absurdity. But I believe that we found a clue to it a little while ago when I was telling you about the concept of resistance, even though what I was saying then was that resistance today should be sought in the drive towards theory. For that something should be done is a belief held by everyone nowadays; what is found to be problematic is when someone decides not to do anything for once, but to retreat from the dominant realm of practical activity in order to think about something essential. Now what I wish to emphasize is the factor of resistance, of refusing to be part of the prevailing evil, a refusal that always implies resisting something stronger and hence always contains an element of despair. I believe that this idea of resistance, then, may help you best to see what I mean when I say that the moral sphere is not coterminous with the theoretical sphere, and that this

fact is itself a basic philosophical determinant of the sphere of practical action.

Perhaps I can illustrate this with something I experienced, a very
simple experience, in the first few months after I returned to Germany
– it is now almost fourteen years ago – from emigration. I had the
opportunity to make the acquaintance of one of the few crucial actors
of the 20 July[17] and was able to talk to him. I said to him, 'Well, you
knew very well that the conspiracy's chances of success were minimal,
and you must have known that if you were caught you had to expect
a fate far more terrible than death – unimaginably terrible consequences. What made it possible for you to take action notwithstanding this?' – Whereupon he said to me – you will all know his
name, but I do not wish to name him here – 'But there are situations
that are so intolerable that one just cannot continue to put up with
them, no matter what may happen and no matter what may happen
to oneself in the course of the attempt to change them.'[18] He said this
without any pathos – and I should like to add, without any appeal
to theory. He was simply explaining to me what motivated him in
that seemingly absurd enterprise on 20 July. I believe that this act of
resistance – the fact that things may be so intolerable that you feel
compelled to make the attempt to change them, regardless of the consequences for yourself, and in circumstances in which you may also
predict the possible consequences for other people – is the precise
point at which the irrationality, or better, the irrational aspect of
moral action is to be sought, the point at which it may be located.
But at the same time, you can see that this irrationality is only one
aspect, because on the level of theory the officer concerned knew perfectly well how evil, how horrifying this Third Reich was, and it was
because of his critical and theoretical insight into the lies and the
crimes that he had to deal with that he was brought to the point of
action. If he had not had this insight, if he had had no knowledge of
the vile evil that prevailed in Germany at the time, he would quite
certainly never have been moved to that act of resistance. But we then
find that this other factor comes into play, the conviction – for whatever reason – that 'things cannot go on like this, I cannot allow this
to happen, regardless of what might happen to me or others in consequence.' This will perhaps help to give you something of an idea
of the complexities of what is meant by moral philosophy in a concrete instance. This feature that I have just described introduces something alien into moral philosophy, something that does not quite fit,
precisely because as a theory moral philosophy tends to overlook
such matters. It is difficult to express this, but there is something
shameful about my standing here in the comfort of a lecture room,

making comments of this sort to you who are all sitting more or less comfortably in your seats, about situations like that of the men of the 20 July – which, God knows, have been the stage on which the moral dialectic of our age has been acted out. When you confront this with practice – and practice is when it hurts, when it really hurts – there is something cynical here that is hard to ignore. This cynicism can also be detected in the concept of moral philosophy as a theoretical discipline which I began by describing, simply because moral philosophy almost compulsively ignores this element that I have just described and that theory cannot accommodate. To that extent we might even say that because the moral involves action it is always more than thought, and that moral philosophy, the reflection on moral questions, stands in something of a contradiction to the object of its own reflections. Moreover, there are situations – and I believe that we find ourselves still living in such a situation – in which the contradiction involved in thinking about something when we should be doing something about it is especially flagrant. But on the other hand, this contradiction is not one we can simply ignore. And when I said to you that our task was to achieve a greater consciousness – and the task of moral philosophy today is above all else the production of consciousness – it was precisely such things that I had in mind. In other words, where we find contradictions, where we find ourselves unable to eliminate contradictions through the stratagems of theory or conceptual devices, what we have to do is to become conscious of them, to generate the strength to look them in the face, instead of arguing them out of existence by more or less logical procedures.

This sense of the inappropriate of which I have been speaking is particularly prominent in the terms 'morality' and 'moral philosophy' which, as you all know, were subjected to scathing criticism by Nietzsche, who may be said to have echoed a discontent with the terms which goes much further back in time. Only a few days ago, to my great surprise, I found the term 'moralistic' being used in a pejorative sense as early as Hölderlin, which shows that the problematic nature of the term goes right back to the age of so-called German idealism.[19] Morality derives from the Latin word 'mores' and 'mores' means, as I hope you all know, 'custom' [Sitte]. In consequence moral philosophy has been translated as 'Sittenlehre' [moral teaching] or 'Lehre von der Sittlichkeit' [doctrine of morality].[20] If we refrain from emptying this concept of custom of meaning from the outset, to the point where the word no longer conveys anything at all, we will doubtless be reminded of the customs that prevail within specific communities, i.e. among specific nations. What I would say is that the reason why the question of moral philosophy has become so very problematic today is that the substantial nature of custom, the possibility of the good life in the forms in which the community exists, which confront the individual in pre-existing form, has been radically eroded, that these forms have ceased to exist and that people today can no longer rely on them. And if we act as if they did still exist, this will only lead to the preservation of specific spheres of life in which a little of the old order still appears to have survived in a provincial form – as if this were in itself the guarantee of a good or moral life. The resistance to the term 'moral' as seen in 'moralistic', that you surely all feel, becomes explicable at this point. It is based on the fact that we all chafe at the narrow limitations imposed by prevailing ideas and existing circumstances and resent the assumption that these in some sense already embody the good life.

Ladies and Gentlemen, as a consequence of this there has long since been a tendency to smuggle in the notion of ethics as a substitute for the concept of morality, and I once suggested that the concept of ethics was actually the bad conscience of morality, or that ethics is a sort of morality that is ashamed of its own moralizing with the consequence that it behaves as if it were morality, but at the same time is not a moralizing morality.[21] And if I may be frank with you, it seems to me that the dishonesty implicit in this is worse and more problematic than the blunt incompatibility of our experience with the term 'morality', an incompatibility that at least permits us to extend or otherwise build on what Kant or Fichte understood by the concept of the moral and thereby to arrive at more authoritative and harder insights. In contrast the concept of ethics in many ways threatens to dissolve – chiefly because of its connection with the so-called concept of personality. Ethos, the Greek word ἦϑος, from which the expression 'ethics' is derived, is very difficult to translate. In general it is rightly rendered as 'nature' – it refers to the way you are, the way you are made. The more recent concept of 'character' comes very close to that of ἦϑος, and the Greek proverb ἦϑος ἀνϑϱώπον δαίμων – the ethos is the daemon, or we might call it the destiny, of man – points in the same direction. In other words, to reduce the problem of morality to ethics is to perform a sort of conjuring trick by means of which the decisive problem of moral philosophy, namely the relation of the individual to the general, is made to disappear. What is implied in all this is the idea that if I live in accordance with my own ethos, my own nature, or if, to use the fine phrase of our own time, I realize myself, then this will be enough to bring about the good life. And this is nothing but pure illusion and ideology. An ideology, moreover, that goes hand in hand with a second ideology, namely the illusion that culture and the adaptation of the individual to culture brings about the refinement and self-cultivation of the individual, whereas culture stands opposed to moral philosophy and is actually open to criticism from that quarter. For all these reasons I believe it is better to retain the concept of morality, albeit critically, than to soften up and obscure its problematic nature from the outset by replacing it with the sentimental concept of ethics. But I think I need to spell out these last ideas more precisely in the next lecture to make certain that you all see what I mean.

LECTURE TWO

9 May 1963

Ladies and Gentlemen,

In my last lecture I promised that I would follow up in greater detail my hurried comments in the last few minutes on the concepts of morality and ethics. This is because we need to gain a better understanding of the general field we are about to explore and perhaps to make it easier to grasp the direction of the subject as a whole. You will recollect that the concept of morality is problematic above all because it has its origin in 'mores', in other words, because it postulates a harmony between the public customs in a country and the moral, ethically correct behaviour, the moral life of the individual. And I explained to you then that this harmony, or what Hegel called 'the substantial nature of the ethical', this belief that the norms of the good are directly anchored and guaranteed in the life of an existing community, can no longer be assumed today. The chief reason for this is that the community has now acquired such overwhelming power in its relations with the individual and that countless processes have forced us to conform so utterly that harmony can no longer be produced between our own individual destiny and what is imposed on us by objective circumstances. However, when I reflect on what I said to you last time by way of criticism of the concept of morality, I find it unsatisfactory because it does not really get to the heart of our feeling of discomfort with morality. The issue is not really the verbal, philological connections between custom [*Sitte*] and individual morality. What is at stake is rather what Simmel would have called the 'cachet' of the term morality. A philosophical concept like morality – and it is important that you should understand this – is not simply identical with its pure meaning. Over and above that it has an aura, a layer of connotations which are not necessarily reducible to that meaning. And the concept of morality is in fact bound up with a particular notion of moral rigour, of conventional narrowness and conformity with a whole series of given ideas that have now become problematic. So if you reflect on the fact that in ordinary usage the terms 'moral' and 'immoral' have come to be associated with questions of sexuality and that these in their turn have long since been superseded by psychoanalysis and by psychology in general, you will have some general idea about the constraints that are at work in the concept of the moral. This has been articulated by Georg Büchner in a very profound and also witty passage in *Woyzeck* where the Captain rebukes Woyzeck, a man who radiates decency with every fibre of his being, for having an illegitimate child, and he goes on to oscillate between the assertion that Woyzeck is immoral and that 'he is a good man'. When he tries to explain why Woyzeck is immoral he finds himself reduced to the tautology 'that he is immoral because he lacks morality'. So in the Captain we find that this notion of morality has become completely separate from the idea of moral goodness. He sees absolutely no contradiction in claiming both that Woyzeck is a good man and also that he is immoral.[1] Nietzsche's entire objection to what is known as morality is based on ideas of this sort. If I were to formulate the matter in Nietzschean terms, I would probably say that the concept of morality has been severely compromised by the fact that, consciously or unconsciously, it carries around a lot of baggage in the shape of 'ascetic ideals'. Furthermore, it is not really possible to find any justification, or at least any profoundly rational justification for these ideals; they are no more than a front behind which all sorts of more or less murky interests lie entrenched.[2] This may perhaps give a clearer idea of the resistance we feel towards the word 'morality' nowadays than the connection with 'custom' which formed my starting-point last time and about which I should like to say more today.

This unwillingness to equate the moral with a restricted, narrow and superseded ascetic ideal is what has given rise to the attempts to replace the term 'morality' with that of 'ethics'. I have already indicated to you that this concept of ethics contains the idea that people should live in accordance with their own nature, and that accordingly such a concept of ethics appears to offer something of an antidote to a morality that is forcibly imposed from outside. I have already suggested that this antidote is not without its own difficulties. At its simplest, this entire concept of ethics contains something that only emerged fully into the light of day with the theory of Existentialism – which essentially regards itself as an ethical, moral movement, albeit in a negative sense. For here the idea of the good life, of right action, is reduced to the notion that one should act in accordance with the way one is anyway. Hence by acting in accordance with one's ethos, one's nature, mere existence, the fact that one is 'constituted' [*geartet*] one way rather than another, becomes the yardstick of behaviour.[3] The roots of this belief can be traced, strangely enough, back to Kant, for whom the concept of personality – which however does have a rather different meaning in his writing, one we shall need to discuss in detail – appears for the first time as a crucial ethical category. I should like to observe at once that in Kant personality means something like the abstract, general conceptual unity of everything that makes up a person. Or we might say, personality refers to all the determinants of the acting human being that do not refer to the person as a merely empirical, a merely existing, natural being, but, following Kantian theory, everything that goes beyond that. Hence personality is everything about the person that is supraempirical and at the same time expresses the universality that should be binding on every person, or, as Kant himself says, every rational being.[4] It is from this point, in the course of a process that would be interesting to reconstruct, that we find the emergence of the personality as the strong human being, identical with himself, complete in himself, that then displaces the concept of the ethical and puts itself in the place of ethical norms. So here, then, we have a realm which is concerned from the outset with tensions and contradictions, namely with the question of how to bring individual interests and claims to happiness into harmony with some sort of objective norms binding on mankind as a whole. What is problematic about this concept of personality is that these tensions are swept aside, spirited away, and that it looks as if all you really need to lead the good life is to be yourself and to be identical with yourself. As I have already indicated, since this identity, this mere identity of the individual human being does not suffice, the concept of culture is introduced in an analogous fashion as a correlative, quite uncritically, as something simply given. Then, in line with this idea of ethics, 'man' – I intentionally use this cliché since we find ourselves in the realm of cliché here – 'man' turns out to realize some cultural values or other on the basis of his identity with himself, his harmony with his own being. This conception of ethics contrives to undercut the question that should form the basis of every deeper reflection on moral or ethical questions, namely the question whether culture, and whatever culture has become, permits something like the good life, or whether it is a network of institutions that actually tends more and more to thwart the emergence of such righteous living. This conception of ethics sweeps away the entire set of problems that came into the world through the writings of Jean-Jacques Rousseau and that were then espoused with particular emphasis by Fichte. They are simply spirited away in favour of these would-be harmonizing notions.

If I were now to reformulate in slightly more ambitious philosophical terms what I have been telling you about this conception of ethics, I would have to repeat what I said earlier on, namely that ethics is the bad conscience of conscience. If I were to offer an interpretation of this statement, I would say that, as Nietzsche was one of the first to make clear, morality has been nurtured on faded theological ideas, and that since the fading of theological categories attempts have been made to recreate something along the same lines. Philosophers have tried to grasp the essence of the moral in merely immanent categories, that is to say, in categories of nature, of the mere existence in which we find ourselves, without any transcendent element, in other words, without trying to go beyond our purely organic, natural being. This turns morality into an aspect of nature. But this direct, primitive identification of categories of nature, of existence as it naturally happens to be, with the moral is invalid. And if humanity has any meaning at all, it must consist in the discovery that human beings are not identical with their immediate existence as the creatures of nature. After what I have said up to now, you may be able to understand rather better why I would say – at the risk of sounding somewhat old-fashioned – that observations of the kind we are making here are better suited to the concept of morality than that of ethics. It is not that I have any desire to justify or reinstate traditional morality in any way at all. I believe that my publications will suffice to protect me from any suspicions on that score. But the concept of morality that has been developed above all and with the greatest incisiveness in Kantian philosophy will be best able to convey the tensions between the general and the particular, between empirical existence and the good, in other words, that aspect of our destiny as human beings that goes beyond our mere existence. In short it will be able to encompass all the real problems and difficulties that arise in connection with the good life, with right action, in an incomparably more honest way than the concept of ethics, and if I may say so, in a much harder-edged and purer way as well. And since my primary concern is to present you with a series of problems in moral philosophy – since there is no point in discussing anything unless it confronts us with problems – it is because we are dealing here with difficulties, with genuine contradictions, that I believe that we will do better to discuss them under the rubric of morality rather than the

would-be harmonious concept of ethics. There is a further factor
here. The question that might be described as the question of the good
life is one in which the concept of morality can boast a long and by
no means contemptible tradition, one that is not contaminated by
trivial, petty-bourgeois attitudes. This is the tradition of the so-called
French moralists that goes back to writers like Montaigne, and whose
most famous representative is the Duc de la Rochefoucauld. La
Rochefoucauld can surely be described as a moralist in the sense that
he analysed the mores, the conduct and customs, of human beings,
but he was certainly no moralist in the pejorative sense of the term.
He was not a preacher or – to cite Nietzsche once more – a 'Moral
Trumpeter of Säckingen'.[5] So much for the question of terminology
that we have been concerned with up to now.

I have been saying that in order to deal with moral problems, the
problem of morality, that is to say, the relation between freedom and
law, in a serious way, we must at all costs avoid smoothing over the
difficulties. We must instead confront the contradictions that emerge
at the point where cosy attempts to smooth over the problems cease.
Now I believe that in this respect I find myself in sympathy with the
way in which the discussion of moral questions arose historically.
We can probably say that moral questions have always arisen when
moral norms of behaviour have ceased to be self-evident and unques-
tioned in the life of the community. Thus morality as a theoretical
discipline – and I would remind you that the task we have set ourselves is to reflect on theoretical issues – arises at the precise moment
– and this brings me back to the concept of custom – when the
customs and usages that obtain and have been generally accepted
within the life of a people have lost their immediate authority. Hegel's
assertion that 'the owl of Minerva only spreads its wings with the
falling of the dusk'[6] applies nowhere more aptly than to the reflection
on moral questions. Plato's philosophy was the first of which it could
be said that its entire philosophical interest was dominated by moral
questions in the sense in which we have been speaking of them. And
it is no accident that its historical emergence should have coincided
with the disintegration of the Athenian polis. Over and above that,
it does Plato no injustice if we say that his philosophy was conservative in tendency, that is, up to a point at least, it represents the attempt
to recreate in thought those codes of conduct and those ideals – if
we may call them that – that had once been the traditional virtues of
Attic society. However, these codes of conduct had ceased to function and Plato's philosophy was designed as a polemic against their
absence – we need only to remember his lifelong disputes with the
Sophists.[7] In Max Scheler's book on formalism – as I mentioned last

time – you can already find the distinction between ethics as a substantial, existing body of rules and maxims which are not made the object of reflection, and ethics as a philosophical discipline. And he remarks quite bluntly, 'Whereas ethics in the first sense' – as a substantive collection of rules – 'is the constant companion of every ethos' – what that companionship amounts to I shall come to in a moment – 'ethics in the *second* sense is a relatively rare occurrence.' Well, I would not say 'rare', but would prefer to call it an occurrence that always makes its appearance at a late stage in a historical process. '*Its origins*', he maintains, '*are invariably linked to the disintegration [Zersetzung] of an existing ethos.*' And he points out that this idea has been discussed at length in Steinthal's book.[8] However – and I think it is worth making the point here and now – we should not understand by this that something old and valuable has been lost, that it has ceased to function in the present, and that the task of philosophy is to conjure it into existence once again. Both here and elsewhere in my view Scheler's theory itself is simply conservative and inadequately worked out. We must add that it is not uncommon for the customs of a nation to assume the form of what the Nazis called *Brauchtum* [usage, custom], and for mores to persist even though the consciousness of individuals and the critical labour of the intellect are no longer in tune with them. But the moment such customs continue to assert themselves in the face of a confrontation with liberated, autonomous reflection, it ceases to be possible to regard them as the vestiges of things that are old, good and true because they then assume the features of something poisoned and evil. In the passage I have referred to, Scheler talks about the disintegration [*Zersetzung*][9] of ethical ideas, an expression I do not at all care for and which his philosophy turns into a theme in its own right – you will find that this expression recurs again and again and particularly in treatises on morality. And whenever you hear it, it suppresses the fact that in all likelihood nothing is more degenerate than the kind of ethics or morality that survives in the shape of collective ideas even after the World Spirit has ceased to inhabit them – to use the Hegelian expression as a kind of shorthand. Once the state of human consciousness and the state of the social forces of production have abandoned these collective ideas, these ideas acquire repressive and violent qualities. And what forces philosophy into the kind of reflections that we are expressing here is this element of compulsion which is to be found in traditional customs; it is this violence and evil that brings these customs [*Sitten*] into conflict with morality [*Sittlichkeit*] – and not the decline of morals of the kind lamented by the theoreticians of decadence.

This repressive element was probably pointed out for the first time in a book called *Folkways*, by the important American sociologist William Graham Sumner, who is scarcely known in Germany and who taught towards the end of the nineteenth century, roughly at the same time as Veblen.[10] And in general, the sociologists have been more conscious of this repressive dimension than the moral philosophers. Durkheim, too, who went so far as to equate the social and the moral, was thinking along the same lines when he remarked that the social could always be recognized by the fact that 'it hurts', in other words, that some collective norms conflict with the interests and claims of individuals.[11] This would include the popular customs that survive to this day in country districts which still possess so-called vigilante courts where outsiders or others who refuse to conform to local customs are ridiculed or attacked or molested.[12] A direct path leads from these customs to the practice of cutting off the hair of girls who fraternize with enemy soldiers in occupied countries – whatever nation the occupying force may have come from – and from there to the persecution of people for *Rassenschande*[13] and to all those other excesses. We can say that the horrors perpetrated by Fascism are in great measure nothing more than the extension of popular customs that have taken on these irrational and violent features precisely because they have become divorced from reason – and it is this that forces us into theoretical reflections.

This example is enough to enable you to recognize – perhaps in a rather crass and drastic manner – what I would describe as the central problem of moral philosophy. It is the relationship of the particular, the particular interests, the behaviour of the individual, particular human being and the universal that stands opposed to it. And I must tell you from the outset – to forestall any misunderstandings – that it would be quite wrong and a crude mistake if in this conflict between the universal and the particular we were to place all the blame on the side of the universal from the outset, and attribute all the good to the individual. Of course in social conflicts it almost always looks as if it is the universal law that oppresses and crushes the individual, while the humane appears to reside in the claims and norms of the individual. But we shall have occasion to see that the universal always contains an implicit claim to represent a moral society in which force and compulsion have ceased to play any role. And on the other hand, we shall see that the very same mechanisms of repression and force are at work in the claims of the individual, in the self-assertion of the individual, that the individual is wont to encounter in his relation to society. At all events, the problem of how the general interest and the particular interests relate to each other in the course of human interaction is the fundamental problem of ethics, and, in a disguised form, it is also the fundamental problem of Kantian ethics, although Kant does not express it in the form that I have just used in my explanations to you. It is the fundamental problem of Kantian ethics for the following reason. – Incidentally, you must forgive me if I sometimes alternate between ethics and morality. I do so because the constant repetition of the word morality simply gets on my nerves, but I think that I have said enough on that score to prevent any misunderstandings. – In Kant, moral problems always circle round the question of the relations between the natural, empirical individual human being and the intelligible human being, who is determined simply and solely by his own reason of which freedom is an essential characteristic. If that is so, then the relation of the universal to the particular is a central feature of that relationship. Ethical conduct or moral and immoral conduct is always a social phenomenon – in other words, it makes absolutely no sense to talk about ethical and moral conduct separately from relations of human beings to each other, and an individual who exists purely for himself is an empty abstraction. Given that this is the case, it follows that the social problem of the divergence between the universal interest and the particular interest, the interests of the particular individuals, is what goes to make up the problem of morality. The two are inseparable, and the question of which came first is less important than one might be tempted to think. In thinking about ethics, the spontaneous understanding of the particular within the universal is that it is the accidental, the contingent, the psychological and as such it has the tendency to soften up and dissolve [ethical] norms simply because of its focus on the particular human being as a natural being. Conversely, where the universal does not simply agree with the particular, it presents itself as an abstraction that fails to include the particular and hence – ignoring its rights – appears as something violent and extraneous that has no substantial reality for human beings. We find ourselves, therefore, confronted by two impossibilities. On the one hand, we see the accidental nature of the psychologically isolated human being who is so conditioned by his inner life that he scarcely achieves anything like freedom. On the other hand, we find the abstract norm that has assumed such an objective reality vis-à-vis living human beings that they find themselves unable to appropriate it for themselves in a living way. And how we are to get to grips with these two impossibilities in their specificity; how we are to think about them and what solutions we might possibly discover – this is what defines the scope of thinking about ethics or morality as a theoretical discipline.

Ladies and Gentlemen, I shall not say any more than this by way
of a general introduction to the subject we are dealing with. I could
follow it up with a list or with an overview of the terrain to be
covered. I could classify the issues as a good scholar should and, start-
ing from the most general concepts, I could proceed systematically to
examine particular questions. It is not my intention to do so. To give
you a reasoned explanation for this would exceed the limits of what
can be achieved in this course of lectures. It would extend the course
into metaphysics and epistemology, and to tell you the truth I would
find such a prospect very tempting. But we would never reach the
point where we could discuss the problems of moral philosophy that
I have promised you. So I must simply ask you to accept as a working
hypothesis that I would rather talk about the neuralgic points that
enable me to tell you about some of the problems and necessary contradictions that go to make up the moral sphere, than to give you a
general overview of the problems of moral philosophy. There may be
some among you whose nerves are so constituted that in the present
situation they might find something slightly comical about any such
overview, any such logical hierarchy of moral propositions. But nor
do I wish to leave our discussions entirely to chance. I have no desire
to fix on a series of problems 'like a rhapsodist', as Kant would say.
A certain organization is needed, as I am sure you all feel. Strange
though it may seem, young people today have a greater need for
organization, for a certain kind of systematic thought than, for
example, I do. For I belong to a generation that grew up in violent
rebellion against the very concept of philosophical systems, and
whose entire way of thinking was defined by that rebellion. You find
the belief in any order and security to be altogether problematic,
whereas we had to break free from too much order and too much
security. If I am not deceived, you have in general a much greater
need for order than I do – perhaps it is only a need for security, I do
not know. But at all events, I would wish to pay you the compliment
of not pretending that this need does not exist. Since I neither can
nor wish to present you with an ethical system – or rather, I could
perhaps do so, but I assuredly do not wish to – it would be useful if
we could at least up to a point orientate ourselves by looking at a
thinker in whose work the question of morality is most sharply contrasted with other spheres of existence, and in whose writings the
antinomies, the contradictions of which we have spoken, make their
appearance in their most tangible form. So to a very considerable
degree I should like to orientate my lectures very strongly towards
Kant, and certain Kantian definitions that I would then propose to
discuss with you. And only when we have finished talking about a

number of the Kantian categories of moral philosophy shall we proceed, in the second part of the course, towards the end, to a number of seemingly more immediate problems, such as the question of the nature of moral norms today, the possibility of the good life today, or the problem of so-called relativism and nihilism. But we shall only do this when our discussions of Kant have enabled us to isolate a number of categories that we can then think about critically.

In this connection it would be good if as many of you as possible could read Kant's two principal works on morality. I do not know whether it is reasonable to expect you all to do this. The demands of these writings are not excessive in comparison to the *Critique of Pure Reason*. We are talking about two works here, the *Groundwork of the Metaphysic of Morals* and the *Critique of Practical Reason*. When you embark on these works you will find that it is not altogether easy to explain the difference between them. Kant himself made it look as if the *Groundwork* were a kind of preparation for the critical standpoint, whereas the *Critique of Practical Reason* was the systematic execution, once that reflective, critical standpoint had been achieved.[14] But you will find that the two things overlap. And in general you find here something that is very often found in philosophy with so-called simple works. It turns out that the simple texts only appear simple because they skate over the real problems and leave you in the lurch at countless crucial points. So I would urge you – and I am thinking here of certain traditions that have become established in connection with examinations when you find candidates who imagine that the *Groundwork of the Metaphysic of Morals* is a kind of easy route into Kant's moral philosophy – so I would urge you all, if at all possible, not to restrict yourselves just to the *Groundwork*, but also to read the *Critique of Practical Reason*. Indeed, I would almost go so far as to advise you that if you can only read one of them, you should start with the *Critique of Practical Reason*, which is much the more profound and rewarding work. I should tell you, however, that in these lectures you will also encounter a whole series of formulations taken from the *Groundwork*. In the next lecture we shall take a look at Kant's starting-point in his discussion of ethics, namely with his question 'What shall I do?', and with the problems that arise from this question, which incidentally is to be found in the *Critique of Pure Reason*, in the 'Transcendental Doctrine of Method'. We shall have to think about this before we enter into the problems of his so-called practical philosophy. – Thank you.

LECTURE THREE

14 May 1963

Ladies and Gentlemen,

I promised you last time that we would provide our discussions here with something of a framework by linking them with Kant's treatment of moral philosophy, and I shall stick to my promise. However, in this context I should like to say a few words about method – not about method in general, but more *ad homines*, and by *homines* I mean me as much as you. In particular, I am referring to a certain difficulty that evidently makes its appearance in connection with my lectures in particular. Outwardly, this difficulty takes the form that people who attend my lectures find they are unable to take notes as they can in other lectures and hence have nothing in black and white to take home with them. I have on various occasions heard and seen that this is the case, and recently it has even found its way – barely disguised – into a novel.[1] I would like to dwell a little on this matter for a moment. I can understand very well that you feel the need to have something hard and fast in your hands, particularly since at the very start of your studies you will not have had much opportunity to reflect on the distinction between mere learning and learning philosophy – which according to Kant is nothing other than learning how to philosophize.[2] On the other hand, you have to be aware that there are some very serious and very considerable difficulties here; and you can take my word for it that the approach I have chosen is neither rhapsodic nor arbitrary, but that if I decline to proceed with 'firstly', 'secondly' and 'thirdly', and if I fail to give you a set of definitive statements, this is bound up with the essence of what I stand for philosophically. Those of you who have taken the trouble to look at my writings beyond what you can learn in this course of lectures will have seen quickly enough why this is the case and why it cannot be otherwise. But I should like to make two further comments, or perhaps a whole series of further comments. I believe that it is good for these matters to be aired, for us to take a frank look at them, rather than letting them fester in a murky realm halfway between whispering and fascination.[3] My view is as follows. Firstly, philosophy consists in reflection on knowledge and not in the immediate transmission of information, and anyone who becomes seriously involved with philosophy – and I assume that this applies to you – has to be prepared to submit to the process of reflection, and to reflection, moreover, conceived as free, without any spoon-feeding, and cannot expect philosophy to provide the kind of solid subject-matter that is normal elsewhere. This applies with particular force in the present situation in which the concept of so-called systematic philosophy has become profoundly problematic. I cannot go into the problematic nature of systematic philosophy here and now, if only because we would never get on to anything else, but I assume that you are all more or less aware of this problem, which was radically formulated as early as Nietzsche who talks about the 'dishonesty of the system' or the 'dishonesty involved in creating systems'.[4] But at all events, in such a situation and especially when one's own thoughts are so critical of the concept of system, it would be inappropriate to clothe one's ideas in a form that in reality does no more than mimic a non-existent system. Instead I at any rate think it the task of philosophical discourse to attempt as far as possible to express *as* discourse – in other words, through the form in which it is presented – something of the content it wishes to convey. It is an essential feature of philosophy that form and content cannot be separated from each other, as is supposed to be the case in the various branches of learning, although it is my view that an expert on German literature, for example, who used phrases such as 'roughly speaking' in his texts would thereby disqualify himself as utterly as any philosopher who indulges in linguistic waffle and thinks it acceptable to talk in phrases and generalities. I have told you that I would think it contemptible were I to formulate my ideas in terms of 'firstly', 'secondly' and 'thirdly', since this would amount merely to the pretence of a systematic treatment that is inappropriate to the subject-matter. What I am trying to do instead is to lead you un-daunted over the rough ground in pursuit of the ideas and reflections which in my view represent the actual movement of philosophical thought.

There is, finally, one other consideration that bears on the form of philosophical lectures and indeed on lecturing in general. I am accustomed to pay very strict attention to forms, and this holds good for the form of lectures too. I would say that the lecture, which came into being in an age when printing had long since been in existence, is in a certain sense an 'archaic form', a point Horkheimer once demonstrated very elegantly.[5] That is to say, it has in a sense been superseded by the written form. Hence if this form is to be retained, if people are to continue to give real lectures, this can only have a meaning if the things that are said during a lecture, and the way they are said, cannot be found in printed form, especially not in the so-called authoritative texts of philosophy. Hence I regard with contempt the idea of simply regurgitating the contents of a book, and rebel against the whole conception. It would also be very foolish, because if it were simply a matter of gaining a knowledge of some theories or other, of opinions or doctrines that have been handed down in the history of philosophy, these are matters that you could indeed learn much more easily by reading them yourselves. Reading them for yourselves would also have the advantage that you could dwell on the difficult passages – and philosophy has no shortage of those – and really sink your teeth into them. That is much better than for me to attempt to expound them here since I would necessarily have to condense the arguments much more and you would find them rushing past you. This is one reason why I have chosen a form that some of you find so puzzling; but it is often the case that if we are baffled by the form in which something is presented, the difficulties frequently arise from the fact that we approach them with false expectations. In this instance you have come with the expectation that I shall deliver something like a system of ethics or a philosophical system, or something of the kind – and you then measure what happens against your expectation and end up feeling disappointed. There is a similar situation in modern music; such music is misunderstood by many people simply because they expect it to exhibit the same kind of symmetrical patterns as 'Twinkle, twinkle, little star', and when such patterns fail to make their appearance they react by saying, 'Well, this is simply not music at all.'[6] For this reason I believe that, if I may give you some advice to make our discussions here easier to understand – something that of course matters as much to me as it does to you – that advice would be not to come to these lectures with those expectations, or indeed with any fixed expectations of the kind you may have acquired from elsewhere in your philosophical studies. Instead you should try merely to give your attention to the matter in hand, and to what I shall try to tell you about it as well or as badly as I am able. You should try and follow the argument and spontaneously think along with it, instead of being constantly on the lookout for nuggets that can be conveniently picked up. If you do that, I think I can promise you that there will be enough to satisfy you by way of subject-matter, for I have no wish to underestimate, or to disparage, the hunger for information. It is the case rather that in intellectual matters, as well as elsewhere, the purely material elements – in other words, the raw data of thought before they have been thought about – have what might be called a certain vitamin content which stimulates the brain. And the need for this stimulation is not without considerable justification. But the compromise I seek is one which – *si parva licet componere magnis*[7] – was chosen by Kant himself. For in his lectures Kant never attempted to teach his own philosophy directly, but always did so in the context of traditional ideas, and in actual fact these were the ideas of the selfsame philosophy of Leibniz and Wolff that were the target of the critique in the title of the *Critique of Pure Reason*. I am using Kant in a similar fashion, namely as a vehicle, in order, on the one hand, to introduce you to the problems of moral philosophy by telling you about his problems and his way of tackling them, and, on the other hand, to lead you to go beyond Kant through my critical and other reflections on him. At all events, that is my intention in the first part of this course. And, as I believe I have already told you, what I wish to do in the latter part of the course is to discuss with you some at least of the burning topics in moral philosophy at the present time.

If we now turn to Kant's moral philosophy, we find ourselves confronted by an astounding fact. This is that his approach is anchored in his theoretical philosophy, in the *Critique of Pure Reason*. This has to do with Kant's own tendency to lean towards theoretical systems, that is to say, with his predilection for inferring more or less everything else that goes by the name of philosophy from certain basic premises, from certain fundamental insights of his so-called transcendental philosophy which are thought to be incapable of being overturned. This includes moral philosophy, which in his thought is grounded in a certain sense in cognition. To this extent there is a conflict between his approach and what I talked about briefly in our preliminary remarks. I said then that the distinguishing feature of the sphere of practice, that is to say, the sphere of action that is covered by moral philosophy, lies in the fact that it cannot be translated without remainder into the realm of theoretical reflection. Now this second aspect is indeed expressed by Kant, albeit indirectly, in a thesis which is astonishing, even paradoxical, for a thinker who insists so strongly on the primacy of reason. It is expressed in the thesis in which he actually credits moral philosophy with primacy over

theoretical philosophy. This thesis states that the so-called supreme
questions of metaphysics as a theoretical discipline – the questions
that figure on traditional lists and include God, freedom and
immortality – are really only relevant as questions of practice, while
theoretical reason regards them with a certain detachment.[8] I can tell
you at once, since I believe it is the key to an understanding of Kant's
moral philosophy in general, that the factor that unifies Kant's theoretical and practical philosophy lies in the concept of reason itself. And
I believe that you would be well advised to try and grasp this if you
wish to gain an understanding of the conception of theory and practice at work in Kant's thought. Reason as the capacity for right,
correct thought, the ability to form concepts correctly, the ability to
make correct judgements and precise deductions, as it is called in
traditional logic – all this is constitutive of both theory and practice
in his philosophy. That this is true with regard to theory is evident,
since reason so conceived is the authority that decides about theory
and Kant – without concerning himself too much about the matter
in detail – endows it with the ability to reflect on itself and its own
scope, and even to set limits to its own jurisdiction. On the other
hand, however, this reason, which is always the same, is the same
reason at work in every part of the Kantian philosophy, no matter
how disparate these parts may be. The reason that we encounter
there, the organ of reason that is sometimes called judgement and
sometimes understanding, is simply the organ of correct thought
and is always the same in Kant. Within the realm of practical reason
that we are concerned with here it enjoys a particular position of
supremacy because practical actions, in so far as they are the object
of moral reflection, are precisely the actions that arise solely from
reason, and that are constituted entirely on the basis of the pure laws
of reason – independently of any perceptions, of any empirical material, of anything that impinges on this reason from outside.[9] Moral
conduct in this sense is conduct that is literally pure. The word 'pure'
has a very profound double meaning in Kant. On the one hand, *pure*
means in accordance with reason, undistorted by any matter in any
way connected with the senses. But also, because it is nothing but
action *purely* in accordance with the laws of reason, it necessarily has
the character of the formal and the abstract that – as you are all aware
– has been the reproach that has constantly been levelled at Kantian
ethics. This may enable you to understand why Kant, in whose
thought the primacy of reason is as predominant as in any
Enlightenment thinker, nevertheless insists on the primacy of practical philosophy. For practical philosophy is the philosophy that exists
in pure conformity with reason, without the need for its laws to pay

heed to any material that impinges on the knowing and acting subject from outside. Morally speaking, such material, and hence too the consequences of my acts, are a matter of indifference in Kant, as compared to their ability to satisfy the laws of reason. When I tell you that in Kant morality is grounded in the theory of knowledge in a very precise way – you will hear more about this in a moment – but that at the same time, morality has primacy even over reason's interest in knowledge, you will feel the full force of the Kantian dualism of which I have been trying to give you at least the flavour. We might characterize Kantian philosophy as a whole by saying that it is the mountain pass linking the motif of epistemological Enlightenment with the attempt to salvage metaphysics, to recuperate metaphysical meaning, which is concentrated for him in the highest universalities not only of knowledge, but also of ideas and hence too of the laws of morality. This will perhaps clarify for you this peculiar oscillation in the relative status of theory and practice. We could no doubt attempt to explain it away somehow or other, perhaps by saying that the theory is the foundation, but that morality, as the loftier, human dimension, stood higher than knowledge, or something of the sort. But in general I find it more profitable – to trail my coat a little – when dealing with complex systems of thought, of which the Kantian system is surely an instance, to reveal the fissures they contain, to chart them and to try and understand their origins and their meaning, rather than to explain such fissures and conflicts away more or less elegantly in the interests of a superficial harmony. In this respect, too, I believe myself to be operating in the spirit of Kantian thought, since his starting-point, particularly in moral philosophy, is the consciousness of necessary and unavoidable contradictions, namely the so-called antinomies.

Now, the problem of moral philosophy in Kant generally, and this is the first point you must grasp, is the problem of freedom, the freedom of the will. What this means in the first instance – just so as not to give you any exaggerated ideas about the question – is no more than a form of behaviour that is not ruled by the causality of nature. That this problem of freedom is the fundamental problem of moral philosophy will be perfectly clear to you. But it is far less obvious how we should think about the definition of this freedom, the definition of causality and the relations between the two. But we shall say more about this once we have obtained an initial clarification of the simple concepts that are involved here. I have said that it is obvious that freedom is the problem of morality in Kant. Very simple and consequently very clear. I have used the word 'I' and I do so with something of the cavalier largesse that was also characteristic of Kant in the same context, since he too did not dwell overlong on what was meant by the word 'I', but simply followed pre-philosophical usage. So it is obvious that I can only act freely if I am not blindly subject to causality in the sense that this book is. For when I drop it, it will fall on the table and perhaps even come unstuck, since it is rather old. It is only then that we can speak of something like moral action, of good and just, right or ethical action, or whatever other terms come to mind. For if I simply act in conformity with causality, I shall not actually be present as the agent that somehow has to make decisions about an action. And it will be obvious to you that all ideas of morality or ethical behaviour must relate to an 'I' that acts. I think that what I am saying here is simply to remind you of something that has even succeeded in establishing itself in the criminal law. For example, take the case of a person who is mentally disturbed and who then wreaks havoc of some kind or other, but only because he is acting under the compulsion of blind impulses that are independent of his reason so that the idea of freedom becomes quite inapplicable. In such a case we say that this man cannot be held responsible for his actions; he is not responsible. This means that in a certain sense he stands outside the problem of good and evil. This problem of freedom is presented by Kant in an intensified form in the doctrine of the antinomies, more specifically, in the third antinomy. I may add that it actually makes its appearance in the fourth antinomy too, but if you take a closer look at the fourth antinomy you will find that it largely overlaps with the third. There is no essential difference between the two, so it makes sense to restrict oneself to the third antinomy when thinking about the antinomy of freedom and causality.

After what I have said about the dual nature of Kantian philosophy, you will perhaps be in a position to think about Kant's doctrine of the antinomies, which we need to examine a little more closely, in a rather broader context, not quite so narrowly as it would appear to you by focusing directly on the text. The essence of this doctrine of the antinomies is that it represents a conflict between that Enlightenment spirit of critical rationalism which I have already mentioned and, on the other hand, the intention of salvaging metaphysics. Because both these impulses – Kant does not speak of them in so many words, but they are well developed in his philosophy – are equally powerful in reason, because they make themselves felt in equal measure in reason, the ambivalence they express leads to insoluble contradictions. You can find a very fine summary of this doctrine of the antinomies as a whole, a really elegant and simple formulation of the doctrine of the antinomies, in the Kant commentary of my old teacher Cornelius, and perhaps I may read you the few relevant sentences that will show you very lucidly just what is at stake. We are talking here about the section of the *Critique of Pure Reason* entitled 'Transcendental Dialectic, Book II, Chapter 2: The Antinomy of Pure Reason'. I shall now quote the passage from Cornelius: 'Wherever a constituent of the world we experience shows itself to be determined by a series of conditions that we are unable to follow through to their endpoint, our thinking becomes entangled in an insoluble contradiction as soon as this series of conditions turns out to be one that *exists in and for itself*' – and, we must add, one that has not been produced by our own consciousness. 'Since this' – that is to say, the fact that we perceive the infinite series of causes in our problem as one that exists in and for itself – 'inevitably happens given our ordinary view of the world' – which Kant calls Transcendental Realism – 'this world view is unable to discover any escape from the contradictions in which it finds itself entangled.'[10]

Now, you can easily convince yourself of this by reflecting that if your thinking is still at a pre-philosophical, pre-critical stage, you will conceive of causality not as a function of our reason, but as a tendency that actually belongs objectively to external objects. Hence you will find that you will trace the cause of a condition, and the cause of its cause, back to what might be regarded as the primary cause. This process goes on to infinity. This infinite regress leads then to the contradictions that Kant treats of in the theory of the antinomies. Kant entitles the entire doctrine of these contradictions in the *Critique of Pure Reason* the 'Transcendental Antithetic'. This is the doctrine of the antitheses in which reason is said to become embroiled. We are speaking here of reason in its unphilosophical usage, that is to say, in the active postulation of an infinite that is itself the product merely of consciousness. Here is the relevant passage from Cornelius by way of further explanation.

'The Antithetic' – this is contained in Section 2 of 'The Antinomy of Pure Reason' – 'does not, therefore, deal with one-sided assertions. It treats only of the conflict of the doctrines of reason with one another and the causes of this conflict. The Transcendental Antithetic' – and it is with this that we are concerned – 'is an enquiry into the antinomy' – that is to say, the necessary contradictions – 'of pure reason, its causes and outcome. If we do not merely put our reason in the service of the principles of the understanding [*Verstand*], and apply it to the objects of experience, but venture to extend these principles' – that is, the principles of the understanding – 'beyond the limits of experience' – that is, the objects of experience – 'then we shall see the emergence of' what he calls '*pseudo-rational [vernün-ftelnd]* doctrines which can neither hope for confirmation in experience, nor fear refutation by it. Each of them is not only in itself free from contradiction, but finds the conditions of its necessity in the very nature of reason – except that, unfortunately, the assertion of the opposite has, on its side, grounds that are just as valid and necessary.'[11]

Ladies and Gentlemen, I should like to underline this motif of the necessary nature of the contradictions in which reason becomes entangled. Kant himself is not quite so unambiguous on this point. Even in the *Critique of Pure Reason*, there are very powerful motifs that cannot readily be reconciled with the idea that the contradictions in which reason becomes involved are necessary. For if this really were necessity in a strict sense, then the kind of resolution of the antinomies that Kant is attempting would not be possible, and nor would the fundamental line of thought that I have sketched to you. This second idea, that is to say, the idea that the contradictions can be cleared up, implies that for Kant the term dialectic – that is, the doctrine of necessary contradictions, or the doctrine of the contradictory nature of theorems in general – is a negative term, a word of abuse. For Kant dialectic is always, necessarily, something false. This is why elsewhere he refers to dialectic as '*the logic of illusion*' [*Schein*],[12] and embarks on the elimination of the antinomies. Of course, this entire line of thinking only gains its profundity from the necessity of the contradictions in which we become involved. That is to say, only when this contradiction is seen as necessary can we understand the actual problem of moral philosophy, the fundamental problem of moral philosophy, namely the problem of freedom or unfreedom as a genuine problem, that is to say, as something arising from the matter itself, and no mere deception that can easily be removed. Incidentally, this motif of the necessary nature of contradictions that Kant derives from reason and nature, but that he then fails to carry through rigorously in his treatment of contradictions, is one of the motifs, and I would say by no means the least trivial one, that forms the starting-point for the concept of a philosophical dialectic. That is to say, the idea of a dialectic as a medium of thought and a way of discovering objective truth acquires a sufficient impetus only when reason necessarily falls into contradiction, and only when it makes advances in the course of resolving contradictions, instead of dismissing them once and for all as errors of logic. And this is why I would like to place such great emphasis on this point. It would be a fascinating task, incidentally – and a task that to the best of my knowledge, has not really been attempted – to follow up this peculiar duality of the Kantian dialectic as a concept that implies necessity, on the one hand, and a mere failure of thought, on the other, and to examine it in the context of a theory of philosophical dialectic.[13] I simply draw your attention here to this problem, which naturally we cannot yet deal with at this stage of the course.

The method Kant chooses to use in this dialectic, this Antithetic, is one he calls the 'sceptical method' – and he thinks of this as standing in extreme contrast to scepticism as such. Kant justifies this by saying that the sceptical method, that is the doubt cast on mere dogmatic postulates and the merely dogmatic, unreflective use of concepts, aims at certainty. The relevant, very interesting, statement goes as follows:

> For the sceptical method aims at certainty. It seeks to discover the point of misunderstanding in the case of disputes which are sincerely and competently conducted by both sides, just as from the embarrassment of judges in cases of litigation wise legislators contrive to obtain instruction regarding the defects and ambiguities of their laws.[14]

So you can see from this approach to moral philosophy that the entire point of view of Kantian philosophy is objective, and that the idea that Transcendental Philosophy is subjective is oversimplified. This is because, on the contrary, Kant's philosophy represents the attempt to salvage the objective validity of the highest and most important propositions by a *reductio ad subjectum*, by reduction to the subject. This fits in precisely with the general thrust of Kantian moral philosophy, since what that amounts to is the reduction to the purely subjective principle of reason in order simultaneously to salvage the absolute, unimpeachable objectivity of the moral law. This makes it possible to say that the supreme principle of morality, namely the categorical imperative, is in fact nothing other than subjective reason as an absolutely objectively valid thing. The extreme opposite of this is the sceptical approach, which denies the existence of any such objectively valid principle. And this distinction between the sceptical method and scepticism as a philosophy is enough to enable you to see something of Kant's moral position. Unlike the sceptics and the Sophists his concern with the subject and human beings is not a strategy to enable him to dispute the universal necessity and binding nature of moral laws, but precisely to reinstate them. His task, therefore, is to demonstrate that the explanation for the misunderstanding lies in a false use of reason. And when this explanation has been found, we then see something that really does remind us of the

workings of a dialectical philosophy. For by demonstrating the negativity of thesis and antithesis, by discovering the nature of the
misunderstanding, to put it in Kantian terms, by eliminating this misunderstanding, we gain access to the positive side, to the higher truth.
In this case we gain access to the explanation for the contradiction
in reason itself, This creates the possibility of eliminating that contradiction through the action of reason itself. You can see from this
that although Kant declares himself to be no friend of dialectic in the
Critique of Pure Reason, in reality he makes a much more positive
use of it, thanks to this sceptical method, than might have been
expected from his own views on the matter. Having said this, next
time we can proceed to a closer look at the third antinomy. – Thank
you.

LECTURE FOUR

16 May 1963

Ladies and Gentlemen,

Today I would like to go straight into a discussion of Kant's third antinomy. Since this is not exactly a simple text for me to present you with as a kind of foundation at a relatively early stage of the course, I must ask you to concentrate your minds somewhat, and to make the sort of effort that the Kantian text expects of us. Let me start by saying something about the method adopted by Kant in the doctrine of the antinomies in general. This method is that of the *argumentatio e contrario*, as the traditional rhetorical figure was called. What he does is to start with a thesis and antithesis that contradict each other and both of which are equally obvious or not, as the case may be, and to prove them by demonstrating the nonsense that their antitheses lead to. Thus both are proved negatively, by their opposites, by their contradictories.[1] This procedure, that may appear to you at first to be rather perverse, this procedure is – like all so-called formal features of respectable philosophy – motivated by its content. It is motivated by the consideration mentioned by Kant at one point in the Antithetic that the two theses cannot be proved positively because as propositions about infinity or about an infinite series they lead to something infinite about which no positive statement can be made. 'Infinite' here is not used in a mathematical sense, but in the meaning it had in ordinary pre-mathematical human reason. Conversely, it is possible for Kant to show that their antithesis leads to nonsense, with the implication that the thesis that thus arises indirectly from this can be regarded as valid.[2] I should just note in passing that this conclusion that the proof of the invalidity of the counter-thesis of an argument entails the truth of the original thesis is by no means all that compelling logically. But we shall have to return to this later on.

I must also tell you – and this is something we must look at in detail, to clear away any preconceptions – that when Kant speaks of causality in the doctrine of antinomies, the concept of causality refers in the first instance – I think this is the easiest way to present it – simply to the concept of causality that operates in the natural sciences. I may remind you, or draw to your attention the fact – I cannot actually remind you, since we cannot deal with the matter here – that one of the peculiar features of the *Critique of Pure Reason* is that the mathematical natural sciences are not deduced from anything, but are somehow presupposed, that is, their validity is presupposed. Kant then goes on to investigate the conditions of their validity, with the consequence that the scientific concept of causality is what counts, at least to start with. This is of lesser importance for the concept of causality than it is, initially at least, for the concept of freedom that is opposed to causality here and which in fact, if I may express myself unacademically, is a veritable can of worms. Let us consider the concept of freedom, and I would ask you to hold on to this idea for the moment: we shall soon have to modify it, but you need to have a relatively simple, straightforward idea to work with; the difficult distinctions will come soon enough. This concept of freedom is merely defined negatively in the first instance, namely as an independence [from the laws of nature] in a series of successive conditions, as an independence from the rules governing such a series that Kant otherwise requires. Initially at least, a positive concept of freedom, freedom in the sense of an 'absolute power to create' – as it was called later on in German idealism – is not involved here, although you will find that in the case of one particular concept that surfaces very quickly at this point, the concept of spontaneity, the transition to such a positive concept of freedom very soon follows. I must tell you, incidentally, that this concept is one that causes particular difficulties in the passage in question because it is not directly applicable to the concept of spontaneity previously employed by Kant, which referred to the production of ideas by the subject.[3] But we can ignore this for the time being. Here I should just like to draw your attention to one point before we look at Kant's treatment of the antinomy, so that you can gain something of an idea of the problems involved. For what I have promised you is to introduce you to the *problems* of moral philosophy, and this means that I shall not just tell you about this fundamental line of thought in Kant, and explain it as well as I can, but I should like to show you that behind these arguments, which may or may not strike you as persuasive, there are a number of conflicting motifs that are hard to grasp and are often incompatible with each other. I regard it as the prime task of philosophical understanding – and every such course of lectures must work towards philosophical understanding – to show you that, beneath the seemingly plausible and coherent propositions, lies a parallelogram of forces that can be thought of as standing in the same relation to any given teachings as the parallelogram of forces in physics stands to its product. This is why I should like to draw your attention here to the concept of a causality through freedom that Kant introduces as early as the doctrine of the antinomies. This concept, which stands on one side of the antinomy, really contradicts the principle of criticism, the general principle of rational critique, according to which causality is a category, that is to say, it is not an attribute of things in themselves, the sphere of the intelligible. Instead, this causality through freedom is conceived as a concept of causality that stands outside the realm of phenomena to which the concept of causality is generally assigned. To understand this, in other words, to understand how we arrive at this highly curious syncopation, this interweaving of the motifs of lawfulness and freedom, and to grasp what impels Kant in this direction, is not just the key to an understanding of the Kantian ethic, but also of the structure of Kantian philosophy as a whole. In all probability it is also the key to what we think of as ethical problems in general. For this interweaving of freedom and necessity and the resolution of the contradictions implicit in it is not just a problem of cognition, but the very real problem that confronts every philosophical account of so-called morality.

All this by way of introduction. Probably the simplest way to proceed now is for me to read out to you Kant's own statement of the thesis and antithesis together with the proof that he then gives. I can then flesh out the individual statements with as much commentary as I think necessary for you to understand his line of thought. I shall set aside any question of criticism for the time being, and only when I have the impression that the ideas have been sufficiently clarified will we proceed to look at their problematic features. Here is the thesis of this so-called 'Third Conflict of the Transcendental Ideas' – and freedom and total determination are to be classed as ideas because to assert them goes beyond the limits of possible experience and into infinity, and so, thanks to the architecture of rational criticism, they belong among the ideas. Hence the title the 'Conflict of the Transcendental Ideas'. The thesis goes as follows:

Causality in accordance with the laws of Nature is not the only
causality from which the appearances of the world can one and all be
derived. To explain these appearances, it is necessary to assume that
there is also another causality, that of freedom.[4]

I shall take the liberty of making one small point, one which
may have occurred to you too on a careful reading of the thesis. This
is that when introducing the concept of freedom the word 'necessary'
has been smuggled in, a term borrowed from the realm of causality.
This indicates that the concept of causality in Kant has developed
to the point where it is capable of different interpretations, and
goes beyond the scientific causality which is what Kant is explicitly
dealing with. On the other hand, we can see that it is a symptom
of the impossibility of eradicating the contradiction we have been
discussing. It is simply not possible for him to prove what he wishes
to prove, or what he wishes to express, because what he wishes
to prove, namely the principle of necessity, is in a sense already
presupposed. This feature, incidentally, is very prevalent throughout Kant's philosophy, and since I have advised you to read the
Critique of Practical Reason, and would be delighted if you were
also to read the *Critique of Pure Reason*, this pointer will perhaps
be of assistance to your understanding of those texts. The fact is
that you will only do Kant justice if you stop believing that everything in him can be deduced from something else. In this respect he
presents a sharp contrast to thinkers like Spinoza or Fichte. When it
comes to the validity of particular concepts, the concept of what is
given [*das Gegebene*] has in Kant a meaning that goes far beyond
what is given to our senses. All sorts of things are assumed to be
given and then neither deduced nor proved nor explained. You may
well think that there is something crude or even primitive about this
procedure when you compare it to the tremendous sophistication
of Kant's immediate successors, above all idealist philosophers like
Fichte and Hegel. But it contains something that is closely bound
up with the very essence of Kantian philosophy, with a claim that
goes to the heart of it. This essence is the fact that in Kant the subject
has not yet become the principle that presumes to be able to deduce
from within itself the totality of everything that exists, including
everything spiritual. Instead, the content of Kantian philosophy, in
so far as it has a negative content, lies precisely in the limits it sets
to the absolute claims of the subject; these limits also imply a limit
to what can be deduced from this philosophy, even though, on
the other hand, it presents itself as a deductive system. To take
this one step further, this curious tolerance of elements that cannot

be deduced from elsewhere, either from other concepts or from any supreme axioms, is a particular feature of Kant's thought. Moreover, this remarkable method does not confine itself, as we might first suppose, to the so-called material of our knowledge, but extends to the very forms of our consciousness which, despite their derivative nature in Kant, have in a sense simply to be accepted, and to be respected. This has the consequence that he can speak of necessity – and necessity is one of the categories in his system – as if it is something given. I cannot provide the evidence for this here; to do so would take us too far away from our present concerns. But I would just like to draw your attention to the so-called 'Deduction of the Pure Concepts of Understanding' in Kant, where you can find a series of statements that explicitly confirm the existence of these givens.[5] Moreover, he even treats as givens things that are actually not given, but are supposed to be pure functions, pure activity.

Let us proceed now to the proof of the thesis *e contrario*. Therefore, let us assume the opposite, namely, that

> there is no other causality than that in accordance with laws of nature. This being so, everything *which takes place* presupposes a preceding state upon which it inevitably follows according to a rule.[6]

Ladies and Gentlemen, what you have in this sentence is the famous Kantian definition of causality, and you should note it as the succinct antithesis to the Kantian doctrine of freedom. In the sense in which it is discussed here, causality is the succession of states in accordance with rules. Therefore, this concept of causality is, as you will have noticed, extraordinarily broad, so broad that it is capable of the most divergent interpretations. You can even – though I leave this to the natural scientists among you – reflect on whether this concept of causality is so general that it even leaves room for the most recent criticism of causality in the natural sciences, namely in quantum mechanics; and you may consider whether the contradiction which is alleged to exist between Kant and modern science is not based on an over-narrow interpretation of the Kantian idea. But this is merely an aside for the benefit of those who have a particular interest in the concept of causality. Kant continues:

> But the preceding state must itself be something which has taken place (having come to be in a time in which it previously was not); for if it had always existed, its consequence also would have always existed, and would not have only just arisen.[7]

Kant's argument here is very ingenious, we might even call it over-ingenious, but it is certainly very rigorous. According to Kant, a pre-ceding state from which the present state must follow causally – in accordance with the proposition that if a particular state has the form A, it must be followed by a state with the form B – must, therefore, be a state that has arisen from something prior. For if that were not the case, if it had existed from the very beginning, then the present phenomenon for whose existence it provides an explanation would itself have to be an original phenomenon that had always existed. In other words, it would have no need to be explained causally by that prior state. That would obviously be unthinkable because it would mean the negation of the phenomenon as something existing *hic et nunc*, as a given in the here and now. Kant continues:

> The causality of the cause through which something takes place is itself, therefore, something that has *taken place*, which again presupposes, in accordance with the law of nature, a preceding state and its causality, and this in similar manner a still earlier state, and so on.[8]

So what we have here is the phenomenon that is familiar to all of you under the name of the causal chain.

> If, therefore, everything takes place solely in accordance with laws of nature, there will always be only a relative [*subalternen*] and never a first beginning, and consequently no completeness of the series on the side of the causes that arise the one from the other.[9]

The expression 'relative' [*subaltern*], which has qualitative, judge-mental overtones, just means secondary or derivative. According to Kant, then, there are nothing but secondary or derivative causes, which for their part, in terms of their own meaning, necessarily point back to a first, primary cause. He explains this as follows, and his explanation may not be entirely convincing: 'But the law of nature is just this, that nothing takes place without a cause *sufficiently* deter-mined *a priori*.'[10] What is meant here – and this is evidently the heart of the argument – is that, because it itself is in need of causal expla-nation, because it is therefore incomplete, this relative cause cannot be a sufficient cause itself, because it would only be a sufficient cause if, without constantly seeking out further underlying causes, it could be made so fundamental that any further questions about its origins would be meaningless. He says, then, 'But the law of nature is just this', and he believes he has established this in the doctrine of cat-egories,[11] 'that nothing takes place without a cause *sufficiently* deter-

mined *a priori*.'[12] In other words, without a complete determination
of the causes. For otherwise the explanation of natural events would
end in a vacuum, or the explanation of nature as a whole, as
a necessity, which up to now Kant has simply taken as given in an
unproblematic way, would be reduced to a mere chance. He goes
on to say: 'The proposition as if no causality is possible save in
accordance with laws of nature,' – he means, the proposition *that*
'no causality is possible save in accordance with laws of nature'
(the meaning is straightforward though the wording is slightly
awkward) – 'when taken in unlimited universality, is therefore self-
contradictory; and this cannot, therefore, be regarded as the sole kind
of causality.'[13] That is to say, if I take this statement at its face value,
its own requirement for a complete determination of causality necessarily remains unfulfilled, and it comes into contradiction with
itself. And he now draws the conclusion from this: 'We must, then,
assume a causality through which something takes place, the cause
of which is not itself determined, in accordance with necessary laws,
by another cause antecedent to it, that is to say, an *absolute spontaneity* of the cause, whereby a series of appearances, which proceeds
in accordance with laws of nature, begins *of itself*. This is transcendental freedom, without which,' – and take note here that he is establishing transcendental freedom on the basis of the causality of nature,
because otherwise it would be nonsensical – 'even in the [ordinary]
course of nature,' – and here he sums the whole thing up once again
– 'the series of appearances on the side of the causes can never be
complete.'[14] What you see here, then, is the astonishing expansion of
the concept of causality to embrace the idea of freedom, so that
freedom, too, is a causality, a causality *sui generis*.

The best way to arrive at an understanding of this remarkable and
surprising use of language is perhaps to reflect on the rather restrictive formulation that Kant has chosen here. He says that there is a
series of appearances that can, as it were, start up of their own
accord, without the need for any knowledge of the infinite conditions
of natural causality. I think it would be as well to tell you what Kant
had in mind here, since one of the principles of philosophical understanding is – and this is a rule that applies particularly to the later
idealists, and especially Hegel – that we truly understand these apparently very formal arguments of the kind I have just given you only if
we do not just follow the train of thought through to its logical consequences, but also succeed in imagining the real situation which
underlies it and provides the model for it. Without a doubt, in this
case the real situation is the individual's own experience, quite simply,
the fact that I can experience for myself – whatever implications this

may have within the framework of a universal determinism – that
I have the ability to set series of causally linked events in motion
through an action that, as Kant terms it, has an element of independence – whatever its objective connections may be with the causality
of nature. Hence, if I once more pick up this unfortunate book, and
drop it again, then the fact that it does fall is a matter of natural
causality, it takes place in the macro-realm, in accordance with the
good old rules of cause and effect. But the fact that I take this decision, however foolish it may be, to lift this book up and drop it, the
fact that I intervene, brings a further element, an independent one,
into this causal chain. We might say that with this decision a new
causal series is inaugurated. And how this series then becomes incorporated into the totality of causal conditions, that is something about
which Kant would say, or rather it is wrong to say he would say it,
because he does say in fact, 'This is a *cura posterior*, this belongs
to a theory of human nature as far as its characters likewise form
part of the empirical world.'[15] But the immediate position for our
own experience, the factor that stands out in opposition to the chain
of causality is this initial act, the beginning of a second series of
determinants which likewise for our own experience is not wholly
determined empirically in its identity with, or its dependence upon,
the universal chain of causes.[16] This is what Kant has in mind at
this point, and he speaks of an 'absolute spontaneity of the cause'
without, however, defining the concept any further at this point.
However, spontaneity here means something like an originating activity, independent activity for which no further conditioning factors can
be positively given in the first instance. Indeed in the *Critique of Pure
Reason* generally, spontaneity is the faculty concerned with the production of ideas, and so represents the productive faculty of consciousness and hence of the human mind as such. As you can read in
the 'Transcendental Doctrine of Method', Kant is, like all respectable
philosophers, no great friend of verbal definitions.[17] He introduces
this concept initially in a fairly restricted sense, limiting it to the ideas.
Because it is a matter of one of the fundamental motifs of subjectivity, and we might even say, *the* fundamental motif of subjectivity, he
takes the liberty, rightly, of applying this activity of mind more
broadly.[18] This is the argument Kant advances in opposition to universal causality and in favour of the causality born of freedom and
hence also of the concept of freedom as the fundamental concept of
ethics.

The antithesis goes as follows: 'There is no freedom; everything in
the world takes place solely in accordance with laws of nature.'[19] You
can see here in the formulation of the antithesis that in defining

causality in contrast to freedom, Kant explicitly equates it – as I have already indicated – with causality in nature. The proof goes as follows: 'Assume that there is *freedom* in the transcendental sense,' – in other words, the freedom which emerges from the proof of the thesis – 'as a special kind of causality in accordance with which the events in the world can have come about, namely a power of absolutely beginning a state, and therefore absolutely beginning a series of consequences of that state; it then follows that not only will a series have its absolute beginning in this spontaneity, but that the very determination of this spontaneity to originate the series, that is to say causality itself, will have an absolute beginning [. . .].'[20] I should explain that on the premise that he is subjecting to criticism here, freedom in the transcendental sense is tantamount to being a category; in this it resembles causality. That is to say, freedom, and this includes action, the course of events independent of laws, would then become a basic category in accordance with which our knowledge and with it the phenomenal world is organized. If we now connect this to this explanation of the term 'transcendental', Kant's thinking is quite simply this: the categories, that is to say, the fundamental concepts, the basic furniture of my mind which I need if I am to be able to bring order at all into my experience, are nothing but the conditions that enable me to organize the world in accordance with laws and hence experience the world as governed by laws. Now if freedom – and this is the *nervus probandi* – is turned into a category, to a transcendental principle, a fundamental precondition of my knowledge of objects in general, this would mean that the opposite of conformity to law would itself be made into one of the categories, that it would therefore form the foundation of lawfulness as such and that freedom would become the epitome of conformity to law, an evident nonsense. This is his basic thought. If you keep this in mind, you will, I think, have relatively little trouble in following the rest of the argument. We shall move on to the second stage soon enough. This means that if I were to accept the idea of freedom in its transcendental sense, freedom as category, then, Kant continues, this will lead to 'causality itself having an absolute beginning; there will be no antecedent through which this act, in taking place, is determined in accordance with fixed laws'.[21] This would mean accepting a principle that would have nothing to do either with a knowledge in conformity with law or with any laws operating in nature.

But every beginning of action presupposes a state of the not yet acting cause; and a *dynamical* beginning of the action, if it is also a first beginning, presupposes a state which has no *causal* connection with the preceding state of the cause, that is to say, in nowise follows from it.[22]

Therefore, this conformity to law that according to Kant ought to follow from the principle of freedom, or that is to be introduced with the principle of freedom, would itself be in contradiction to the concept of conformity to law.

> Transcendental freedom thus stands opposed to the law of causality; and the kind of connection which it assumes as holding between the successive states of the active causes renders all unity of experience impossible. It is not to be met with in any experience, and is therefore an empty thought-entity.[23]

What he has in mind here is obviously the old idea of an ultimate, original creative principle as handed down by Aristotle and the Scholastics. The ultimate root of this idea is the Aristotelian doctrine of the ἀκίνητον πάντα κινοῦν, the unmoved mover of all things,[24] that would be assumed and that would for its part fall outside the causal series in order to provide causality with a foundation. In consequence it would stand opposed to the principles of conformity to law. In this line of argument, then, the argument in support of the antithesis, Kant speaks as the consistent and rigorous man of the Enlightenment whose whole striving is to eradicate the last vestiges of Scholastic, and ultimately Aristotelian and ontological, ideas from philosophy. And as a correlative to that, the argument in support of the thesis aims at the rehabilitation of the metaphysical principle. And when I told you last time that these two impulses are in permanent conflict with each other in Kant's thought, we can now see that this conflict has become thematic in the doctrine of the antinomies, that is, it is articulated literally in the relation between thesis and antithesis. Kant continues in the spirit of the Enlightenment principle: 'In *nature* alone, therefore, must we seek for the connection and order of cosmical events. Freedom (independence)' – and this is very interesting, and I would ask you to take careful note; it is something we shall have to discuss in greater detail next time – 'from the laws of nature is no doubt a *liberation* from *compulsion*, but also from the *guidance* of all rules.'[25] In other words, the moment I wish to introduce the principle of freedom in a positive manner, and liberate myself from the compulsion that has been brought about by the system of categories of causality – and here we have Kant's underlying thought – nature would turn out to be a chaos – and it is against this that the entire thrust of the *Critique of Pure Reason* is directed. 'For it is not

permissible to say that the *laws* of freedom enter into the causality
exhibited in the course of nature, and so take the place of natural
laws. If freedom were determined in accordance with laws, it would
not be freedom; it would simply be nature under another name.
Nature and transcendental freedom' – he formulates this in a very
extreme way – 'differ as do conformity to law and lawlessness.
Nature does indeed impose on the understanding the exacting task
of always seeking the origin of events ever higher in the series of
causes, their causality always being conditioned' – in other words,
they lead to further causes – 'But in compensation it holds out the
promise of thoroughgoing unity of experience in accordance with
laws. The illusion of freedom, on the other hand,' – and here speaks
Kant the determinist and champion of the Enlightenment – 'offers a
point of rest to the enquiring understanding in the chain of causes,'
– just as metaphysics holds out the promise that we can become conscious of the absolute and find in it a point of rest – 'conducting it
to an unconditioned causality which begins to act of itself. This
causality is, however, blind' – and blind, here, means that it does not
form part of the framework of laws which govern knowledge – 'and
abrogates those rules through which alone a completely coherent
experience is possible'[26] – in other words, experience is entirely left
in the hands of chance. I think that after these explanations, you will
all have understood the argument, so that next time we can take a
look at the difficulties lying beneath the surface of the text.

LECTURE FIVE

28 May 1963

Ladies and Gentlemen,

I am still in the process of convalescing, but did not wish, despite that, to cancel the lectures today and Thursday because the semester is dreadfully short as it is, and much has to be cancelled anyway.[1] I would also like to ask for your forbearance as far as the precision of my expression is concerned, and above all for the clarity of my speech, since I have had a throat infection and still find speaking a little difficult.

Ladies and Gentlemen, let us return to the treatment of the third antinomy, and I should like to try to pick up the thread where we left off in the last lecture. The main idea of this chapter is very plausible and I would even say relatively simple. If we assume an ultimate, absolute cause, we offend against the postulate implicit in the principle of causality, namely its universal applicability. In other words, if we arbitrarily break the series of causes to be sought we violate the principle of causality itself. According to this everything that exists [including any cause one might discover] must itself have a further cause, because something falls within a lawlike context of experience only by virtue of the universality of the causal principle. If that is not the case, if anything is excluded from this universal framework of laws, this represents a failure of the lawful order that Kant has proclaimed to be a quasi-divine or rather human world-order, and basically does away with the idea of ordered experience as such. In the same way you should hold fast to one of the motifs of the *Critique of Pure Reason*, one that is commonly not emphasized so strongly. What I have in mind is what might be called 'the fear of chaos', a motif of great importance for the entire grounding of moral philosophy in Kant.[2] So nothing *should* remain outside, there should be nothing that disrupts the total framework of laws. Conversely, however, if such an ultimate cause is not presupposed, then there is no complete causality, but only what Kant called a 'relative', in other words a secondary, causality – I expect you will recall the passage. In that event we offend against the rule that nothing may happen without sufficient reason; in a sense, we break off prematurely, by failing to look for such an ultimate cause. In both cases the error is a failure to satisfy the logic of the principle of causality. In the first instance because the principle claims universal applicability: we are unable to discover an ultimate, absolute cause simply because this would mean suspending the desire for universality itself. The alternative is to decline to assume the existence of such a cause, and act as if there is no such thing as an ultimately accessible cause, but only a secondary cause, so that the concept of causality remains forever unfulfilled. It is important, therefore, and I wish to emphasize it as strongly as I can – you may perhaps regard this as a somewhat formalistic point and be tempted to ignore it – but believe me, I have my reasons for making such a meal of it. What I am concerned about is that you should understand from the outset that the contradiction we are confronted with is not, as Kant would have us believe in the 'Solution', a contradiction that results from our inadequate use of causality, but is, rather, a contradiction that arises because things in the world by their own meaning necessarily become caught up in this contradiction.[3] This is why I have tried to show you the two sides of Kant's argument, so that you can see how on both occasions, that is, by following the logic of the two antinomic theses, or antitheses, you end up violating the meaning of the principle of causality itself. In proceeding like this I have not done violence to Kant in any way, because Kant himself proceeds in exactly the same way as I have just done. That is to say, on both occasions his method makes him confront the meaning inherent in causality itself, and in both cases he shows that you end up violating the meaning of the concept. It is a matter of indifference whether you take your search for causes to the point of infinity, thereby renouncing the search for an ultimate, conclusive cause, or whether you decline to do this and hence break off the search arbitrarily: it is the hypostasis of an absolute cause or an absolute process of causation that leads to such contradictions.

Now Kant believed – and this is the crucial point – that in reality we are simply confronted here by a mistaken usage, that we are applying the concept of causality beyond the limits of possible experience, and that if we were to moderate our demands, and refrain from making such excessive claims, we would not land up in these antinomies. The habit of thinking Kant displays here is one that later on was to become characteristic of Positivism as a whole. Positivists say 'Well, then, if you have to impose such exaggerated demands on knowledge, you will end up in all sorts of difficulties, so it would be better to settle for less right from the start, and content yourselves with your daily bread. Behave from the outset like bureaucrats who refuse to lift a finger to do any work that is outside their department, and you will never come to any great harm.' However, let us assume that what I have told you is correct, and that, as I believe is implicit in the Kantian line of thought, these antinomies actually arise from confronting the application, the possible application, of the category of causality with its meaning. In that event this would show that the rather comfortable construction that Kant puts on the matter – one which tends to stay within the framework of the existing division of labour in the spirit of 'Dwell in the land and lead an upright life'[4] – that this interpretation contradicts the depth of understanding that he has himself achieved at this point.[5] The most powerful support for this interpretation in the text itself is Kant's repeated assertion – perhaps on finding himself driven further by the truth than his system would ideally have liked – that reason necessarily finds itself entangled in such contradictions. There is a subsequent passage, one crucial to his entire practical philosophy, that is, the entire *Critique of Practical Reason*, in which this process of being impelled towards infinity, into the sphere of the intelligible, is actually equated with the realm of the practical.[6] Kant came very close there to an understanding of the problem that I am talking about today, but failed to draw out its full logical implications because of what we might call his architectonic need to keep the two spheres of pure reason and practical reason neatly segregated in different compartments. Instead of reflecting on this contradiction and using it as his starting-point, he left it in place and accepted the existence of two different spheres that were independent of each other in principle. Thus we have two approaches, one in which contradictions are distributed, as it were, in a compartmentalizing spirit, in which they are assigned to two different spheres, and one which confronts the contradictions squarely and attempts through this confrontation to penetrate to the heart of the matter. The difference between them is precisely the contradiction between traditional thinking – or what Hegel calls 'reflexive' thinking [*Reflexionsdenken*] – and dialectical thinking. And when you have succeeded in familiarizing yourselves with the problem that I have been outlining, you will have no difficulty in grasping this. So Kant is concerned to confront the strict meaning of a concept, or perhaps I should rather say, the demand that is implicit in the concept of causality itself, with its consequence – and if a necessary conflict arises then we find ourselves involved in a dialectical process. At this juncture Kant says 'The dialectic arises from an error.'[7] Hegel would say, on the other hand, 'If this dialectic, this conflict, turns out to be inevitable in the sense implied in Kant's argument, then we are not confronted by an error, but by a contradiction in which necessity is itself entailed.'[8] And this means that in reality as well as in the progress of our thinking, contradictions acquire a dignity of a completely different order from what they have in Kant, who remarks in a harmless and naive way, wholly in the spirit of traditional logic: 'Where there is a contradiction, there must be a mistake.'[9] Just as if we had a firm guarantee, as if there were no room for doubt that the world is organized *a priori* in such a way as to be as free of contradictions as the extensional logic that we have simply superimposed on our chaotic and difficult world in order to bring some sort of scientific order into it.

Ladies and Gentlemen, I should like to draw your attention to a further important point. Kant was also poised on the threshold of another problem, one that might be called the problem of the *prima philosophia*, or better, the problem of the very first thing. For as we have seen, he shows both that the assumption of an absolutely first cause leads to contradictions, and conversely, that the problem cannot be resolved by the refusal to make any such assumption. And in so doing, he shows that the concept of any such primal cause itself leads to very great difficulties. On the other hand, however, Kant was a Cartesian in that, like Descartes, he searched for a residue of absolute certainty and at the same time, for a second – free – element[10] that one could hold on to firmly and from which everything else followed. And he did this in preference to drawing the conclusion that is really implicit in the doctrine of the antinomies, namely that the search for any such primal cause might itself be a fallacy.[11] You see here once again the peculiar Janus-face of Kantian philosophy, and you see it moreover at the very source of his practical philosophy. You can see, on the one hand, how he is driven by his own analysis to the realization that giving any such absolute status to the primal thing – whether it be the category of causality or that of the freedom that necessarily precedes it – leads inexorably to contradictions that prove to be insoluble. On the other hand, he nevertheless refuses to relinquish the idea of something absolute and primary.[12] This leads him – and this is why this issue is so important for practical philosophy – by a *coup de main* to establish freedom as a law *sui generis* that then stands absolutely at the beginning, conferring a sort of primacy on practical reason. For you shall learn soon enough that

within the Kantian system there lies hidden a dominant factor that
later on comes to the surface in Fichte in a rather crass fashion.
This is the idea that practical reason, that is, action, is accorded
an absolute priority over theoretical knowledge. Kant finds himself,
therefore – like Hegel, incidentally – in a precarious situation. On the
one hand, thanks to the extraordinary vigour with which he pursues
his philosophy of origins, he comes up against the outer limits of that
philosophy, that is to say, the fact that the concept of the prime mover
is antinomic; while, on the other hand, he clings to the idea while
refusing to follow through the logic of that antinomy. Those of you
who will move on to the study of Hegel will discover that this
contradiction remains intact in Hegel – it is not resolved there either,
but is simply taken over as it stands. For all his dialectic, Hegel
too – just like Kant – accepts something like the dominance of an
absolute prime mover, only in his case it is the infinite subject, Absolute Spirit.[13] We might perhaps consider the issue in more general
terms, by saying that there is a *first thing* as an aspect of the immediate, but really only as an *aspect* – for what has been caused, what
has become, is always mediated precisely through its having become
something, and the *causa* itself is likewise mediated, since the *causa*
can only be the cause in so far as it is the cause of its effect, and not
a cause in general – but this element or moment of immediacy, this
first cause of something given cannot be an immediate given in an
absolute and positive sense. This dialectical consequence is one that
can likewise be inferred from the Kantian doctrine of the antinomies.

Even if we set aside these considerations that I have attempted to
distil from the doctrine of the antinomies, there remains a great
mass of difficulties. These difficulties pertain in the first instance to
the relations between the concepts of causality, law and freedom that
Kant introduces. I believe that most of you will have registered the
difficulties that I have in mind quite simply and straightforwardly by
noting Kant's curious linguistic usage, in particular when he talks of
a special causality, a causality born of freedom [*Kausalität aus Frei-
heit*]. For according to the ideas that we commonly associate with
these concepts, causality means the strict and regular determinacy by
causes; it is the very antithesis of what we normally understand by
freedom. In fact the pivotal issue here – and for any concept of moral
philosophy, not just Kant's – is how to bring these concepts of law
and freedom together. The point to make first – lest you imagine that
Kant's curious treatment of these concepts of freedom, law and causation involves a complete surrender to arbitrary whim and caprice
– is that in Kant the concept of causality is extraordinarily broad. In
the light of developments in the problem of determinism in modern

science, I think it is very important to reflect on this. In the scientific discourse where Kant has formed a starting-point, for example, in the debates about Einstein's relativity theory, and even more strongly in the debate about quantum mechanics, the Kantian concept of causality, Kant's doctrine of causality, has consistently been interpreted in too narrow a sense. In Kant himself the concept of causality is in fact extremely broad. That is to say, his definition is highly formal, and for my part I believe that in the famous debate about relativity theory Ernst Cassirer was not altogether in the wrong when he maintained that thanks to its formal nature Kantian philosophy would be in a position to encompass relativity theory.[14] You will perhaps recall the formula that I read out to you earlier that 'everything *which takes place* presupposes a preceding state upon which it inevitably follows according to a rule'.[15] This phrase 'inevitably follows according to a rule' can only mean that a universal law tells us that if a particular state has the form A, it must be followed by a state with the form B. Kant would be the first to add – and with this we are on strictly Kantian terrain – that 'if that turns out not to work, if something else follows, then we need to search for a further, higher rule that explains why this was not the case'.

What strikes us first about this concept of causality – and I am appealing here to your everyday consciousness, one uncontaminated by philosophy – is a particular kind of externality. By speaking of externality I intend no critical or polemical view of Kant, but am referring to a feature of the *Critique of Pure Reason* that is very pronounced and that has to be understood if we are to understand Kantian philosophy in general. Kant was critical of rationalism of the kind espoused by Leibniz and Wolff because he vigorously opposed the principle of an inner causation – that is, a causation of things or objects in themselves, independently of the subject that confers on them the laws of causality. He launched an extremely sharp critique of the idea that we can know the internal nature of objects and hence their inner determinations in a very important note to the chapter entitled 'The Amphiboly of Concepts of Reflection'.[16] Perhaps you will recollect for a moment that, apart from the dynamic categories, one of the general theses of Kantian philosophy that is known to all of you is that things in themselves are obscure and unknowable by us. We are only able to construct these objects by virtue of our apparatus of categories and the evidence of our senses, in other words, we only construct objects, as it were, from outside and with the assistance of our own consciousness; we cannot enter into them. If you recall this, it will be obvious to you that Kant must likewise reject the idea that we can observe the process of causation or dynamic interaction of objects in themselves. It would probably even be enough to remind ourselves that Kant defined the object as something constructed by us in order to exclude the possibility that we could take these objects that are our own products and of whose inner nature we know nothing and go on and ascribe to them an internal existence of the kind conjectured by the preceding rationalist philosophy. But this very exteriority itself has something unsatisfactory about it because the entirely formal framework of rules is capable of subsuming all sorts of things in itself that may well be wholly incompatible with anything that we might conceive of under the title of causality. It is by no means a bad rule in philosophy that it is inadvisable to give the concepts that you use meanings that are merely derived from your own philosophical system and that are completely different from those in use in everyday speech and which the reader has in a sense a right to expect. So in the spirit of such a set of rules, if we ignore the chronological sequence of cause and effect, the statistical regularity found in quantum mechanics today would come within the scope of Kantian causality just as well as anything else.[17] But of course it would do so at the cost of what we all understand by causality. The answer to this on the part of the progressive sciences is simply that our minds have not advanced beyond the level of mythology, that in our everyday consciousness we are lagging behind the stage reached by scientific criticism and that we are still operating with a basically animistic conception according to which things have an inner soul and an inward determinacy, conceptions which have ceased to be tenable now that the concepts of knowledge have been filtered as they have in philosophical criticism. This so-called external nature of causality, which incidentally is something that the whole of later scientific thought and the whole of Positivism shares with Kant, and which, as in Hume, has been taken incomparably further than it was by Kant himself, arises from the fact that causality does not reside in things in themselves. It is, rather, an ordering principle according to which the subject combines successive states with each other.[18] This means then that causality has nothing to do with the explanation of motivation, which sets out to further our understanding of successive events from within. It aims to achieve this on the basis of our inward awareness in which subject and object, that is, our experience of ourselves and we ourselves as the thing we experience, coincide, or are supposed to coincide so that the problem of the opposition between inner and outer disappears. In consequence of this – and this is a motif that was brought up in criticism of Kant, particularly by Schopenhauer[19] – it was claimed that there was a special form of causality that Kant had really ignored, namely a causality from within, and this was in fact what motivation was.[20] However, in Kant – and this is why I have made so much of the remarkable breadth of the term 'causality' – the concept of causality, that is, this sequence of states in accordance with rules, is broad enough to leave room for something we can call motivation. This remains true even without taking any such coincidence of inner and outer into account. That is to say, there is space for subjective certainty or immediate certainty to explain why two states should follow on from one another. Why this should be the case is not a matter that Kant reflects on, but he does draw certain inferences from it nevertheless. For example, he says that causality has a number of possibilities – we might put it in scientific terms, and say that there is a special case of causality in which the kind of externality of which I have told you does not exist, but that instead there is a kind of causality in which we can instigate a series of events linked by cause and effect from within our own consciousness. What Kant has in mind here – he does not say so explicitly, but there is no doubt about what he meant – is simply the basic fact of some decision or other.[21] I may remind you of the hapless book that from time to time I have dropped on the table and by means of which I intervene on my own initiative, beginning a new causal series into which a kind of caesura is inserted at this juncture. I am trying to express myself very cautiously here[22] for in this very difficult grey area, Kant himself expressed himself anything but clearly, and for the very good reason that it is very hard to be clear about it. So Kant obviously assumed that within the framework of this universal causality there is something like a point at which the subject may intervene and from which it may set the primary conditions for an entire causal series. He believed, further, that within this realm of practice, of practical action, the point at which this new causal series begins could be specified. For this reason he thought that we can speak of something like an exceptional situation in the realm of practice, that is to say, in the motivated behaviour of human beings. Now Kant was an extraordinarily honest man and just as sharp in his thinking as he was honest, and he by no means overlooked the question that is on the tip of your tongues at this point. This concerns the fact that an action initiated in freedom, in which I independently intervene in something, thereby enters for its part into a new causal chain. So if I may come back once again to this idiotic example of dropping a book, this is in the first instance my own free decision. But it may at the same time be regarded as the product of a whole series of other events. For example, I find myself under the necessity of demonstrating to you this phenomenon of a so-called free act, and have nothing else to hand but this accursed book. So I drop it and this can in its turn be referred back to all sorts of other things such as the internalization of the concept of duty and God knows what else – so what I want to say is that major factors and trivial ones are all tied into each other in the strangest way.

Kant would not deny any of this and there is a passage – we shall look at it closely – in which Kant readily concedes that so-called free actions are themselves subject to universal determination.[23] But Kant's way of dealing with this question, and indeed with a number of other, analogous questions elsewhere in his philosophy, is to proceed phenomenologically, to use a term that came into being very much later. What that means is that he is not concerned to make a final, definitive statement about the nature of such an action – in this respect, too, we might say that he would cultivate a certain externality. But instead what concerns him is that at this particular moment I have this particular experience: *I* can drop the object *now*; that is an immediately given reality – and it is quite different from my turning a tap on and as long as it is on the water pours out. No matter how we may think of these two events within the total or universal network of causality, there is a real distinction at the level of personal experience. So there is in Kant – I have already said this, and perhaps you can see here why it is so important for an understanding of his philosophy – something over and above the systematic impulse, the desire to construct as coherent an overall totality out of discrete units as is possible. There is in addition, and you come across it in all sorts of places, this respect for given realities – for everything that cannot be inferred from something else. In fact, in his practical philosophy he treats freedom, or rather its supreme principle, the moral law – which demands nothing other than that I act purely in accordance with reason – as such a given. He treats it as something that in a sense cannot be inferred from anything else, simply because it is identical with the very same principle of reason which alone would be capable of drawing such an inference. Ladies and Gentlemen, the reason why I attach such great importance to explaining these rather complicated matters to you here is that they really are important if we are to lay the foundation for a moral philosophy. This is because my affirmation of the principle of freedom would achieve precious little in practice if we simply persisted with the assertion that in an absolute sense something like freedom exists, but as soon as I enter the limited realm of experience, the finite sphere of experience, I find it under the domination of causality and there is no freedom in sight. For practice is always the practice of empirical human beings and it pertains to things given in empirical reality.

Here, too, Kant finds himself caught up in a certain contradiction. On the one hand, he has strictly to maintain the distinction between the intelligible and the empirical. For the fact is that if he were to tie the intelligible or absolute to empirical conditions, it would be at the cost of its absolute character and its absolute authority. But on the other hand, if these two spheres are absolutely separate and have nothing in common with each other – and indeed this seems to be what Kant is saying elsewhere – then it would be quite impossible to speak of any morality and any such distinctions between right and wrong behaviour. This is because everything that pertains to real action would simply become part of the empirical chain of cause and effect. For this reason Kant has to conduct a desperate search for something like a realm in which the two coexist – I won't say simultaneously, but a realm in which I am justified in speaking of the given nature of what would be inconceivable simply as a given within our experience because it is something infinite, something that transcends the boundaries of possible experience. What we are referring to here is simply that possibility of initiating a causal series in some sense or other. I am telling you this – and shall then explicate it in connection with the relevant chapters of the *Critique of Pure Reason* – because in the fully developed practical philosophy of Kant this has the very great consequence that it results in a very curious theory that we shall have to look at more closely. This is the idea that while it is true that all my actions are conditioned by my character from which they necessarily flow, this character is one that I give myself through a free act.[24] The only possible meaning that can be given to this free act is what I am tempted to call the purely epistemological one that as human beings we are able to initiate causal series which are not automatically included in the universal network of causality. In the light of our empirical knowledge today about the considerable importance of early childhood experiences for the conditioning and formation of our character, it is evident that the theory that I am supposed to have conferred my character on myself will encounter the very greatest difficulties. But that is not something we can consider here. What I wanted to show you here is, firstly, why Kant arrives at this construct of a causality born of freedom and, secondly, how he gets into difficulty as a consequence and sets about seeking a solution.

Let me close by reminding you briefly why he insists on a causality born of freedom. We could start by saying: 'Well then, he wants causality because on the basis of the doctrine of categories, causality is a universal law to which absolutely everything is subject and which tolerates no exceptions; and he wants freedom because without freedom there would not really be anything like reason and

humanity.' But this account is too superficial. What lies behind it –
and this is hinted at in a passage in the doctrine of the antinomies
that I shall perhaps discuss briefly in the next lecture – is the idea
that behaviour that is quite devoid of causality and is therefore
absolutely free, in other words, behaviour without any rules at all,
would be simply chaotic. In that event an amorphous, unformed
nature would in fact triumph over the principle of reason to which
Kant quite unambiguously confides the task of resisting that same
chaotic disorder of nature in a number of passages in the *Critique of
Judgement*. On the other hand, if the law is universal, then this puts
an end to the possibility of anything higher than nature. That means
in its turn that human beings are nothing but a piece of this blind
nature and are unable to escape from it. Therefore, reason requires
something like a universal conformity to law, because only if there is
such a conformity to law can reason resist this blind, amorphous
force. By the same token it requires freedom because in the face
of the amorphousness of nature freedom is the only possible
countervailing force. This twofold difficulty, the fact that the sphere
of the human can exist neither in absolute conformity to law, nor in
absolute freedom, is the true and profound reason why Kant finds
himself forced into this paradoxical construct of a causality born of
freedom.[25] Thank you.

LECTURE SIX

30 May 1963

Ladies and Gentlemen,

I must start with an announcement. I shall have to cancel the lecture in two weeks' time because I am taking part in the Europa Symposium in Vienna.[1] There will be no lecture the following Thursday anyway because of the holiday on Corpus Christi, so we shall next meet in three weeks' time.

I should like to begin by summarizing some of the things I may have said a little too hurriedly at the end of the last lecture, and shall then use the rest of the lecture to take a relatively close look at Kant's text in order to say a few things about the relation between theoretical and practical philosophy in Kant. The first point, then, is that I should remind you that the difficulties we have been experiencing with Kant's doctrine of the antinomies can be traced back to the fact that Kant's philosophy has a dual character. On the one hand, there is a critical strand of thought, that is, the dissolution of dogmatic ideas that had simply been handed down and that he overcomes by recourse to a constitutive subjectivity. At the same time he sets limits by establishing that the knowledge the naive consciousness tends to think of as the knowledge of things is in reality knowledge that arises merely in the subjective mind and cannot therefore be said to be the direct knowledge of existence. On the other hand, opposed to this and at least as powerful, there is the other strand of thought according to which he would like to try to salvage the objective character of thought through this subjective analysis. Moreover, he aims to go even further than this since he strives to rescue what before him was known as ontology, and what we are again inclined to call ontology today. And he hopes to rescue it in a particular sphere, namely the sphere of the intelligible – and this means for him the sphere of morality or freedom. This dual character is what actually motivates the strange attitude that Kant adopts towards the problem of freedom. If we assert that the doctrine of causality and freedom in the *Critique of Pure Reason* has been presented in an 'antinomic' manner, we do not entirely do justice to the situation, since the final result of the analysis of the third antinomy does not take the form: it can be like this or it can be like that. Instead, given the general thrust of the analysis in the *Critique of Pure Reason*, the situation is rather that the discussion of freedom and conditioning is broken off. It is as if Kant were asserting that for me to put the question in those terms is itself to make an error that prevents further progress. The implication is that if I am debarred from putting the question, I shall remain trapped in the empirical realm in which causality rules, and that the only claim I may not make on behalf of this causality is that it is absolutely valid in the realm of empirical objects. Notwithstanding this, in the *Critique of Pure Reason*, at least in the doctrine of the antinomies, the crucial decision was really made in favour of causality, in the spirit of the theoretical use of reason – only with the caveats we have already discussed.[2] In contrast to that, the other side – what we can call the ontological side, or perhaps the preserving, salvaging side of Kant, or indeed the side that opposes the universal scepticism of a consistent nominalism – is expressed in a teaching that does not actually occur in the doctrine of the antinomies in this form. This is the doctrine that the moral sphere is in principle separate from that of knowledge and, positively, that it is the sphere of freedom. Or as Kant himself phrases it in a very prominent passage, 'in the realm of morality freedom is a fact of experience'.[3] I tried to show you last time what meaning can be given to this strange thesis about the experience of freedom, when we set out to examine aspects of the concept of motivation and the dual character of law. But at any rate we can summarize once more the meaning of the doctrine of the third antinomy, the antinomy of causality and freedom. If causality rules absolutely, if, in other words, there is nothing but the law of cause and effect, this would make an absolute of the laws imposed by human beings on the things in themselves of which they actually know nothing, that is, of everything that is needed to control nature, both human and extra-human. This would confer on that absolute the same quality of blindness and externality which, as I explained to you last time, is characteristic of causality in nature and knowledge in terms of the categories as developed in the spirit of Kant. The domination of nature – and we might well say, as blind domination it means mere nature – would itself become an absolute.[4] If, on the other hand, there were nothing but freedom, or as Kant puts it, 'freedom without guidance', without a law that could organize the phenomenal world, it would be a form of freedom that is quite devoid of any element of law, and hence it too would signify a relapse into a mere state of nature, namely into the natural chaos of a purely arbitrary state of affairs. It is interesting to note that on the one hand, in his critique of the consequences that the doctrine of absolute freedom would have, Kant uses the same expression 'blind' that he also used when he was speaking of the exclusive dominance of causality.[5] His philosophy as a whole is opposed to both. It is opposed to the making absolute of the mechanical principle – and the critique of this making absolute of the mechanical principle forms the essential content of the *Critique of Judgement*; and it is no less opposed, on the other hand, to the amorphous, accidental and arbitrary. For his part Kant never deviates for a single second from his conviction that the unity to be discovered in our reason must also be ascribed to things in themselves, if those things are to be otherwise than truly chaotic, a relapse into utter blindness and disorder. I do not wish to discuss here the idea that the unity imposed on the world by the organization of the rational logos must necessarily also constitute a determination of the world itself. But it does appear to me that at this point there is a crucial fallacy in the Kantian philosophy itself, one which had a calamitous influence throughout the whole of post-Kantian philosophy. It arises because the category of absolute unity was hypostatized and conflated with the absolute. And this was something against which the most significant and the most free-spirited of the German idealists made the most energetic protests – what I have in mind here above all is what might be called the philosophical substance of Hölderlin's thinking. He, foremost among others, interpreted this idea of the absolute nature of the One and of unity in such a way as to insist that the true unity was the reconciliation of the many, and not a mere identity which came into existence by riding roughshod over the many of which it is composed.[6] This inflection of thought is self-evidently of the very greatest significance for moral philosophy because it leads beyond the pervasive theme in Kant and Fichte that reality is nothing but the raw material for realizing the unity of a merely human reason. But for the moment I do not wish to pursue the very far-reaching implications of this idea for moral philosophy any further.

The Kantian construct at any rate is, as you can perhaps recognize, a construct created from its *terminus ad quem*, that is to say, the entire doctrine of the antinomies is designed to bring together the idea of conformity to law and unity on the one hand, and freedom on the other. Moving on from the attempt to prove this basically self-contradictory thesis, we can explain the signs of the further contradictions to which the doctrine of causality and freedom lead, although at the same time we cannot but acknowledge the fact that Kant's greatness manifests itself in the completely frank and open way in which he makes these contradictions explicit. I have said that this dialectic is not just a dialectic which exposes our false use of reason, but a dialectic inherent in the situation itself. We can see this plainly in one of the later chapters of the *Critique of Pure Reason* that I would like to discuss in some detail, partly because its fundamental significance for Kant's grounding of his moral philosophy has been extraordinarily underestimated. It is to be found in the '[Transcendental] Doctrine of Method', and the chapter bears the title 'The Canon of Pure Reason'. This entire second part of the *Critique of Pure Reason* is in general far too little studied; the relevant section here is entitled 'The Ultimate End of the Pure Employment of Our Reason' [ch. II, § 1, pp. 630–4]. This doctrine of the ultimate end of pure reason makes a major contribution to the doctrine of contradiction and our understanding of the contradiction with which we were concerned in the previous lectures because the ultimate end of the pure employment of our reason turns out to be practice, action, and not theoretical knowledge or what Kant consistently refers to in this section as 'speculation'.[7] This is how the strange and genuinely contradictory element arises, even more contradictory than the contradictions of the doctrine of the antinomies. In the spirit of the doctrine of the antinomies we can say that causality triumphs, because in the realm of experience we can only think causally – because once we go beyond the realm of experience we end up in insoluble contradictions, regardless of whether we affirm causality or deny it. Whereas here, from the standpoint of the primacy of practice, the triumph of freedom, if you will allow me this strategic trope of speech, gazes out at us in an equally unambiguous way. We can say, therefore, that while Kant criticizes the antinomies of pure reason, the necessity of these antinomies becomes manifest in the Kantian theory itself. It does this because his own philosophy amounts to the statement that in the realm of theory causality is dominant, while in the practical realm only freedom counts. The contradiction this implies is never resolved other than in a remote and vague hypothesis. So we have the situation that the antinomies that result merely from the false use of our reason have seemingly been resolved to everyone's satisfaction, but they then turn out to have the last word since each side of the antinomy reappears in the very constitution of the two principal spheres of philosophy, namely in theoretical and practical philosophy.

So much by way of introduction. I would like to pass on now to this chapter in the 'Doctrine of Method'. Kant speaks here of 'the ultimate end of the employment of our reason'. He says:

> Reason is impelled by a tendency of its nature to go out beyond the field of its empirical employment, and to venture in a pure employment, by means of ideas alone, to the utmost limits of all knowledge, and not to be satisfied save through the completion of its course in [the apprehension of] a self-subsistent systematic whole.[8]

When we read here in Kant of the 'tendency of its nature', if we understand correctly the concept of nature as Kant borrowed it from the eighteenth century as a whole, and especially from Rousseau, we realize that it means more than something psychological – more than the idea that our 'nature' is such that we ourselves impel our reason to the point of the absolute. Instead, 'nature' here has to be taken in its strict sense to mean that reason is impelled by its own essence to go beyond the possible limits of experience. This thought, Ladies and Gentlemen, is in fact extraordinarily plausible and extraordinarily illuminating. If you cast your minds back to Kant's treatment of the third antinomy, you will recollect that it amounts to breaking off the argument that would run on into infinity. It is, if we can put it idiomatically, in a way Kant himself did not scorn to express himself on such occasions, it is a little as if he were to say to reason – in a laconic way, this is an aspect of bourgeois thrift – 'Dwell in the land and lead an upright life' and 'Don't incur any excessive expense, otherwise you will run up debts that you are unable to pay off and you will end up in bankruptcy.' However, there is something unsatisfactory about restricting the argument in this way because there is a sense in which it runs counter to reason. Breaking off the rational line of argument is incompatible with the requirement of reason that it should be allowed to run its course, that it should not be suspended by any external factor. This is the case because the corollary of reason is the idea of truth. Reason is essentially the embodiment of consciousness which has truth as its goal – or so we might define it. If it is interrupted, broken off, suspended, and if it is told that it has to surrender its own true purpose: the search for truth, then reason is prevented by pure rationality, in order to make it see reason, from satisfying the requirements of its own nature. In fact that is precisely what happens in the doctrine of the antinomies, and if that doctrine is not entirely satisfactory, and if Kant goes on to consider the sort of arguments we have been examining, then underlying this is the recollection that any such arbitrary interruption, any obstacle blocking[9] the path of the search for truth, really is incompatible with the concept of reason for which the idea of truth is an absolute. This is why, Ladies and Gentlemen, I believe that Kant's frequent repetition of such phrases as 'the tendency of nature' or the 'contradictions in which reason is caught up' have to be taken extremely seriously. That is to say, this interruption of the progress of reason that Kant is calling for is just as hard to reconcile with reason as its unrestricted progress, and leads just as certainly to contradictions, as he has so plausibly argued. I believe that it is only when we examine this other side of the entire problem of the antinomies that we properly understand what is actually at stake here.

He speaks here, without comment, of the 'speculative interest' of reason, when it is really a matter of a theoretical interest, although we may say of his terminology that he always calls theoretical reason 'speculative' when it goes beyond the realms of possibility, when it is used transcendentally. This means that the concept of the speculative has for him pejorative, contemptuous overtones, whereas his successors reinstate it – and perhaps you will be able to understand why. It is because they realized, Fichte and Hegel, that the self-limitation that Kant here expects from reason, is actually incompatible with its own concept. He goes on to say that he wishes 'to leave aside . . . the success which attends pure reason in its speculative exercise', that is, in its reference to transcendental ideas, and sets out instead to enquire whether or not these ultimate concepts: God, the freedom of the will and the immortality of the soul, have any theoretical interest at all. He formulates the issue as follows, and this may perhaps give you some idea of what I meant earlier on by the hypostatization of unity in Kant:

> I shall, for the moment, leave aside all question as to the success which attends pure reason in its speculative exercise, and enquire only as to the problems the solution of which constitutes its ultimate aim, whether reached or not, and in respect of which all other aims are to be regarded only as means.[10]

He goes on to make an astonishing statement that he completely fails to follow up:

> These highest aims must, from the nature of reason, have a certain unity, in order that they may, as thus unified, further that interest of humanity which is subordinate to no higher interest.[11]

You can see that here he takes the principle of unity that is inherent in reason and hence lies on the subjective side of things, and transfers it to the outside world in the form of a postulate about the absolute. In other words, we are looking here at something like a unified world order based on the unified will of a creator. In a sense this is the suture joining Kantian philosophy and the Christian theology which in fact comes to permeate the closing sections of the *Critique of Practical Reason*. He says then that the final result of speculation concerns 'three objects – freedom of the will, the immortality of the soul and the existence of God' – and he adds the very remarkable consequence of this that I should like to read you now:

> In respect of all three the merely speculative interest of reason is very small; and for its sake alone we should hardly have undertaken the labour of transcendental investigation – a labour so fatiguing in its endless wrestling with insuperable difficulties – since whatever discoveries might be made in regard to these matters, we should not be able to make use of them in any helpful manner *in concreto*, that is, in the study of nature.[12]

This passage is so very remarkable because it introduces into Kantian philosophy, at least into his theoretical philosophy, a highly unusual pragmatic tone that is perhaps the last thing we might expect to encounter in Kant, although it may be more explicable when we recollect that the *Critique of Pure Reason* is preceded by a motto from Bacon, from whom we would sooner expect to hear sentiments of the kind I have just read out to you. Nevertheless, this is the situation: Kant defines the realm of theory in the *Critique of Pure Reason* as that of theoretical physics and mathematics, in other words, the mathematical sciences as a whole. It is a little paradoxical that this sphere should turn out to be synonymous with practice in the somewhat narrower and more restricted sense, we might almost say the more philistine sense that prompts such questions as 'What's the use of that?', 'What can I do with that?' or 'How can this take me any further in the technique of mastering nature?' For this is very much in the spirit of the empirical sciences and the ways in which the possibilities of controlling nature are defined in Bacon's *Novum Organum*, a work which I recommend that you should inform yourselves about. These two concepts of practicism and the domination of nature converge here to the point where – and here we see the paradox emerging clearly – it is theoretical reason in its preoccupation with the knowledge of nature that is linked in a particular sense in Kant's philosophy to the measuring-rod of practice. The sense in which this is true is indicated by such questions as 'What's the use of that?', 'How does this take me any further?', 'What do I get out of the whole thing?' In my opinion, it is very beneficial for us to distance ourselves from Kant sufficiently to obtain a clear view of such consequences and to see that they lead him to make an extremely remarkable statement, one that is really quite astounding. He says in effect: 'Very well, then, the existence of God, the possibility of immortality and the freedom of the will – since I can do nothing with these things in the world of experience, they can be a matter of perfect indifference to me.' This view of things completely ignores the fact that if death is the ultimate reality, if there is nothing but the brief life that we have, and if we surrender entirely to a blind principle, or rather a non-principle, a dead end, then our lives are exposed to a degree of meaninglessness of which modern philosophy, even in its less rigorous variants, has made an all too liberal and all too popular use. What I mean to say is that my inability to make any sense of God, freedom and immortality, cannot blind us to the fact, Ladies and Gentlemen, that our entire life, every moment we are alive, assumes a very different complexion depending on whether or not this is all there is. It is barely comprehensible that a thinker of Kant's insight into metaphysics should have simply ignored this basic reality, while the wicked, anti-moral and anti-Christian Nietzsche should have drawn attention to it with his assertion 'But all joy wants eternity'.[13] In other words, Nietzsche was aware of the crucial insight that what happens in the world is dependent on immortality – if I may express it like this – and conversely, we might add, the theory of such ideas is bound up with what we experience here. But this is really the heart of this Kantian line of argument, namely the belief that these ideas are a matter of indifference to us because we cannot do anything with them in terms of our knowledge of nature or the domination of nature. Hence we find in Kant only the sphere of the knowledge of nature, in the sense of an unrestrained pragmatism which asks 'What can I do with this?', on the one hand; while, on the other, there is the sphere of morality which is a sphere in which the laws of reason hold absolute sway. But these two spheres are so far apart from each other that, thanks to this split, even genuinely simple and urgent questions like the ones I have just told you about sink without trace as if into a pit, and are lost to view.

Ladies and Gentlemen, many of you may have already have come to philosophy with the expectation and hope that you would discover answers to such questions as 'Is that everything, then?' or 'What will come next?' – questions which Kant has dismissed as irrelevant for theory. These hopes have now been dashed. I shall not be so bold as

to offer you anything better, but I can at least show you at this point
the mechanism that has led to this disappointment. It is that even in
Kant – who is one of the thinkers from whom you can rightly expect
the very greatest things – this strange division into pure practice and
pure natural science, which is conceived as the pure domination of
nature, spirits away these matters of essential interest: he simply does
not perceive them and even says explicitly: 'God, in so far as we are
thinking about theory, is of no concern to us; but as far as our
practical behaviour goes, well, we do need Him there as a working
hypothesis.' However, on the question of our practical behaviour we
are no longer concerned with knowledge, but only, as he remarks
later on, with the question 'What shall we do?' This has the consequence that at the very point where we are faced with the most crucial
interest of reason conceivable, the system of philosophy he has constructed leaves us high and dry. If you wish to complain about philosophy, and you may be justified in so doing, you can at least perhaps
see what motives and mechanisms within philosophy itself – and after
all, Kant and Hegel *are* philosophy – have led to this disappointing
outcome. This is why I have dwelt on this point at such length, for
it is one thing to be naively disappointed, and quite another to reflect
on the reasons for this disappointment and to achieve a critical understanding of why philosophy should, to remain within the figure of
speech, give us stones rather than bread. Kant speaks wholly in the
spirit of scientific determinism when he says 'The will may well be
free' – which means 'if the will be free' – 'this can have a bearing
only on the intelligible cause of our volition.'[14] And here, as we have
argued at length, 'the intelligible cause of our volition' is incompatible with the concept of freedom.

> For as regards the phenomena of its outward expressions, that is, of
> our actions, we must account for them – in accordance with a maxim
> which is inviolable, and which is so fundamental that without it we
> should not be able to employ reason in any empirical manner what-
> soever – in the same manner as all other appearances of nature, namely,
> in conformity with unchangeable laws.[15]

I should like to add to this, Ladies and Gentlemen. The structure
of the argument that Kant produces at this point seems to me to
contain a mechanistic element. It is as if he were saying 'All right,
then, let us suppose that I introduce the element of freedom somewhere or other, whether in an original free action on the part of the
intelligible character, or in the original free postulating of God. But
even if I do this, the principle of causality remains utterly intact for
the entire realm of experience.' Now, if it is really true that the prin-

ciple of causality can lay claim to the universality Kant ascribes to it, we might well enquire at this point whether the whole system must not come crashing down if we are forced to concede the existence of the minutest gap, the smallest exception. Because if there is just the tiniest amount of freedom, just a little corner, then this must mean that the entire business of a chain of cause and effect has a hole in it and in that case I can no longer ascribe universality to it. For in that event it is quite unclear why there should not be an element of freedom in countless other places. But this question, that certainly seems on the face of it to be a question of knowledge, or, as Kant calls it, of speculation, is simply swept under the table, when he remarks 'Causality remains in force in the realm of experience, even if somewhere – in far-off Turkey, where nations come to blows – in the realm of the absolute there is an element of freedom.'[16] Well, modern science appears at this point to have paid Kant back in full for his strange procedure, by proving to him that in the realm of our progressive understanding of nature, in other words, precisely at the point where he supposed the laws of cause and effect to be absolutely inviolable, this concept of universal causality no longer holds good in the traditional manner.

I have now told you a certain amount about the attitude of indifference that characterizes the speculative interest according to Kant; and I have also said that no matter how we act, nothing is more important for us than those ideas which Kant claims are *only* of significance for our actions. In certain circumstances, for example, they may prevent us from taking any action at all, and the concept of action may fall by the wayside, as is the case with monks of various kinds, with quietist movements, or else with Schopenhauer's philosophy. So these are ideas that can no longer be sustained. Kant then goes on to say: 'If, again, we should be able to obtain insight into the spiritual nature of the soul' – while in the chapter on paralogisms in the *Critique of Pure Reason* this was the very thing he had doubted – 'we could make no use of such insight in explaining [. . .] the appearances of this present life [. . .]'.[17] So no particular inference could be drawn from this because, in so far as the soul is the object of our knowledge and therefore a part of the world in space and time and bound up with the world in space and time, it cannot be thought of as an absolute. Now, we might well say that there is a vast difference, even for theoretical propositions about the possibility of immortality, between saying, on the one hand, that the very idea of the soul is a mere idea, a hypostasis, that we merely assign an absolute status to the synthesizing of phenomena in conceptual form, and, on the other hand, asserting that such a synthesis is the necessary precondition of the plurality of souls. In other words, these so-called metaphysical questions are crucially dependent on the theoretical definition of the term 'soul'. And the attitude of indifference that Kant supposes to exist between these ideas and theory, an indifference felt on both sides of the equation, is anything but dominant.

Finally, he says in connection with God that we can indeed take the idea of 'a supreme intelligence', as he somewhat coyly terms it, from which we would be able to 'render what is purposive in the constitution and ordering of the world comprehensible in a general sort of way, but we should not be in the least warranted in deriving from it any particular arrangement or disposition, or in boldly inferring any such, where it is not perceived'.[18] Now this third assumption makes a legitimate critical point, but it is one we can set aside here, since it is really aimed at a very limited form of rationalism of the kind that was formulated in the so-called Wolffian philosophy, that is, in the systematic adaptation of Leibnizian rationalism for pedagogic purposes. In Wolff the premise of a central monad and a supreme intelligence was used in a direct, naive and narrow-minded way to show how all sorts of natural phenomena were purposively arranged for the convenience of human beings. Thus Wolff actually states that 'the moon shines at night in order that men should not find everything so dark'.[19] So it is obviously illuminating and plausible to find such ideas repudiated here, but it has no bearing on the question of whether the existence of God has any relevance for theoretical reason.

Once again, it is necessary for you to think of what has happened here from its own *terminus ad quem*. For this entire, really rather strange line of argument with its dallying over genuine abysses can really only be explained by pointing out that what he wants to say, come hell or high water, is that these three cardinal terms – the existence of God, freedom and immortality – are not necessary for our knowledge, that is, in theory. In other words he wishes to assert that they do not need to interest us in theory, but at the same time 'they are strongly recommended by our reason', and therefore he states that 'their importance, properly regarded, must concern only the *practical*'.[20] And with that we have reached one of the pivotal points of Kantian philosophy in general. This concerns the so-called metaphysical ideas which he cannot salvage for theory, nor can he accept that they have a constitutive importance for theory. Instead he introduces them simply and solely because they are postulates of practical reason. This means that according to the Kantian doctrine the moral law is given to me, it is a fact; experience teaches me that I

should act morally. But lest this experience lead me into inconsisten-
cies, it also contains the implication that I should reckon with the
existence of these metaphysical entities so that – and this is one of
the great paradoxes of Kantian philosophy – I cannot act freely for
the sake of the existence of God, but that God exists only in order
that I should act freely.[21] This relationship has been completely
inverted, and in consequence practice has gained the absolute priority. That is the actual justification for the thesis that I have developed
here, namely the idea that in the philosophy of Kant practice has
priority over theory. But we can continue this discussion in the next
lecture. Thank you for your attention and I hope you have an enjoyable holiday.

LECTURE SEVEN

18 June 1963

Dear Colleagues,

I hope that we shall now be able reach the end of this semester in a very concentrated way without further interruptions. I shall certainly do my utmost in this respect, now that the Whitsun holidays are behind us, and even though I was forced by a prior commitment of long standing to cancel one hour, to my very great regret.[1] I think the best way to pick up the threads of our previous argument without regurgitating the whole thing once again, would be for me to use this hour to explain again – or rather not again, but in principle – the structure of Kant's moral philosophy in the sense that I wish to give it here, and to do so in conjunction with the text from the 'Doctrine of Method' that we have begun to interpret, but without making much progress up to now. So I want to kill two birds with one stone, and both reiterate what we have said from the point of view we have been unfolding and at the same time take the argument a few steps further. I should like to remind you, then, that the three cardinal propositions that Kant regards as the cardinal propositions of ethics are those that maintain the existence of freedom of the will, the immortality of the soul and the existence of God. According to Kant, these three propositions have their decisive meaning not in theoretical philosophy, in other words, not in our knowledge of what is the case, but in practical philosophy. This means that, following the Kantian theory, they are strictly, necessarily bound up with the question 'What shall we do?' and can really only be understood and explained in connection with what we should do. Last time I explained in some detail that the separation of this question from the realm of theory seemed to me to do violence to the problem, that is to say, Kant's disclaimer that theory has no interest in these propositions does not seem to be entirely convincing. For if anything matters to a man in his own life, aside from his actions, then it must be the question whether or not everything comes to an end with his death. I do not wish to repeat this entire complex of arguments here, but would just like to remind you that I criticized this distinction in the last lecture, or one of the earlier lectures. Kant says, as you will recollect, that the theoretical interest in these propositions is very slight. I should like now to attempt to interpret Kant's argument in a perhaps more faithful sense than I did in the last lecture. His claim that the theoretical or speculative interest in these cardinal propositions is slight may possibly be interpreted to mean that there is no real connection between these propositions and our scientific experience together with the foundations of our scientific experience. The question of interest relates simply to the idea that these propositions fall outside the framework of theoretical knowledge, and that it is in fact a matter of indifference to us what their status is. What Kant's way of formulating the matter leads to can indeed be linked to the general tenor of Kantian philosophy, and specifically, with the priority he gives to practice. In such a context knowledge that has no consequences may well appear nugatory. But it is probable that Kant would not have spoken quite so insistently on this point as I did last time and that all he meant was that theoretical reason, that is, our knowledge of nature, has no great interest in those propositions because it could not hope to provide a proper explanation of them. There is something in Kant's philosophy that intimates to us that the ideas that we have been discussing are matters that we should not concern ourselves about, that it cannot be in our interest to pursue questions that appear insoluble from the outset in the sphere to which we have assigned them. I regard this line of thought as highly problematic. In the course of the development of modern philosophy it is this line of thought that has increasingly led to the elimination of those questions worthy of human beings, the questions that have led people to philosophy in the first place. And while in this way what we might call the process of converting philosophy into a science has advanced inexorably, philosophy itself has increasingly declined in 'interest', to use Kant's term, that is, it refuses increasingly to make any statement or judgement on those matters about which we expect philosophy to have something to say. Now this rejection of the three crucial propositions, the three cardinal propositions, relates both to experience itself and to the constitutive forms that organize it. In other words, according to Kant, we can neither obtain any answer to these questions from our experience, nor do they really enter effectively into the apparatus of our categories, that is, the preconditions in whose absence it would not be possible for us to experience anything at all.

This in its turn brings a particular difficulty in its wake. This is the difficulty that our practical philosophy cannot really be separated from experience in any absolute way because it is related to our actual actions, which are inevitably concerned with the material of experience. You will all of you have the obvious riposte on your lips: 'Of course, if anything at all is connected with experience, it must surely be whatever has to do with my own actions.' And you are all aware that in the realm of ordinary behaviour we are accustomed to talk about our experience, for example, when we make distinctions between good and evil. That is to say, if you are inexperienced, as it is called, you may do all sorts of things that turn out to be highly dubious, whereas convention would have it that if you are experienced and able to grasp a situation as a whole, you ought to be in a better position to act rightly – including in a higher sense. I need not enter into a discussion about whether or not there is any truth in this piece of popular wisdom. I would only point out to you that here as elsewhere the rationale of moral philosophy in Kant does make formidable demands upon us. Kant, however, would be opposed to this entire line of argument. Nevertheless, we could well imagine that just as there is such a thing as the form and content of knowledge – a distinction Kant makes – so too there could well be form and content in the realm of practice. That is to say, I cannot imagine any action that does not, by the very fact of becoming an action, relate in some way or other to empirically existing beings, be they things or people. I mean to say that even the noblest, most sublime action is only possible because, in becoming the sacrifice of the man who carries it out, it presupposes his sacrifice as an actual empirical person; and the very worst action involves empirical realities in the same way. Thus if someone wishes to commit a murder he needs firstly a person he can kill, and secondly some such implement as a hammer with which to carry out the deed. So the separation of form and content, this absolute separation, seems to be just as problematic in the realm of practice as it is in that of theory, where, according to Kant, the forms of knowledge only retain their validity to the extent that they relate to the material of experience, to living sensation. To put it rather less loosely and irresponsibly than I have just done, action has both a form and a content. We can speak of the form and content of moral action in the much weightier sense that here too there is a distinction between universal rules, the universal norms in accordance with which we act, however problematic they may be, and the specific action that results and that then, precisely because it is a specific action, necessarily entails the principle of individuation, that is, it includes some concrete element of the material of experience. If this is correct, then the distinction Kant makes between speculative or theoretical interest and practical interest is by no means so radical. In this connection it is perhaps worthwhile my reminding you that he could only arrive at this radical distinction because he had once decided come hell or high water to deny any theoretical interest in these cardinal propositions. It is always valuable to be able to construct such aporetical situations, that is, to clarify for oneself what difficulties there are, on the one hand, and to discover the *thema probandum*, on the other, that is to say, what Kant actually wished to demonstrate. I believe that after these brief remarks you will have understood both.

What is at issue here is the way in which Kant extricates himself from this entire situation when he talks of practice – and you must recollect that when Kant speaks of a critique of practical reason he has a very definite and highly tendentious idea of practice in mind. Practical reason in Kant always means practical *pure* reason, in other words, the *a priori* ability to distinguish between right and wrong, good and evil, and not what we mean when we say of someone that he is a practical or an unpractical person. In this highly tendentious sense that the words 'practice' and 'practical' have in Kant it is as good as laid down and stipulated from the outset that this kind of practice has nothing to do with experience. This exclusion of experience of which I have told you and the difficulties that come in its train are so organized in his philosophy that if he were here amongst us, and if he did not disdain to explain himself to us – and it is my belief that Kant would be the last person to think it beneath him – then I think he would probably say, 'Indeed, what you mean by practice is utterly different from what I mean; when I use the term "practice" in this precise way, I would say quite simply that it is defined by the fact that it is independent of experience.' And I believe that if you are to understand this entire complex of problems that we are concerned with in this semester, you should try to give an account to yourselves of the significance of this undervaluation of the role of experience, something we might also claim for Kant's treatment of it in the realm of theoretical reason too. In short, we might ask what significance it has within the Kantian system as a whole. The material of my feelings, therefore, and indeed everything that comes to me from outside, everything that is not me in the sense of being my own reason, is really no more than a stimulus, a view that is given a much blunter and more radical form in Fichte, his immediate successor. An action is supposed to be the direct product of my mind and must be independent of any material that is tied to it. And I can only conceive of it as practical if it is independent, if it is my own act and is bound to nothing that is not determined by me as a thinking, rational being. Regarded socially, what that means – and it will perhaps be of assistance to you to think of these rather abstruse ideas in slightly more concrete terms – what that means is that something like a supreme metaphysical principle has been created out of the idea of the emancipation of the bourgeois individual – the idea of bourgeois autonomy. Humanity at the end of the eighteenth century was caught up in a struggle for bourgeois emancipation from tutelage, and it is as if this struggle were reflected in philosophy in such a way that this freedom, the freedom that had yet to be achieved, became the supreme principle, the principle in which philosophy reached its pinnacle and was equated with reason. You can only understand Kant and particularly Kant's practical philosophy properly once you realize that for him freedom and reason are actually the same thing. And similarly, the entire construction of the categorical imperative, about which we shall perhaps be able to say something today in this context, can only be understood if the very strange coupling of freedom and law that is contained in the categorical imperative is arrived at in such a way that the principle of freedom should itself be nothing but reason, pure reason, and that it should not be subject to constraints by anything external, alien to it that is itself not rational. And the kernel of the Kantian idea here is that everything that I do not recognize as a purely rational being, and every rule that is not derived from my own reason actually restricts the principle of freedom. It does this because it binds me to something that is not myself, something that is alien to me and upon which I make myself dependent. Kant's so-called rigorism, the massive and almost inhuman harshness and severity with which Kant excludes from his moral philosophy everything to do with happiness and everything that came to be regarded by his successors as an integral element of practice, all of that is excluded essentially for the sake of freedom. You have this very curious and paradoxical construction in Kant that in a certain sense the two conflicting impulses of moral philosophy, namely the idea of freedom and the idea of suppression – no better word occurs to me – the suppression, above all, of every natural impulse, the suppression of affection and the suppression of sympathy – both are really suppressed for the sake of freedom. The entire realm of impulses and interests, all of that is suppressed by Kant with a theoretically very cruel harshness, and really only so that I should not make myself dependent on anything that is incompatible with the principle of my own freedom, my own reason. I should draw your attention *en passant* to the fact that this system is predicated on the idea that we live in a world in which the fulfilment of my natural impulses or whatever we may call them – my need for happiness, affection and everything else – is incompatible with reason as a universal principle. And all this happens without his ever really asking himself whether the absolute making real of reason does not entail the fulfilment of all the desires that have been suppressed. This problem only really surfaces in Kant in an extremely indirect and tortuous manner, namely in the conception of immortality, which is one of the three cardinal propositions.[2] It emerges here when Kant finally does concede that the world would be a hell[3] if it were not possible to achieve – and were it only in a transcendental realm – something like a unity of reason and the impulses it has suppressed. It would be a hell if this were not to lead to the absolute elimination of that dualism which reflects in Kant's philosophy the antagonistic, dualistic nature of the world in which we live. Therefore, if as acting human beings we make ourselves dependent on some material factor or other, if my action does not depend solely on my idea, and more particularly on my idea of the universal law, then it really ceases to be practical; it is no longer free. Thanks to this line of argument the sphere of morality in Kant is in general construed as the sphere of freedom, because it would otherwise come within the sphere of mere nature in which, as you have now heard at some length, causality holds sway to the exclusion of freedom and which for that reason belongs entirely to theoretical reason and not to pure practical reason. With that in mind, Ladies and Gentlemen, we can consider a sentence from the chapter we are examining here, 'The Ultimate End of the Pure Employment of our Reason', from section 1 of 'The Canon of Pure Reason'. You will perhaps be in a better position to understand it now since if you did not carry in your minds the arguments I have put before you it might well appear somewhat forced, but now, following the work we have put in on it, I hope it will be quite transparent to you: 'By "the practical" I mean everything that is possible through freedom.'[4] If you now think through what I have said then this statement will be comprehensible to you as a cornerstone of Kantian philosophy in general. There are, of course, certain difficulties with it, logical difficulties, for the situation in Kant is that the material of theoretical reason, in so far as it is mere material, is supposed to be quite indeterminate; it only assumes particular shape through me as a thinking being, thanks to the apparatus of the categories. This contradiction can itself only be explained in terms of the tension we have repeatedly returned to between the Enlightened strand of thought in Kant that desires to expand the frontiers of nature as far as possible, and his wish to reinstate an earlier state of affairs, to call a halt to Enlightenment in which nothing would remain but blind nature and the blind domination of nature.

The entire problem that Kant's moral philosophy now finds itself confronted by is how to derive from his practical philosophy those three cardinal propositions or principles about which I spoke to you at the outset. I should draw your attention to the fact that Kant is continuing here a historical trend that began with Descartes. In this tradition the absolute itself, the existence of God, is not placed at the very starting-point of philosophy, but instead has to be inferred from that initial philosophy. In short, the existence of God has to be proved. This has the truly remarkable consequence, one that strikes the unprejudiced observer as paradoxical in the extreme, that the very thing that ought to be the πρῶτον, the very first thing in the hierarchy of ideas, is reduced to the status of something secondary and derivative.[5] Now if you pause to think about what lies behind the concept of reason in Kant, namely the freedom of human beings in action, then we can truly say that in this entire philosophy the existence of God is made to depend on the human principle, namely the principle of human reason. And ever since philosophy has concerned itself with providing proof of its supreme metaphysical principles, that is, with making them commensurable with reason, as was already the case with the classical Thomist doctrine of the *analogia entis*, from that time on there has been an inherent tendency in philosophy to make its first and absolute principle dependent on something that should really be secondary. For reason cannot itself be conceived of except as something abstracted from finite human beings and made corporeal in them. From this vantage-point you can assess the programme that Kant embarked on when he stated that 'If, then, these three cardinal propositions are not in any way necessary for *knowledge*, and yet are strongly recommended by our reason, their importance, properly regarded, can concern only the *practical*.'[6] This remarkable sentence that 'their importance can concern only the practical' really means, even though it is not expressed as bluntly as I have here, that because they are important for practical reason, they must follow from practical reason, or, as it is stated later on in the same chapter, 'be proved through experience'.[7] Kant now lands himself in a terribly difficult and disagreeable quandary, as happens not infrequently to us philosophers when we try to grapple with such matters. Remember that these three cardinal propositions or principles may not be inferred from pure thought alone. You have to think back to the structure of the Kantian system which on its negative side consisted of a critique of the philosophy of Leibniz and Wolff. They had set out to deduce the existence of just such entities as God, freedom and immortality from pure thought alone, that is, from the pure principles of reason. Now in the entire negative part of the *Critique of Pure Reason*, Kant showed in great detail that this was not possible, that it leads to contradictions. And I have discussed at length the decisive contradiction, the one relating to the idea of freedom, in connection with the third antinomy. On the other hand, however, these principles – and this is not something we need to discuss further – cannot be taken from experience either, for we are dealing with absolute principles, and to derive these absolute and universally valid principles from experience would mean making absolutely permanent, eternal, necessary and unchanging principles dependent on experiences that were themselves accidental and contingent. In the philosophical tradition we are dealing with here, and given the nature of Kantian philosophy itself, this would be a highly paradoxical demand that Kant could not accede to in any circumstances. In order to understand that in Kant ethics is constructed as an aporetical construct, that is to say, as a system that arises from the difficulties inherent in its initial situation, you need to understand how Kant extricates himself from this dilemma. He does so by establishing the principle of ethics – and we may say, in anticipation of what comes later, that this principle of ethics is none other than the moral law, that is, the categorical imperative – as a principle that is neither deduced from reason, since that would place him in the camp of the rationalists, nor from experience. Instead he says, 'The moral law is a fact, the moral law is a given.'[8] And this is the point on which the entire argument hinges. I have already told you of a number of pivotal points in Kant, but this is probably the most important of all; it is the decisive crux in the entire structure of moral philosophy in Kant. You will only be able to understand the *Groundwork of the Metaphysic of Morals* and the *Critique of Practical Reason* once you have grasped why he has to regard it as a given and with what justification he does in fact regard it as given. The further element of the argument is that if the moral law is a given, that is, if it simply exists and resists any further question as to its origin, its source, if in short it is an ultimate reality that underpins all knowledge, then it cannot dispense with those three principles or entities – God, freedom and immortality – if it is to be valid. And that is precisely the point which I drew to your attention in connection with Descartes, who likewise demonstrated the existence of God from the idea of the logical coherence of reason. Because for Descartes too if we were deceived in this regard it would be incompatible with the logical coherence of reason – and that is why we are in need of God. Naturally, this is only one side of the very complex argument about God in Descartes who at this point also has recourse to another traditional idea about the existence of God, namely the ontological argument.[9] At any rate, this is the point at which Kant lapses into the rationalist tradition of philosophy. If the moral law truly is a given, if, therefore, there is an absolute, unambiguous obligation 'so to act that the maxim or the supreme principle of my action could at the same time be made the principle of a universal law',[10] then – and I should like you to take note that, once you have entered into the spirit of this Kantian tradition, these things do obey a very strict logic – the conclusion about freedom does follow in a very strict way, because this irresistible injunction to act in accordance with the categorical imperative would be quite senseless unless I also had the ability to act as I am required to by this simply given and absolutely existing moral law. For if I did not have that ability, Kant would maintain, the existence of this moral law would be nothing more than a demonic, blind accident.

The problem – and for us today, this is a very serious and relevant problem – is whether there might be a real contradiction between such a law, between the idea of a good and moral action and the ability to put it into practice. However, the question of whether there are circumstances when that ability is not available is simply absent from Kant's theory. Whereas for us, if we can be permitted to regard Kafka as a philosophical writer, we can see that one of the chief subjects of his writing starts at this point and from there it has moved into the so-called philosophy of Existentialism. In Kant, on the other hand, there is no sign of the absurdity that the idea of the good can exist, and the obligation to do good and act in conformity to the law likewise, but that human beings might be denied the possibility of so acting by the general social context from which they cannot escape. When Kant says, 'I must be free so that the moral law can be fulfilled', he is expressing an indescribable and to our ears almost naive optimism that is in fact the optimism of the early bourgeoisie. We can hear it in the music of the young Beethoven which also contains the idea that 'Indeed, everything is possible, and if the good must exist then it must also be possible for it to be put into practice'.[11] Here we encounter the magnificent, fascinating and we could almost say inspiring aspect of this Kantian philosophy that dwells side by side with its naivety, its limitation, that is so evident today. And you can see here how this utterly serious philosophy, a philosophy that always seeks out the hardest possible route, nevertheless finds itself ·

embroiled in a terrible conflict. This conflict has nothing to do with any cheap relativizing of its principles, but arises instead from the fact that contradictions emerge between these different principles – between the principles of freedom and determination, for example. These contradictions are intensified and reproduce themselves, even though Kant imagined that he had done away with them once and for all by combining freedom and necessity in the concept of reason. By such means he believed that he had excluded from the outset the possibility that the demand for the good life could lead us into insoluble contradictions.

Now the idea that the moral law can be a given is itself a curious matter. All of you, especially if you have some experience of philosophy, and particularly of epistemology, will be bursting to raise an objection at this point. You will say to me 'You have not told us, or rather you have now given us an interpretation of Kant' – and believe me, I have been faithful to Kant on this issue – 'according to which the practical is pure behaviour, pure freedom, that is, a mode of behaviour that is supposed to be absolutely independent of all experience. But damn it all, is not the concept of givenness the very essence of the concept of experience? Hasn't empiricism, the whole empiricist philosophical tradition always insisted that it proceeds from facts that are givens, the data of immediate sense experience that it bases itself on? And hasn't it always claimed that anything that is not so given, but has been created by the subject, and produced, is supposed to be no more than an optional extra?' This objection will have occurred to all of you, and you will all want to say 'Kant starts off by making a huge fuss about throwing out everything to do with experience. But he then goes on to claim that a moral law that absolutely transcends experience is itself no more than a given, and in saying this he smuggles experience back in through the back door.' And if you are feeling malicious you will add 'These philosophers are a fine lot to present us with tall stories like this and try to pull the wool over our eyes.' Ladies and Gentlemen, there are all sorts of things that can be said about this. To this day we do not have a really adequate account of Kant's concept of the given. I believe that my colleague Wilhelm Sturmfels at one time worked on such a study. If I am correctly informed, this project was never completed.[12] It would be of the greatest importance for this concept of the given to be properly investigated – if there were any real Kant research going on that went beyond questions of a philological nature. Schopenhauer was perhaps the first to point out that the given is not limited to sense-data, but in some fashion also contains the deity who is supposed to have been the cause of whatever is given.[13] To that extent, then, the concept of the given has other roots than just the empirical. And I should like to conclude by saying that this concept of the given does not of course refer to immediately given sense-data, but refers to quite a different order of things without its being in any sense a mere sham. I shall attempt on Thursday to discuss this concept of the given more thoroughly. – Thank you.

LECTURE EIGHT

20 June 1963

Ladies and Gentlemen,

You will perhaps recollect that last time we at least made a start with our examination of the concept of the given in Kant with its manifold meanings, and above all of the problem that arises when the moral law, which he formulates in a highly general way, is presented as a given. Now you will remember no doubt that I began by saying that in moral philosophy what Kant regards as 'given' is in truth nothing but reason itself and to that extent the adversary of experience, even though it is only through experience that I can know of the existence or givenness of this reason. This is the famous problem – one that constantly recurs in Kant's philosophy – of the division into the consciousness, which is observed, reason which is to be observed and the reason which does the observing. This is a problem that only became fully thematic with post-Kantian philosophy. To act morally, according to Kant, means as much as to act in accordance with pure reason. What is meant by this sphere of the given nature of the moral law and ultimately of reason itself can perhaps best be expressed in terms of the structure of the system as a kind of neutral zone between *a priori* knowledge and experience. What is meant, on the one hand, is the given nature of reason; reason is given in the sense that it cannot be pursued any further, it is irreducible to anything else. On the other hand, however, what is also meant is the attempt to justify this givenness by saying that just as with other experience I am supposed to be able to appropriate reason and its laws directly. So if you will permit the image, we are talking about a kind of no-man's-land between *a priori* and *a posteriori* knowledge.[1] It contains the entire thematic contents of post-Kantian idealism, which strove to synthesize *a priori* and *a posteriori* in one, and laboured with equal consistency to synthesize the two realms of theoretical and practical reason, which Kant had likewise separated, and to unite them by virtue of their common root in what then became known as spirit [*Geist*]. Underlying this in Kant there is an unfathomable problem, namely the problem of how to justify *a priori* knowledge itself, the problem of how I know about *a priori* knowledge. This problem is intractable because I can only obtain *a priori* knowledge through experience, by apprehending some form or other, even though the rightful source of this *a priori* knowledge, namely experience, is incompatible with *a priori* knowledge. It might be said that this is not the least of the very many forces impelling the Kantian philosophy in the direction of dialectical thought. We may summarize the problem in this way: on the one hand, the concept of knowledge *a priori* precludes experience because *a priori* knowledge is a kind of knowledge that is absolutely independent of all experience, but on the other hand, I can only obtain a purchase on this *a priori* knowledge through experience, through perception of one kind or another. And here we have a contradiction that cannot be resolved by the procedures of ordinary, traditional logic. The consequence of this is that philosophy can have no other recourse than to make this contradiction a theme in itself. For if I may attempt to define dialectical thought from this standpoint, we might say that it is the refusal to accept the denial or elimination of contradictions – if these contradictions make their appearance as forcefully as this – but instead it makes contradiction into an object or theme of philosophical reflection itself. And in this instance you can see how powerfully we are driven along this path.

To act morally, according to Kant, means in effect to act in accordance with pure reason; and the supreme determining feature of pure reason in Kant is the *a priori*, the synthetic judgement *a priori*. A synthetic judgement *a priori*, and thus the shape in which we apprehend the *a priori*, is defined for Kant by two qualities – you must forgive me here if I take you back to a fundamental definition from the *Critique of Pure Reason*, but you will soon see that it stands in a very compelling relation to practical reason. These two characteristics are necessity and universality.[2] If we transfer these two principles of necessity and universality to practical reason we then arrive automatically at that feature of Kant's practical philosophy that he introduced under the name of the categorical imperative. From this point of view the categorical imperative is simply the maxim governing action, the supreme principle of every practical action that combines the two elements of necessity and universality with each other. It must be universal, and the *a priori* judgement is universal because it may not be restricted by anything individual or particular. We should remind ourselves here that for its part any determinate individual phenomenon only becomes individual in time and space, that is, as a thing that contains something material or a sensation in itself. This contradicts the principle of purity to the degree that it is tied to such material, that something is given to me as material which is distinct from me as a pure form of consciousness. As for the concept of necessity, this is implicit in the concept of law. That is to say, reason generally makes its appearance with the claim of deductive necessity, with the claim that everything it implies follows in accordance with the propositions of logic. And this element of necessity already possesses an affinity – I phrase this cautiously – with the causality that is supposed to hold sway in the realm of empirical phenomena. If Kant transfers the principle of necessity to reason itself in the shape of the idea of making inferences in accordance with rules, this means that in a sense the principle of causality is now to be found in the intelligible sphere, that is within a realm independent of experience, whereas it had previously been confined, in the *Critique of Pure Reason*, to the realm of appearances. This fact may help you to understand, Ladies and Gentlemen, the otherwise very troubling contradiction that arises because he speaks constantly of conformity to laws, even though moral philosophy and morality is actually defined by him as the sphere of freedom. This may also help you to understand that the whole of Kant's moral philosophy is tied to the concept of autonomy which is regarded as the realm where freedom and necessity meet. What this means is that the moral laws are indeed the laws of freedom – because as a rational being I give them to myself without making myself dependent on any external factor. At the same time, however, they have the character of laws because rational action and rational deduction cannot be understood except as acting and thinking in conformity with laws and rules. So this is perhaps the first point to be made about the given nature of the moral law, what we might call a second-order givenness. It should be regarded as the existence of reason – the presence and registering of reason as such and not of any experiential content it may possess – and this implies also its two aspects, necessity and universality, whereby the concept of necessity instantly implies the opposite of necessity, namely freedom, since this reason is defined by Kant as the organ of freedom.

The entire question has a further aspect – and this is connected with the fact that Kant asserts that this freedom and this moral law are both givens. This concept is peculiarly elusive. You will see at once that this second meaning is linked to the first, but it is essentially more problematic than the extraordinarily disembodied construct of *a priori* knowledge that I have just attempted to expound to you, and hence correspondingly difficult to attack. The fact is that, in the practical philosophy, givenness is based on obligation, that is the coercion that proceeds from moral principles. In the crucial transitional section in the *Critique of Pure Reason*, to which we shall turn our attention in a moment, he constantly produces statements to the effect that 'we have the fact of freedom or the fundamental principle of practical philosophy as a given'. And if he makes such statements, this is not just based on the memory of this second-order givenness, in other words, on the fact that we have something like reason, but on something even more specific and substantial. What he has in mind – I believe he would deny it, but when you look at the texts you will find it hard to draw any other conclusion – is the element of compulsion that is exerted by moral principles. In its simplest terms what this means is that as empirical beings we experience the obligation to perform certain actions, or to leave them undone. At the basic psychological level, he is thinking simply of the whole realm of experience summed up in the word 'conscience'. If we constantly speak of the fact of the moral law, a very considerable role is played in this by the phenomenological or descriptive discovery that human beings act in accordance with obligations of this kind, that there are things that they respect, however much they may find themselves in opposition to particular moral ideas or systems. I only need remind you of the fact regurgitated *ad nauseam* by complacent philistines that even in the world of crime there is supposed to be a definite moral code, and that for the real criminal – at least that is what we read in books – there are particular actions that are simply precluded by his code. From this every moralist infers a justification for his own moralism; for even absolutely amoral people are supposed to have a morality of their own – as if such a morality could provide a justification of other, superior moral codes. But that is merely an aside.

What needs to be said here is that, empirically, Kant is in the right when he appeals to obligation, something he does repeatedly in the *Critique of Practical Reason*,[3] and that this obligation is supposed to represent the most powerful reason for us to recognize the moral law and to acknowledge that some such thing as conscience really does exist. The only problem that arises here is that the actual existence of conscience – and here Kant falls into a trap of his own making – and the actual existence of compulsive behaviour of the kind that is commonly covered by the concept of conscience tells us nothing about the legitimacy of this authority. When I say that Kant has fallen into a trap of his own making, what I mean is simply this: if he desires to exclude every empirical element from his foundation of moral philosophy – and that is his aim – he cannot then appeal to the empirical existence of the so-called moral compulsion in man himself because this compulsion is itself an empirical fact. In Kantian terms, it is a mere fact of psychology which therefore lacks the dignity he must give it. I say 'must give it' because the fact of this moral obligation is the most powerful argument in favour of the idea that something does exist that I must respect. This is one of the points at which empirical science has made a definite advance over Kant, and as the man of Enlightenment that he was, he would surely have been the last to deny this. Psychoanalysis in its strict form has shown that these compulsive mechanisms that we are subject to are phylogenetic, that is to say, they are internalizations of actual power, internalizations of dominant social norms. These norms are transmitted to us through the family and we generally appropriate them by identifying with father figures. By the strict form of psychoanalysis I mean its Freudian version and not the adulterated versions, the attempts at depth on the part of people like Jung and Adler which result only in greater superficiality. Moreover, psychoanalysis has shown something that would not have been to Kant's taste at all. This is the idea that the authority known to psychoanalysis as compulsive character, or in Freud's later writing as super-ego, is irrational in so far as it is pathogenic. That means that this compulsion tends to be transmitted to things that are irreconcilable with reason. An instance, I suppose, would be when a man can only go to sleep once he has performed a certain ritual like smoothing out the pillows, or the kind of compulsive actions performed incessantly by particularly pedantic, sadistic or miserly people in the name of an orderly life.[4] In short, the unity of moral obligation and reason that Kant insists on is not altogether unproblematic if we reflect a little more deeply on this obligation; indeed it becomes highly dubious. Needless to say, Kant would himself resist this argument. He would reply: 'I can concede all that as far as it concerns the empirical world and as long as it fails to touch the absolutely valid formal shape of the moral law as such.' However, this formal, abstract shape of the moral law is itself detached from these actual obligations, and when we find it assuming a somewhat more tangible form in the *Critique of Practical Reason* under the name of 'duty', we can see its origins all too clearly. If every connection with the real modes of behaviour expressed by the ideal of duty were absent, that would also do away with the essential content of what Kant meant by obligation. On the other hand, it can scarcely be denied that the obligation Kant

postulates as absolute, as formally absolute, is not itself unconditioned, as it seems to be in his work, but contingent. It cannot,
therefore, be regarded as the rightful source of the moral. Moreover,
these perceptions owe nothing to modern psychology; they are
rather the discovery of Friedrich Nietzsche and it is not the least of
his merits that he was able to articulate them so incisively in the
course of a purely philosophical analysis. He had a keen eye for the
limitations of Kant's concept of duty and an incredibly sure instinct
for the element of heteronomy at the heart of Kant's so-called
doctrine of autonomy.[5]

Having said all this by way of introduction, Ladies and Gentlemen, I should like now briefly to examine the text we have been considering. I believe that these remarks will have made it much easier
for you to understand, that is to say, I can now read you the relevant
passages while referring you to what we have said. In the first place,
you will now know what is meant by the statement, 'By "the practical" I mean everything that is possible through freedom.'[6] This
is because freedom means nothing more than a form of behaviour
that is guided simply and solely by reason, and because action in the
strong sense is characterized solely by that; whereas action, in the
fully subjective sense of acts determined exclusively by subjectivity,
ceases to exist the moment an act becomes dependent on anything
other than subjectivity. Kant then continues:

> When, however, the conditions of the exercise of our free will are
> empirical, reason can have no other than a regulative employment in
> regard to it, and can serve only to effect unity in its empirical laws.
> Thus, for instance, in the precepts of prudence, the whole business of
> reason consists in uniting all the ends which are prescribed to us by
> our desires . . .[7]

This passage is not easy to understand if only because we tend to
read it as if Kant had meant to say – and it would make a lot of sense
– *because* 'the conditions of the exercise of our free will are empirical'. For the fact is, Ladies and Gentlemen, and here we touch on the
cardinal point of disagreement between Kant and Hegel, the conditions of the exercise of our free will are empirical. Thus if my free
will leads me to set a house on fire, the exercise of this act of will is
tied to the existence of the house, the courage I need to carry out the
crime, the availability of fuel, and similar empirical factors. But to
interpret Kant in this way would be to misunderstand him since the
nub of his conception of the sphere of morality is precisely that
the moral is something that is absolutely independent of empirical

conditions. Kant would say: 'To the extent that my moral or immoral acts are related to empirical conditions this can detract from the effect of my will.' But if I leap into the water to rescue a man who was attempting to take his own life, and am myself unable to swim, it may end up with both of us drowning. However, Kant would say to this: 'This effect, which depends on empirical conditions, is itself merely empirical and is quite independent of the fact of morality. Morality is simply and solely a matter of the free will' – in other words, of my absolute autonomy, or as Kant himself phrased it, 'a matter of my conviction' [*Gesinnung*]. And this will enable you to understand why in a significant sense Kant's ethics is an ethics of conviction, in contrast to what has been called an ethics of responsibility in which empirical conditions have to be taken into account. This is because the effect of my actions is treated as a determining factor in the moral act of freedom. In this way, then, Kant makes a distinction between the pragmatic laws of free behaviour, that is, everything that could be described as a means–ends relation, and the moral law proper. And the entire pragmatic sphere, that is, the entire sphere in which moral behaviour, however nobly motivated, makes itself dependent on empirical conditions and empirical ends, is one he rejects. He has only one concern and this is that the moral law as such should be obeyed, and the effects of any resultant actions are excluded from consideration. This is the ultimate explanation for the fact that Kant's ethics has been described, not without a certain justice, as rigorist. He goes on to say:

> In contrast laws of this latter type, pure practical laws, whose end is given through reason completely *a priori*, and which are prescribed to us not in an empirically conditioned but in an absolute manner, would be products of pure reason.[8]

I am certain that after what I have told you, you will have no difficulty in understanding these crucial statements without further elucidation. 'Such' – and by this he means pure practical laws – 'are the *moral* laws; and these alone, therefore, belong to the practical employment of pure reason, and allow of a canon.'[9] That 'they alone belong to the practical employment of pure reason' is a little ambiguous; we might surely believe – when we recall our discussions of earlier passages – that they rightfully belong not to theoretical reason but entirely to practical reason, but after what we have heard and understood, we see that something else is intended. Namely that the moral laws proper are only those that are valid for the practical employment of pure reason and its canon. What are not valid, on the other hand, are the pragmatic laws of action that ultimately are only the laws of prudence and are therefore heteronomous. This is because they bind us to external conditions and external consequences, and for that reason they make us unfree in a certain sense and dependent on something that is not our own reason. Kant continues: 'The whole equipment of reason, in the discipline which may be entitled pure philosophy, is in fact determined with a view to the three above-mentioned problems.' – These, you recall, are the problems of God, freedom and immortality. – 'These, however, themselves in turn refer us yet further, namely to the problem of *what we ought to do*, if the will is free, if there is a God and a future world. As this concerns our attitude to the supreme end,' – and this supreme end is the moral law – 'it is evident that the ultimate intention of nature in her wise provision for us has indeed, in the constitution of our reason, been directed to moral interests alone.'[10] Ladies and Gentlemen, you have here the explanation of everything that, as early as the *Critique of Pure Reason*, can be described as the primacy of practical reason. For if our reason is in general only directed at the moral and everything else is no more than what might be called a stimulus for reason, then according to this theory practical reason must have priority over theoretical.

In the process we witness the remarkable internalization of the old teleological belief that the world is rationally organized which was to be found in Leibniz's philosophy. This takes the form of the belief that our reason is so arranged that it shows us the way to right action, that it suffices in itself to tell us what we should do. Thus here we have a system of ethics that is radically internalized, radically subjectivized for the first time, and in it the teleological thinking of classical rationalism has been given a new function. This does, however, give rise to a remarkable inconsistency that I should not wish to pass over without having brought it to your attention. The question is raised suddenly about what we are to do if God exists, if my soul is immortal and if I am free.[11] However, this stands in a real contradiction, one that cannot be explained away, to Kant's own principle according to which these three elements are supposed to follow as the postulates of practical reason, and to act as the 'guarantors of the moral law', as Kant phrases it at one point in the *Critique of Practical Reason*.[12] Therefore, they cannot be treated as the preconditions of the moral law. Rather, they are what is conditioned by it, and I have already pointed out that in this respect Kant is to be found in the mainstream of modern rationalist thought because he infers even the existence of God from reason, which is identical with the moral law, and does not postulate God as an absolute. But if that is the case, it is hard to explain why these three elements should be able to tell us anything significant about *what* I should do, since what I *should* do follows from the absolute, namely the moral law itself, and not from something that might be discerned from a great distance as its possible alternative or its possible guarantor. Now I believe that this is one of the first points at which the element of heteronomy creeps into the Kantian ethic. For by reinterpreting freedom as the freedom of the unconfined and absolute employment of reason and at the same time, as the law that I have to obey and in accordance with which I must act, this philosophy at once acquires an authoritarian aspect. It is as if the appeal to reason alone might not suffice to enable the moral law to prevail, even though it coincides with reason, and there actually are passages in Kant's ethical writings, particularly in the *Groundwork of the Metaphysic of Morals*, where he points out that in order to act rightly there is no need for philosophy and that it is possible to lead a good, honest life even if you have not studied the *Groundwork of the Metaphysic of Morals*. Of course, this takes us back to the healthy, old, rustic virtues of the peasant, and in a sense constitutes a restriction of the rationality contained in the concept of reason. For if the concept of reason is the supreme authority, and nothing is moral but reason, then it follows that all action that does not result from the employment of reason is immoral – I am speaking now in the spirit of Kant himself, of immanent critique. The moment he fails to acknowledge this, he himself, by attempting to preserve the authority of the moral law, introduces into his own philosophy an element that contradicts his own concept of autonomy. But if that is the case, then the moral law is in fact not sufficient on its own to induce human beings to behave morally. Here again – in so far as we are arguing pragmatically, in the realm of moral experience – Kant is in tune with the psychological observation that has taught us to accept the reality of something like conscience in the sense we have already discussed, and the existence of what we called obligation. But at the same time the resistance of the instincts to this secondary, derived aspect of the super-ego that has been imposed on us is so powerful that it makes our own attitude problematic to the point where we are constantly tempted to break out. In this respect Kant is an authentic spokesman of bourgeois society and its discipline, above all, of the bourgeois work discipline – and wherever we speak of bourgeois morality we think in the first instance of bourgeois work discipline. For he evidently feels it necessary to mobilize assistance in order to din into people the need for strict adherence to the moral law because the appeal to pure reason does not suffice on its own. And this explains the remarkable statement, one which is truly heteronomous in Kantian terms, about 'what we ought to do, if the will is free, if there is a God and a future world'. This statement is not so very far removed from the heteronomy of religion which warns the poor peasant woman not to pick up even a single potato that does not belong to her, since, if she does so, she will go to hell. You can see how in Kant's philosophy the most sublime motives sit cheek by jowl with the most narrow-minded ones – I do not mean this genetically, but in their own immanent meaning. 'Freedom', he goes on to say, exists 'in this practical sense only.'[13] And at this point Kant really does say something that sounds highly paradoxical at first sight, but that I hope that my interpretation has made completely clear to you, namely, '[The fact of] practical freedom can be proved through experience.' And he goes on to explain:

> For the human will is not determined by that alone which stimulates, that is, immediately affects the senses; we have the power to overcome the impressions on our faculty of sensuous desire, by calling up representations of what, in a more indirect manner, is useful or injurious [. . .][14]

Here too we find an important point, namely the possibility of controlling the id, the instincts, through the ego when they come into conflict with reality. 'But these considerations, as to what is desirable in respect of our whole state, that is as to what is good and useful, are based on reason.'[15] So here we find it clearly stated that the so-called empirical proof of our freedom is provided by the fact that reason is given us as the faculty by means of which we can test reality. It is extremely interesting and once again provides proof of Kant's immense honesty that in this passage, when it comes to the crunch, he does not postulate reason as a logical faculty floating in a vacuum. Instead, his thoughts here are very much empirical thoughts concerning the actual employment of reason as a faculty that enables us to test reality and, if necessary, to defer certain gratifications if they conflict with our overall interests. You see, then, that here, where he really has to argue in order to demonstrate the existence of reason, he ignores the absolute antithesis between the pragmatic laws of reason and the actual moral laws. He ignores it because he is perceptive enough and truthful enough to realize that reason as the pure organ of truth and reason as the organ of our self-preservation are not two absolutely separate things that have nothing to do with each other. He can see that the reason that makes itself autonomous and focuses entirely on truth is a dialectical product; it is the child of the selfsame, self-preserving practical reason in the ordinary sense which he had tended to dismiss as merely 'pragmatic' in the preceding section. 'Reason therefore', he continues, 'provides laws which are imperatives, that is, *objective laws of freedom* which tell us *what ought to happen* – although perhaps it never does happen,' – you see here his indifference towards effects – 'therein differing from *laws of nature*, which relate only to *that which happens*. These laws are therefore to be entitled practical laws.'[16] I have only quoted these somewhat paradoxical statements of Kant's in order to highlight and confirm the interpretations I have given. I hope that these laws will now begin to be transparent to you and to acquire as much meaning as I have attempted to suggest to you in my discussion of them. – Thank you.

LECTURE NINE

27 June 1963

Ladies and Gentlemen,

Our lecture course has had to be interrupted once again, but you may remember that we were in the middle of our reconstruction of Kant's approach to moral philosophy, and I want simply to continue where we left off.[1] I should like to start by reminding you of the assertion that 'Reason provides laws which are imperatives, that is, *objective laws of freedom*'.[2] This statement contains a contradiction in a compressed form, for according to Kant freedom is precisely something that is not subject to laws, and this will perhaps help you to grasp the starting-point of dialectics for which I wish also to prepare you. For I have been attempting to show you again and again, from the most varied angles, that what dialectics does is to take such a contradiction as we find compressed in a single statement here and to follow out its implications and resolve it. Thus one of the merits of Kant's philosophy, and this is the reason why I place such great stress on such contradictory, such glaringly contradictory statements on Kant's part, is that it enables us to achieve clarity about the dialectic; you can see that it represents the attempt to unfold such glaring and therefore static contradictions instead of simply allowing them to manifest themselves in what might be thought of as a kind of syncopation. And these *'laws of freedom'* – and with this phrase you have Kant's entire moral philosophy in a nutshell – are laws 'which tell us *what ought to happen* – although perhaps it never does happen – therein differing from *laws of nature*, which relate only to *that which happens* [. . .]'.[3] Kant attempts here – and this is of crucial importance for the aporetical nature of his moral philosophy as a whole – to master this contradiction between freedom and law – and

I would ask you to pay close attention to this, since it really is the pivotal point of his entire moral philosophy – by bringing these two elements of law and freedom together in this one sentence and resolving them so that the element of law does not apply to what exists, but only to what ought to exist. As such, however, it should do so with absolute stringency, absolute rigour. Nevertheless, it is left open to the individual human subjects at whom these imperatives are directed to decide whether to comply with them or not – and this distinguishes them sharply from the laws of nature – so that it does not need to be established whether in the empirical world anything is ever done in conformity with these laws or not. This stands in contrast to the laws of nature, which were simply the laws governing actual events in nature. I would ask you to note this so that you will have a better grasp of what now follows. Kant now goes on to restrict his conception of the sphere of freedom, and this restriction is itself very remarkable for a number of reasons. In the first place, it shows once again how conscious Kant was of the problems at stake here, and how candidly he confronted them. In the second place, however, there is a certain ambiguity implicit in this restriction. I must read this out to you as well, Ladies and Gentlemen, since we can only do these questions justice if we examine them in the context of specific texts, and it pays to focus on relatively concise, crucial and concentrated texts and then to scrutinize them as if through a magnifying glass. I believe that the only fruitful approach lies in the collaboration between such a micrological method and the construction of a philosophical system, whereas the 'average' comprehension of so-called larger relationships within a system contains the risk of an over-deferential attitude from the outset. At all events, Kant continues:

> Whether reason is not, in the actions through which it prescribes laws, itself again determined by other influences, and whether that which, in relation to sensuous impulses is entitled freedom, may not, in relation to higher and more remote operating causes, be nature again, is a question which in the practical field does not concern us, since we are demanding of reason nothing but the *rule* of conduct; it is a merely speculative question, which we can leave aside so long as we are considering what ought or ought not to be done.[4]

I should begin by pointing out that Kant not only subjects the solution he himself proposes to a further condition here – we shall come back to this directly – but also, and this is highly significant for Kant, he breaks off any further interrogation at this point; he stops his interrogation short. This peculiar tendency to interrupt his own analysis is something we shall have to return to. What Kant means here by these 'other influences', and whether '[freedom may not] in relation to higher and more remote operating causes, be nature again' is capable of two mutually opposed interpretations. The first – and we shall have to decide this from the context as a whole, the literal phrasing here does not suffice – is one that is consistent with the Kantian argument as a whole: he may have in mind here a more remote intention on the part of nature, one which coincides with the kingdom of freedom. According to this, if nature had fully disclosed itself to us, if our incomplete knowledge were to yield to the kind of knowledge that according to Kant is proper only to an absolute, divine consciousness, then in knowledge of that kind the kingdom of ends represented by morality would coincide with the kingdom of means represented in our knowledge of nature. Moreover, they would coincide because Kant finds the divergence between the two intolerable. This is the probable meaning if we examine this passage in the light of the Kantian system as a whole. However – and this is often the case – if you cleave to the literal phrasing of the text, then a second interpretation emerges, one that we have already touched on. This interpretation depends on the ambiguity of the term 'nature' in Kant and implies that for their part these laws of freedom belong in the general framework of nature as part of the general system of determining factors. In other words, then, the moral law is a given, a ready-made thing we find ourselves faced with, what Hegel calls something that has grown, has originated and that in its origins is subject to the causality of nature. We may compare it with the situation in psychoanalysis where the super-ego, the conscience, can be explained in terms of the dynamics and the economy of the drives, in terms of a mechanism of identification, that is, by means of categories that themselves belong in the realm of nature. It is an open question whether in this way Kant opens up the *Critique of Practical Reason* to what might be said to lie below, or to one side; in other words, whether he is prepared to extend the universal validity of the moral law in a nominalist spirit so as to include ontic, actually existing determinants, or whether, on the contrary, he imagines that the resolution of the contradiction between the sphere of freedom and the sphere of nature is to be sought in a higher concept of nature, namely in a divine, and, for that reason, benevolent nature.

Ladies and Gentlemen, you might well ask me – and I may well be advised to spend a moment or two on this methodological question – why I should take the trouble to consider this second possibility at all, if for the connoisseur of the Kantian system the overwhelming probability is that what Kant meant to say was what I have called the first interpretation.[5] Apart from the fact that the problem we are dealing with seems to point impartially in either direction, I should like to take the opportunity to say in principle that I do not share the attitudes of the philologists – attitudes which I am sure that very many of you will hold to be absolutely valid and which you will have been taught to respect so utterly that it will give you quite a wrench to have to jettison them. In particular I do not share their view that products of the mind can in essence be elucidated by an appeal to the will and intention of their creator. I believe that a whole series of possible sources of error is involved in such an appeal, one of which, perhaps the crudest of all, stems from the fact that the author's will and intention cannot be identified with absolute certainty, any more than it is possible to infer the so-called intention of the legislator in interpretations of the law, an idea that, if I am correctly informed, still haunts legal experts. But behind this lies an even deeper consideration: in arguments about such serious and responsible matters as those of which we are speaking, what is at stake is not just what Kant wanted to say, but the fact that the ideas he proposes – and it is here, I would suggest, that we see the greatness of a philosopher like Kant – transcend whatever subjective opinions he may have espoused. Instead, their substance consists in the objective movement of the concept, that is, in the objective rigour, the objective plausibility of the argument. I believe that in general it is a prejudice going back to what might be called the intellectual version of the middle-class parlour, according to which the products of the mind are the property of the great thinkers, poets and composers, and so forth, whose plaster busts used to grace these parlours in the old days. They may have disappeared now, but may well survive in spirit, invisibly, and to even more disastrous effect because of that invisibility. We should prefer to say that a significant product of the mind is the result of a union of the mental effort of its producer and the objective ideas that are involved, and this is the ideal of mental activity in general. Moreover, Ladies and Gentlemen, this objective substance is moral in nature, and I should like to offer it to you almost as a maxim. The essence of a mental product is that in it the will of the individual thinker is submerged in the subject-matter, in the coercion exerted by the subject-matter, to the point where that will disappears entirely. Intellectual products are not the expression of intention and of the person who creates them, but represent the extinction of that intention in the truth of the objective matter in hand.[6] And this is why I believe that this objective matter has a force and a weight even in the texts themselves that is greater, particularly in significant texts, than the force of whatever the author's own purposes may have been. In consequence I would say that the task of a philosophical interpretation of a text is to do justice to this product of conflicting forces as it happens to be formulated, rather than to anything the author may have thought on the subject, since these thoughts represent no more than a particular, and in a sense ephemeral viewpoint. This is why I have been concerned to explain this matter at such length and I hope at the same time that it will also shed some light on my interpretative approach in general.

I have told you that what Kant seems to be concerned with is the higher intention of nature whose objective is the union of the two dualistic principles themselves. But I have also said that the other interpretation may also have been intended. You will then have realized that the decision about which interpretation is correct will depend on the meaning we give to the term 'nature'. And it would be a matter of great importance for someone to investigate the different meanings of the concept of nature in Kant's philosophy and to show what he means by nature in general – a piece of research that would be primarily philological and which we have not had the benefit of up to now. Kant's concept of nature is ambiguous. You may perhaps find a clue to this ambiguity in the ambiguity of the word 'thing' in Kant. On the one hand, it means the *Ding an sich*, the thing in itself, that is, the unknown, so-called cause of all the things I perceive as phenomena. Thus it is something transcendent, something never fully given to me. On the other hand, a thing is something constituted, an object which comes into being as something that endures through the interaction of my sensations, that is, of the material of existence with my forms of perception and thought. If nature is nothing but the embodiment of everything that occurs in the realm of things, or if nature is a world concept, to use the term Kant employs in the essay on Enlightenment, then the same dualism that applies, as is generally known, to such concepts as the thing in itself, could also be extended to the concept of nature.[7] This would mean that in his philosophy nature would be as ambiguous as the world viewed as the totality of all things, which as such is never present to me. Therefore, nature in Kant is on the one hand that which is constituted, conditioned, the embodiment of experience. And in 'Religion within the Boundaries of Mere Reason', as an internal human principle, the faculty of desire, it is even bluntly equated with radical evil.[8] On the other hand, however, as a thing in itself, it is the very foundation of existence, if you will permit me this rather kitschy expression. In other words, it is the absolute that holds sway in us all and is supposed to indicate to us what is good and what evil. And these indications are themselves equated with the good because they have their origins in what characterizes mankind as such, namely his reason. In this context you must recollect that in Kant reason is itself the organ of the good and in his moral philosophy there is no organ of the good other than reason. It follows that reason cannot be divorced from self-preservation, from the satisfaction of human needs. For reason is supposed to provide us with the law that according to Kant is unconditional and absolute – and Kant is the last person to have deceived himself about this, given that the entire history of philosophy in modern times has asserted it – I need only remind you of Spinoza and his extreme opposite, Hobbes. The essence of that reason is self-preservation. We can even hear this principle of self-preservation in the Kantian concept of the ' "*I think*" that must *be able* to accompany all my representations',[9] even though here it appears sublimated into the purely logical principle of identity, the idea of self-preservation, of the preservation of an identical self. On the other hand, this same self-preservation is actually denounced by him as an inferior principle. There is a celebrated passage in the *Groundwork of the Metaphysic of Morals* where he describes the efforts to preserve one's own life as wise and rational, but as non-moral in an exalted and even absolute sense because they do not follow purely from the moral law.[10] So here we have the contradiction that, on the one hand, reason cannot be separated from the interest in preserving one's own life because reason is really the identity of the self-preserving subject, while on the other hand, reason should be able to oppose the interests of self-preservation. This simple, even flagrant contradiction will perhaps enable you to see clearly why Kant cannot tolerate the dualism of the two concepts of nature which we have been discussing, and why he feels impelled to sublate them [*aufheben*], to use a term that came into use subsequently, into a higher concept. It is not so much the need for harmony or synthesis in a higher principle or unity, or any of these things about which the histories of philosophy regale us with such platitudes by way of explanation. It is rather the case, quite simply, that he finds himself confronted by the ambiguity of the concept of reason – as something that is based on the model of self-preservation, on the one hand, and on the need to restrict the particular manifestations of that self-preservation, on the other, because of the calamitous consequences and contradictions it leads to. And this ambiguity compels us to go beyond that dualism and at least to consider carefully whether such a procedure would suffice to eliminate this entire glaring contradiction. In other words, the element of reconciliation arises not so much from the famous need for harmony or for a coherent system or anything of the sort, as from the fact that a contradiction of the kind I have been describing is intolerable to the process of rational thought and is simply not to be endured. But now that Kant has carried through this line of thought with a rigour whose workings I hope I have been able to show you, he dismisses the matter with a gesture, as much as to say 'Thus far and no further', and then adds 'Well, perhaps just a little more', and this is when you reach the specific bourgeois element of Kant: 'This is of no practical importance to us and hence we have no need to concern ourselves with it further.'

Now I should like to say a few words about this process of 'breaking off', of rupture. First, because it is such a ubiquitous feature of the structure of Kant's philosophy and because it is precisely this aspect of Kant that his successors rebelled against. For I would say that if we wished to summarize the distinction between Kant and Fichte and all succeeding idealists in a single gesture it would be this moment of rupture, the moment when Kant says, 'This need not concern us', that they were unable to stomach. And what they said was, 'What you have said about this being of no concern to us is precisely what concerns us most.' Moreover, the reason I have given you for this rupture is not even the most important one, for in essence it is the entire structure of his moral philosophy itself that is founded in a decisive way on this rupture, that is, on his insistence that the given nature of the moral law should not be open to further questioning. In this respect it reminds us, somewhat paradoxically, of the situation with sense-data such as 'red'. For here, too, no further debate is possible when it manifests itself, simply because it is there. This gesture of breaking off is so pivotal for the structure of Kant's entire moral philosophy that we need to dwell on it for a few moments, for it represents a condensed version of highly complex elements. What will strike you at once after what I have said already is the authoritarian gesture that asserts that when the moral law tells you to do your duty, you must not dither, or as Kant is wont to express it, you should not quibble [vernünfteln] further, but should treat it with the same respect that you would show to any other given fact, in other words, you should just 'dwell in the land, and lead an upright life'. This should not be taken to mean you should just obey the moral law and not bother your head about why it is there. It means rather that the fact *that* it exists is actually the most powerful proof of its validity. Of course, we must be entitled to ask not only about the nature of its prescriptions but also about its legitimation. If, *horribile dictu*, a psychologist were to scrutinize Kant's argument at this point he might say, not unreasonably, that we are in the presence of a defence mechanism. We perceive that Kant feels a little queasy when he contemplates the origins of duty and conscience because here at the heart of autonomy an element of heteronomy has become entrenched. It is for this reason that he reacts defensively and says, 'For God's sake, let's stop here, otherwise my entire effort to rescue universals will slip into the realm of what ought to be, and that will wreck the whole top floor of my carefully constructed philosophical hierarchy.' We might go on from there to a critique of all the mechanisms of coercion whose validity Kant simply takes for granted. Indeed at a time when psychoanalysis really did provide something like a social critique, as opposed to a technique of psychological massage, at that time it really did object to the idea that all ethical norms should be granted recognition merely because they existed, as opposed to making them transparent and providing them with a rational justification. To that extent we might say that Freud's psychologism was more Catholic than the Pope, that he was more consistently Kantian than Kant himself, whom, incidentally, he presumably never read. But this is not the end of the story. This Kantian rupture also contains an element of truth. To start with, Kant, unlike his successors, possessed what we might call in shorthand the consciousness of non-identity – a feature of great importance for his moral philosophy. The Kantian system of transcendental philosophy – and I am speaking here of Kant's philosophy as a whole – does not presume to deduce everything from some supreme principle, as Fichte did in a quite strict sense. For since knowledge in Kant's view is composed from a deducible and a non-deducible element, the interaction of these elements and the embodiment of knowledge and the embodiment of action cannot themselves be deduced in any pure manner. So Kant's curious attitude of resignation when faced by things that positively exist, the given world, does not just contain this element of heteronomy. Viewed from the other side it contains the idea of setting limits to the absolute claims of reason, in so far as reason makes the claim that everything that exists and every action is nothing but its own product. Paradoxically, then, even though Kant criticized heteronomy so fiercely, everything that is non-ego, and is thereby heteronomous, is more revered in a certain sense and is allowed to assert itself more powerfully than in the idealist philosophies. The latter do indeed concede a greater recognition of the non-ego than does Kant, but since they absorb it into the ego, in effect they dissolve it there and hence strive to vindicate and legitimate it as rational.

But there is a different, an even more profound aspect of this rupture. This aspect is one that I mentioned at the very beginning of this course of lectures, but it has its rightful theoretical place here.[11] I do not know whether you will recall it, for I undoubtedly intro-

duced it prematurely; it was the assertion that the division into theoretical and practical philosophy implies that moral action cannot be
wholly translated into its theoretical determinants without remainder. If we were to attempt to set up an absolute law and to ask the
laws of pure reason to explain why on earth it would be wrong to
torture people, we would encounter all sorts of difficulties. For
example, the sort of difficulties many Frenchmen have encountered
in Algeria where in the course of the terrible concatenation of events
in this war their opponents did resort to the torture of prisoners.
Should they follow this example and torture their own prisoners,
or should they not? In all such moral questions, the moment you
confront them with reason you find yourself plunged into a terrible
dialectic. And when faced by this dialectic the ability to say, 'Stop!'
and 'You *ought* not even to contemplate such things!' has its advan-
tages. For example, consider the moment when a refugee comes
to your door and asks for shelter. What would be the consequence
if you were to set the entire machinery of reflection in motion,
instead of simply acting and telling yourself that here is a refugee who
is about to be killed or handed over to some state police in some
country or other, and that your duty therefore is to hide and protect
him – and that every other consideration must be subordinated
to this? If reason makes its entrance at this point then reason itself
becomes irrational. And the idea that an action, that which we
do, is not fully coextensive with theory because we would never
reach the point of performing a right action unless that action contained an element of the absurd – this idea is expressed in this Kantian
principle. I believe that we can only think meaningfully about the
entire sphere of moral philosophy if we are conscious of its twin
aspects: first, that the entire sphere must be permeated by reason and
second, that notwithstanding this, reason is not the sum total of
morality. This aspect is expressed in the commandments of religion,
as contrasted with philosophy, and I would say that this happens
from a purely philosophical motive, namely because it represents
the frontier of reason in the realm of the moral. It follows that,
however problematic their moral norms may be, there is something
valid in the religions, and the injunction 'Go, and do thou likewise'[12]
contains something that, formally at least, is no less essential a part
of moral theory than the rationality that requires me to be able
to explain why I should go and do likewise. Moreover, I believe
that it is appropriate particularly for a secular and enlightened
philosophy not simply to undermine such [religious] ideas by subjecting their authority to critical scrutiny, but also – in the course of
reflection on the nature of thought – to salvage them as ingredients

of moral action and to incorporate them into one's actual conduct.

In the passage that I have read out to you, you can see very clearly the element of shock [*Erschütterung*] and absolute self-certainty in pure autonomy. These are features that Kant would subsequently, in the *Critique of Judgement*, bring together in the concept of the sublime. You can see how this becomes intertwined with its exact opposite, namely with an element of bourgeois narrowness and insularity. I would almost be tempted to say that this insularity of the bourgeoisie, to which Kant himself belonged, this limitation of the feeling of sovereignty which people acquired, rightly or wrongly, in the post-Kantian period, was something like the precondition for ethical philosophy, as indeed for morality itself. We should enquire whether in the absence of this insularity such things as moral philosophy and moral action are even possible if we are not able – and I hope I have no real need to add this – to turn back the wheel of history, to conjure up this narrowness by main force and hold fast to it, now that it has been swept away by the movement of mind, by what Hegel called the 'fury of destruction'.[13] Hegel himself, for example, foresaw the coming catastrophe that lay in the removal of this narrowness, but his reaction – and this is by no means to his credit – was to try and justify it as a growth in freedom. This landed him in a contradiction which cannot be salvaged as a dialectical contradiction. This brings me to the point that Valéry has perhaps expressed more succinctly and magnificently than anyone with his question 'Is morality itself growing old?'[14] In the same spirit we feel that the concept of virtue has taken on an archaic sound that it certainly did not have for Kant. This in its turn prompts the question of how we can still respond to this entire Kantian moral philosophy, now that the concept of virtue is obsolete. I owe it to you to give you at least some explanation for the historical dialectic to which the concept of morality has been subjected. In so doing, I shall ignore the obvious facts, visible to you all, and in particular, the progressive concept of Enlightenment to which more and more allegedly eternal moral categories have succumbed. I have in mind here Nietzsche's critical analysis of the idea of an eternally valid moral law.[15] What this means, I believe, is that such things as moral philosophy or virtue are only possible in a circumscribed universe, in contrast to the immeasurably expanding universe of today which is incommensurable with our experience. This is because it is only where our universe is limited that something like Kant's celebrated freedom can survive. In the immeasurably expanded world of experience and the infinitely numerous ramifications of the processes of socialization that this world of experience imposes on us, the possibility of freedom has sunk to such a minimal level that we can or must ask ourselves very seriously whether any scope is left for our moral categories. Particularly since, even if someone were to live his life as an individual in the spirit of the categorical imperative, it is extremely uncertain how far even such a moral life would be able to assert itself given the objective snares and entanglements of modern life. Let me conclude by illustrating this with an aesthetic analogy. The situation in music is that as long as there had existed something like prescribed, established, given forms that corresponded to the prescribed, established, given forms of bourgeois life, it was possible for musicians to improvise. The less this was the case, the more these pre-established forms were eroded, the more the freedom of the artistic subject, and especially the freedom to improvise, was restricted. This restriction was particularly evident in music, an art close to my heart, and efforts to revive it of the kind we have witnessed in our own age have remained without force. Thus music that is seriously contemporary and that no longer tolerates the pre-established forms which were the precondition of absolute freedom finds that it is no longer confronted by defined objectivities. In consequence its freedom to improvise, its freedom to behave as it wishes, has shrivelled to the point of no return. It is my belief that something similar has taken place in the realm of morality. After all, to concern oneself with moral philosophy and reflect on these matters means also that we must give an account of the historical status that questions about moral action and a moral life possess today. Compared with the status they enjoyed in the age of the great philosophers, their importance has been infinitely reduced in magnitude today. – Thank you.

LECTURE TEN

2 July 1963

The[1] consciousness of the paradox implicit in experiencing what we call freedom as an apparent natural cause has been conceded by Kant in his statement that 'a problem remains between freedom and necessity, between the kingdom of nature and the realm of practical reason'.[2] In other words, Kant finds the dualism we have discussed unsatisfactory and, according to his own argument, incapable of resolution. I believe that I must dwell on this a little in order to explain why it is unsatisfactory. For you – or many of you, and especially those among you whom I would like to think of as my pupils – will rightly object at this point and say 'Well, why is this dualism unsatisfactory? Must everything fit neatly into a formula? Must everything be integrated into the same system? Is it not true that in reality there is something akin to two separate realms, the one that governs the knowledge of what exists, the other concerned with what ought to exist? Why are we so obsessed with the need to unify the two realms *à tout prix*? Does this not point to a superstitious belief in system for its own sake?' It is my belief that if you were to take this view you would be doing a grave injustice to the seriousness and complexity of the problem we have been discussing and of which Kant was himself fully conscious. And going beyond this formal statement, I should like to try and show you in substantive terms why the dualism that Kant encountered really is unsatisfactory and why it is so hard for theory to tolerate it. Let us assume first that the determinism of nature is total, that is, everything in nature is determined by cause and effect, in conformity with laws. In that event Kant's assertion that the moral law is a given, an ordinance, something that irresistibly imposes itself on us, would itself – if I may be allowed this extreme formulation – be profoundly immoral. It would be immoral because it would make demands on people which, because they are empirical beings, they could not possibly satisfy. You must bear in mind here that in his critique of the psychological paralogisms, instead of proposing a rational theory of the soul that would have turned the basic determinants of the soul into something non-empirical, Kant insisted that the soul, in so far as it is embedded in the world of time and space, is an empirical phenomenon. Unlike Plato, Kant does not accept that a part of the soul can exist without forming part of the natural world. As an adherent of scientific method, Kant would not have agreed that there is any part of the soul that is not subject to science and hence to psychology and the laws of cause and effect. For example, let us suppose he had wished to establish something like a psychology of thought, that is, to study the psychological factors that condition the supreme logical modes of behaviour of the subject in so far as these modes of behaviour involve real reactions of the human subject to the external world. In that situation he would have refused to define some faculty or power of the soul as something positively given and present in the world and yet assign it to the intelligible world. If it is in fact the case that these two realms are irreconcilably opposed to each other, then by positing the moral law as a given, he would impose a burden on mankind whose demands would be beyond them from the very outset. I might add that this excessive demand would itself be a kind of unreason that would be quite incompatible with what for Kant is the vantage-point, the τόπος νοητικός of the ethical, namely reason itself. Conversely, however, if empirical subjects really can act freely, then because they are themselves part of nature, the Kantian unity of nature, founded on the categories, will be destroyed. Nature will then have a gap, and this gap will violate the unity of our knowledge of nature to which, according to Kant, the natural sciences aspire. He rightly claims that what characterizes the natural sciences is their search for unity, that is, their striving to reduce the largest possible diversity of facts to a minimum of functional equations. Let me say at once that in explaining the intolerable aspect of this dualism I have emphasized the excessive demands placed on the human subject. In so doing I find myself on terrain that is actually not very far away from Kant's own. For this kind of excessive demand lies in the nature of the entire Protestant tradition to which Kant belongs, a fact that has been rightly emphasized on numerous occasions and that is particularly relevant to Kant as a moral philosopher. The irrationality of being the chosen recipient of divine grace, and accompanying this the belief that the subject may perhaps be the beneficiary of grace if he strives unceasingly to do his duty without placing any limits on it, without being able himself to influence the outcome, is in a certain sense the hidden, unexpressed model of that paradox that Kant has stumbled on here. But, on the other hand, he is also a critic of theology because he refuses simply to accept the theological paradox and instead, in the spirit of Enlightenment, can see how dubious it is rationally. In general we can see the complexity of his relationship with theology. For, on the one hand, his philosophy undoubtedly strives to salvage the theological values that have been undermined by the progress of the Enlightenment. On the other hand, however, he wishes to salvage them by recourse to pure reason, in other words to philosophy, to thought. The very fact that the theological transcendent realm is made to depend on rational analysis enables us to perceive the principle that undermines theology as such. You will have to give some thought to the very complex and unresolved nature of Kant's relationship to theology if you wish to acquire an adequate grasp of the complexities of his moral philosophy with which we are dealing in this course of lectures.

If we are not satisfied with such explanations as those I have briefly pointed to, we shall doubtless need to have recourse to the experiential core of what Kant had in mind with his theory of two worlds. I would ask you not to push the term 'experience' too hard; it is not the empirical concept of experience that I have in mind here. It is easier to explain the matter by example than by drawing your attention to a general methodological principle. What I mean by experience here is simply a matter of what he saw, thought and noted; it is a matter of what occurred to him and what inspired him to think this remarkably contradictory and dualistic conception through and at the same time allow it to stand. You can have the same experience – using the word in this sense – if you think of yourselves as spiritual beings. Such beings do exist – or so I hope. Just think for a moment, consciously as it were, of your own consciousness of yourselves. That is to say, do not think of any principle of objective or absolute spirit, completely separate from the individual, nor even of the transcendental concept of constitutive principles. If you think of yourselves in this way, then this experience of spirit will have arisen, somehow or other, in the context of nature. Notwithstanding this, the spirit itself will, as I once formulated it in a conversation with my late teacher Adhémar Gelb, stand out a little bit above and beyond the natural world.[3] The spirit has no wish to exist entirely in vain, it has no wish simply to be a piece of nature itself, since what we call nature is defined through its opposition to our mental experience. In other words, the idea that we have, the epitome of all our ideas can be something that is not fully reducible to that natural context even though all their elements derive from existing reality, that is, from the natural world. We can imagine things that do not yet exist, and even though all the elements of our ideas come from the given world, existing reality, they are not reducible to their origins in nature because our mind organizes them or, to put it another way, disposes of them freely. And I believe that if you want to go back to the origins of what Kant actually meant by freedom, if you want to obtain a precise picture of the model that underlies his concept of freedom, a concept which in general we use in a fairly casual, imprecise manner, then it will turn out to be simply this remarkable faculty that enables us to organize in our imagination the various components of the natural world or of existing reality, and to rearrange them in different ways from those in which we found them initially and in which they exist in reality. This fact, this readily observable fact, that in its origins and its content mind points back to nature, but at the same time is not reducible to it, is, I believe, what Kant probably means by this entire doctrine of freedom in the midst of nature. Moreover, this is something that cannot be expressed adequately in a logic devoid of contradictions of the kind Kant advocates, an either-or logic, since in such a logic this situation can only be contradictory. It can only be expressed adequately in a dialectical logic in which the product of thought does not resemble the premises from which it sprang. I would say, incidentally, that this is the crucial distinction between a dialectical mode of thinking and that of the *prima philosophia* or ontology. And one implication of the dialectical method is that the primacy of origins, the primacy of the first thing, if I may express myself a little paradoxically, is not deferred to in the sense that I have just illustrated with my simple little model. Now this projecting element, this little piece of our nature that is not nature, is in actuality identical with consciousness of self. It thus stands in contrast to delusion [*Verblendung*], which is the category that designates the state of being utterly in thrall to nature. The truth is that we are no longer simply a piece of nature from the moment we recognize that we are a piece of nature. I think that it is not possible to express this more emphatically, for delusion is really nothing other than that stolid, blinkered pig-headedness that lacks the capacity for self-reflection and that succumbs to the delusion that all is natural conditioning precisely because it does nothing but set out in pursuit of immediate ends, immediate activities. It is not for nothing that delusion is also a category of myth, the category by means of which human beings are represented, as they are in myths, as beings unable to transcend nature. Moreover, any being that stands outside nature and might be described as a human subject can be said to possess consciousness of self, the capacity for self-reflection in which the self observes: I myself am a part of nature. By virtue of that fact the human subject is liberated from the blind pursuit of natural ends and becomes capable of alternative actions. These are ideas that underlie Kantian ethics, in an unexpressed and objective manner. They can also be found in a later stage of Kantian thought, in Schopenhauer, albeit in a very definite, even problematic form, specifically in the idea that ties ethics to the 'negation of the will to live'. I would rather not say anything further here about the negation of the will to live. Or perhaps I should just note that something of what Schopenhauer meant by it is contained in the idea of 'tearing down the veil of Māyā', that is to say, of recognizing one's own blindness and thereby escaping from it.[4] This in turn comes very close to what I am talking about here, even though I do not think it is necessary to follow Schopenhauer's logic to the point of sharing the positive identity-philosophy or metaphysics he deduces from this.[5] Only one point calls for mention here. I said that what transcends nature is nature that has become conscious of itself. Kant himself says this in a way, but at the same time the idea is alien to him because for him the domination of nature by means of the category of reason (which is the master category as far as the domination of nature is concerned) is itself something absolute and self-evident. And in general all the categories he uses in ethics are really nothing but the categories by which the domination of nature is achieved. It can be said, albeit with some licence and by departing a little from the literal meaning of the text, but without, I believe, distorting his intentions, that the categorical imperative itself is nothing but the principle for achieving the domination of nature, raised to a norm, elevated into an absolute. This means that if I am so to act that I am dependent on neither any external nor any internal agency, but solely on the universal laws of reason, this is tantamount to the total domination of nature, just as reason itself is in fact the most abstract statement of the principle of the domination of nature. Hence in the spirit of this domination Kant is now compelled to treat spirit *qua* freedom as an absolute. This means that he is not really able to take the step I have attempted to explain to you that would lead to a possible solution to the dilemma in which he and philosophy find themselves here, namely to regard reflection or freedom as nature becoming conscious of itself. This is the point at which Kantian philosophy can be said to be bewitched, as the fairy-tales would say. If it became aware of this, if it knew this itself, then his entire philosophy would be transformed; it would be changed into something completely different. This explains why the concept of self-reflection has no place in his thought and why in all theories of this kind the concept of self-reflection is avoided like the plague. This even includes Heidegger who through his concept of authenticity denounces reflection upon the self and its conditioned form, namely death, as a mere process of brooding or gazing at death transfixed.[6] And since authenticity is actually supposed to consist in a blind 'Being oneself toward death', Heidegger lapses here, in a very dubious fashion, in my estimation, into the tradition of idealist philosophy.[7] This then is the reason why Kant is unable to treat spirit as the principle governing the domination of nature in the spirit of dialectical mediation; that is, why he is unable to treat it as the self-reflection of nature in man and is forced instead blindly, unconsciously, as it were, to make it into an absolute – as if this principle of domination were a thing with an independent existence – and why he is unable to advance beyond this dualism of spirit and nature. The reason, we might say, is that the concept of mediation does not exist for him. Mediation here is not to be understood as a middle term, but in the sense that through the mediation of two diametrically opposed moments the one becomes conscious that it necessarily implies the other. In this sense we may argue that through this blind domination of nature in Kant what is constantly reproduced is that portion of nature that is not illuminated. In other words, we may say that Kantian morality is at root nothing other than domination.

Ladies and Gentlemen, now that I have confronted you with these perhaps rather difficult ideas, albeit ideas that I believe are indispensable to an understanding of our present project, I would like to revert to an earlier promise that I would explain why I have kept so rigorously to the Kantian texts. It is my belief that there is a fruitful tension between the construction of a philosophy of the kind I have undertaken and the literal interpretations or the interpretation of verbatim passages which frequently say very different things and are able to articulate very much more than they would if they were merely inserted in a general context where their effect is often dissipated. I would like to say that the kind of philosophical speculation that succeeds in going beyond the general intellectual context and that manages to articulate the thought-structures that are being investigated and enable them to speak is not one that distances itself from the literal specificity of the text. That is to say, it is not a method that conveys the general spirit of a philosopher as Dilthey does to a simply unbearable degree, but nor is it like Ernst Troeltsch's book on historicism, an otherwise reputable work.[8] The situation is rather that a close examination of a particular formulation, or the scrutiny of a passage like the one we have dwelt on at such length in this

particular chapter in Kant, is far better suited to giving you an understanding of the so-called great ideas that go beyond individual
insights than a straightforward survey of what can be found in Kant's
theory of ethics. I must add, however, that I cannot spare you that
survey since I recognize that you have a legitimate need to gain a
precise knowledge of what Kant's ethical doctrines actually are in the
course of these lectures, even if you only pick that knowledge up by
the way and in a relaxed and playful manner.

I should like to move on to an exposition of Kant's moral philosophy itself. Now that I have, as I believe, given you a fairly thorough
account of the questions of principle, I can concentrate more on
specific aspects of his moral philosophy. Perhaps the most suitable
way to begin is for me to explain to you why I decided to focus on
Kant's moral philosophy almost against my own will. The fact is that
we might say that Kant's moral philosophy is moral philosophy *par
excellence*, moral philosophy as such. Because it rules out empirical
reality from consideration, this *chorisis*, this extreme segregation of
the realms of nature and morality, is what makes possible something
like a fully articulated and logically consistent philosophy of morality. It is not by chance that none of Kant's successors – with the exception of Schopenhauer whom we have already mentioned – had
anything like an explicit moral philosophy, and the explanation for
this is that they were not minded to accept the dualism that has
been preoccupying us. The difficulties that I have outlined to you
induced them to abandon this dualistic system. This in turn made it
impossible for them to construct a moral sphere as such within their
philosophies. This was the criticism that Kierkegaard levelled at
Hegel at a later point in time. Kierkegaard saw it as a particular
defect, without realizing, however, that this mediation between the
different realms characteristic of a thoroughgoing idealism no longer
permits the construction of a moral philosophy in its true sense. But
this has the grave drawback that as a result the idealist tradition surrendered to a relativism that subsequently contributed to very sinis-
ter consequences indeed. The attempts to purify the Kantian ethics
that you find in neo-Kantianism bear the marks of impotence precisely because they are attempts at purification. And since they are
anyway linked, in Hermann Cohen, for example, to the philosophy
of law, this casts the shadow of heteronomy over them, particularly
when they are compared to the Kantian insistence on autonomy.[9] If
Kant is so bent on the radical exclusion of everything empirical as I
have suggested, you must not interpret this as the monomania of a
man obsessed with the concept of purity as he developed it in the *Critique of Pure Reason*, with *a priori* knowledge, and universal valid-

ity. You must instead be clear in your minds that empiricism is identical in its basic stance with scepticism. When you come to study the
history of philosophy, when you prepare for an examination on
Hume, for example, you will at some point realize that Hume's philosophy is essentially sceptical. But I believe that you would be well
advised to reflect on the meaning of scepticism in its relationship to
empiricism. It means that the more you admit empirical conditions,
the more you rule out the possibility of any objective definition of
the good life and of moral action. For example, if you follow the
arguments of a vulgar empiricism and demonstrate that the sanctity
of individual human life is not respected in certain empirically existing cultures, among the fashionable Trobriand Islanders, for example,
or elsewhere in the South Seas, this will lead you to the inference:
'Indeed, if all these norms are merely empirical in nature, then we
have no authority to insist on their universal validity.' And the
Kantian formalism that Kant was always being accused of is partly
to be explained by the fact that he wished to preserve the possibility
of a universally applicable formulation of the ethical despite this
aggressive empiricism and despite the scepticism associated with it.
His aim was to achieve such a high degree of universality that it
would disqualify sceptical arguments to the effect that the values
under discussion had to be regarded as the product of mere empirical conditioning. Now, you might well interject here: 'But if his conception of the ethical or the content of the ethical is nothing more
than the idea that I should act in accordance with laws that I have
presupposed as universally valid, then that is really terribly feeble and
in the practical life with which Kantian philosophy is concerned it is
not likely to be of the slightest interest to anyone.'

From this angle you will perhaps be able to understand another
feature of Kant's philosophy which has attracted only slightly less
criticism than that of formalism. This was the objection of excessive
rigour, which may indeed be seen as the correlative of formalism, if
I may put it in that way. Kantian ethics are rigorous in the sense that,
even though their universality and necessity are not indeed a matter
of natural fact, the ethical commandments will not allow the smallest concession. In particular, every action performed out of inclina-
tion is regarded as heteronomous and, if not simply condemned out
of hand, it is at least treated as something outside the realm of ethical
decision. And this is the feature of Kantian ethics that gave rise to
the earliest objections. As you probably all know, Schiller espoused
this particular deviation, even though he was in other respects a faithful follower of Kant, and we find in his writings something that Kant
only hinted at, namely the idea of a union of the otherwise opposed

principles of nature and freedom. This union could be said to have
been accomplished within the world of Kantian thought by means of
the argument that if freedom is the end of nature, then nature cannot
be the embodiment of radical evil in a moral sense. There is in short
a nature that can be called good, and this good nature can be said,
in the shape of art, to have an ennobling effect on humanity. It may
be said, therefore, to have an ethical effect, and so we are able to
credit nature with ethical qualities. This is a thesis that represents a
blunt deviation from Kant himself, who replied to it by saying – and
this is a good example of Kant's own rigorist approach – 'that vice
and evil are only too ready to sneak into the retinue of the Graces'
– whom Schiller defended against him.[10] I do not wish to bore either
you or myself with the trivial assertion that this Kantian rigorism is
linked to the ascetic ideals of Protestantism and is moreover an
ideological reflex of the so-called bureaucratic mentality, as the
sociology of knowledge has urged in criticism of Kant. Such trivial
objections were raised above all by Nietzsche and since then have
degenerated into a kind of infantile sneer. Such matters can be safely
ignored here. I believe that it will take us further and be more
profitable if we attempt to explain this so-called rigorism in terms
of the complexion of Kant's thought itself – a procedure I have
attempted to adopt with all these concepts. If you recall for a moment
that I explained Kant's formalism, that is, the extreme reduction to
universalities, as a kind of last-ditch stand against scepticism – as
the very bourgeois attempt to keep a grip on something like a moral
minimum that is protected against relativism of every kind – then
Kant's philosophical genius must surely have been fully aware that
the sort of definition he gives here really is a little feeble. His rigorist
zeal acts as a complement to this. That is to say, the only way in
which these formal definitions go beyond their own formalism, the
only way they develop any depth, is through the fact that they
absolutely refuse to tolerate any exceptions whatsoever and that
Kant ascribes to them what he terms their categorical character,
the summons that simply cannot be ignored. If you think back to the
concept of duty, you can see that we may think of it here as the
expression of the moral law in all its rigour. You will notice at once
that this irreducible minimum, this situation from which I am quite
unable to retreat, confers on this extreme moral formalism a kind of
concrete specificity. In particular, there is the fact that it is defined at
any moment by the exclusion of all desires, impulses and indeed
everything to which this norm applies. Thus the formal nature of the
ethical obtains its contents negatively through everything that stands
opposed to the moral law by virtue of this prohibition on everything

heteronomous, and what it means in concrete terms can always be identified by these opposed elements. The abstraction or formalism we have discussed here – and this is my final point – is itself the expression of the radical separation of the principle of freedom or reason from that of nature. This formalism, then, has a foundation in the content of the doctrine. This is no formalistic thinking; instead, formalism arises from the content of the theory, for theory excludes every specific moral content on the grounds that such contents arise from mere existence, the merely empirical sphere. It is external, alien to morality, something that does not just dwell in the freedom of my mind. Since it is quite impossible to imagine anything that did not refer back to empirical reality, then thanks to this *chorisis*, this dualistic principle in Kantian ethics that I have now expounded to you at some length, it becomes necessary for this principle to be proposed as something quite formal. Fundamentally, it is nothing but the identity of reason with itself. On the other hand, however – and this is what is so remarkable about it and something I can only mention to you in passing – thanks to its being intertwined with the rigour of the Kantian theory, that is, with the stringency and the inexorable nature of the concept of duty, these characteristics almost come to assume a kind of concrete specificity against Kant's will. In consequence his ethics ends up being rather less formal than it seemed at the outset. This is a point to which Julius Ebbinghaus[11] has rightly drawn attention, even though he failed to note that there is a peculiar dialectic at work between this concrete specificity and the strictly formal character of Kantian ethics. However, I have no time in which to discuss this further today. – Thank you.

LECTURE ELEVEN

4 July 1963

Ladies and Gentlemen,

I have tried in a number of ways to make clear to you that the principle of moral action in Kant is really nothing but reason itself, reason, moreover, that has freed itself from all the restrictions of particular ends and that in general proceeds only in accordance with the most universal matters of substance. Now of course this has a very long tradition and consequently a whole series of implications on which we should dwell for a few moments at least. The most important of these traditions, although admittedly not one that always lies closest to the surface, is the one history ascribes to Socrates. As you know, no texts by Socrates have come down to us and his philosophy contains a number of highly controversial issues. Nevertheless, following arguments formulated by Plato, his teaching has been expressed in the idea that right knowledge determines right action. In Plato's hands this was converted into the idea that virtue or moral behaviour is capable of being taught.[1] This theory, which is usually referred to as the rationalist foundation of moral philosophy, is preserved in Kant, and if anywhere this is the point – I would add, the only point – at which he can accurately be described as a rationalist philosopher. This rationalist theory has been widely discredited because it conflicts with the doctrine of the pure heart, the feeling that speaks for itself. In Germany, especially, this idea has assumed the virulent form that moral action is the result of immediate impulse and quite distinct from reason; it is an idea that finds its ultimate, shabby expression in the ghastly concept of 'nobleness of heart' [*Herzensbildung*], or sensitivity, which is what your family used to hold up to you as a model if you insisted too much on the importance of rationality. It survives today, if at all, only in wedding announcements. I have not succeeded in getting to the bottom of what is actually meant by this concept; it would be an interesting task, albeit more for an empirical sociologist than for a philosopher, to take a representative sample of the ways the term is used in order to find out just what this 'nobleness of heart' is supposed to mean. It is of the very greatest importance to be clear in your minds that on this central point Kant was at loggerheads with the entire German tradition, a tradition that presumably went back to Pietism and that regarded moral behaviour as a matter of purity of heart, of pure immediacy. Admittedly, his immediate successor of equal stature, Fichte, at once regressed to the earlier standpoint with his conviction that morality is always self-evident. Ladies and Gentlemen, you will know that Fichte not only regarded himself as Kant's successor; he also thought of himself as a strict Kantian, and actually believed that he understood Kant's philosophy better than Kant himself, a claim that is by no means as absurd as it appears to be to commonsense. For in many respects Fichte really does carry Kant's ideas to their logical conclusions.[2] It would be a valuable exercise to explore whether these two apparently contradictory statements are really as utterly incompatible as they seem. That is to say, the claim that reason is the guarantor and the only guarantor of the good, and the opposing claim that the moral is self-evident. Now that I have attempted to guide you down the narrow defile to the entrance to Kant's moral philosophy, I should like to venture the mental experiment of explaining why, on closer inspection, these two principles are not really as mutually exclusive as they appear to be. For on the one hand, the Kantian principle of morality is reason, a form of action that accords with reason absolutely and without any reservations. It thus ignores the particular nature of the particular ends of the individual and confines itself to the universal structure of rational rules. On the other hand, however, because reason is conceived as the universal, that is, as the faculty that is identical in all human beings, it can also be argued that reason and its conformity to law, which, as we have seen, Kant claims to be something immediately given, can be said to be something immediate. Thus what is needed for right action is not any reflection about reason, but immediate action in accordance with reason and the logical consistency of reason. It follows that from this point of view it is possible to interpret Kant as meaning that the moral is self-evident. I would like to believe that for all his resistance to Fichte's theory of knowledge, he did not object to this aspect of Fichte's doctrine. And I am not aware of his having raised any such objection as a matter of historical fact.

Of course, what is problematic about this identity of knowledge and virtue is – and I believe it is necessary to state this even if it is not my intention to link it to 'nobleness of heart' – that a decisive element in moral action disappears. That element is the transition from moral consciousness to moral action. Thus one substantial objection to the identification of morality with reason is that the fact that I have the right consciousness does not at all imply that I shall act in accordance with that right consciousness. Moreover, the more an antagonism develops in society between the interests and ends of particular individuals and the interests and ends of society as a whole, the harder it is to postulate the existence of any such immediate identity. At the very outset of the bourgeois age, a play was written in which the category of the bourgeois individual, the autonomous, independent individual, can be said to have appeared for the first time. I am thinking here of Shakespeare's *Hamlet*. It is not by chance that this play contains a character in whom right consciousness and right action enter into an irreconcilable contradiction. It is Polonius I have in mind here. He gives his son the very best advice – even though this advice is in the spirit of what Kant would call prudential advice, rather than of the categorical imperative – and yet he acts like an utter buffoon. We may say in general that this discrepancy, this divergence of consciousness and action constitutes the central theme of *Hamlet*. This theme can be said to be reflected in Polonius as in a concave mirror, whereas Hamlet is the figure who is destroyed by this conflict between knowledge and action – between the consciousness of the task imposed on him, of what the laws, the moral laws of his time, require him to do, and the possibility of carrying out this task.[3] What I want to say about this famous problem of theory and practice – which has again become such a burning issue today – is that wherever people possess, or imagine that they possess, a true theoretical consciousness they find that they are prevented from following its logic through in practice, partly, at least, because the problem has its own historical implications. That is to say, the problem of the disjunction between consciousness and action only comes to the surface in a world in which the individual is a being for himself who has become clearly detached from objective social reality and even stands out as its antithesis. We can see this clearly in the great artistic products of the Renaissance. When that happens this disjunction is accompanied by all those problems of suffering under the burden of knowledge that are not the least significant factor in the subsequent formation of European irrationalism. What I am referring to here is the fact that people suffer from their knowledge because they discover that no direct path leads from knowledge to practice. Instead they stand in need of a third thing, namely that injection of irrationality, of something no longer reducible to reason which I have now mentioned several times during this course of lectures. But as we have seen, this problem does not arise until the modern age, until the emergence of the antithesis between individual consciousness and the given historical reality of the society into which that individual enters. I am certain that this problem is one that very many of you will find very troubling because there really are very many situations when you really do not, and cannot, know the answer to the question 'What shall I do?' Nevertheless, despite its relative modernity, it is a problem that has a long prehistory, one that is deeply rooted in our society and its structure. Moreover, it is probable that it will only disappear once we achieve a reconciled society. You will all realize that by reconciliation here I am not thinking of any peace or compromise between necessarily antagonistic interests. But in contrast to this line of reasoning, we have to hold fast to the idea that there is some truth in this Kantian conception of the rational nature of right action – notwithstanding its blind spot, the defect that simply cannot be eradicated. The element of truth is, as I attempted to explain to you last time, that only insight, non-blindness, in other words, only self-reflection is capable of raising human subjects out of their purely natural context.

There was one further point I wanted to make.[4] This element of non-identity between the consciousness of right action and right action itself is also made explicit in Kantian philosophy, specifically, in a thesis that we have touched on elsewhere, but which I should like to clarify further here. What we discover is that the Kantian distinction between the kingdom of freedom and the kingdom of necessity contains an extremely important insight.[5] More specifically, we discover that we can pinpoint the element of non-identity by saying that in practical philosophy, that is, in Kant's writings on moral philosophy, the moral law is indeed conceived as a strict law, but as a law that merely prescribes what should be the case, and says nothing at all about what is in fact the case. Accordingly, we find that even in the theory the gap persists between moral law and moral practice that I have just been attempting to represent to you as a necessary component of the theory. It is to be found in those assertions in Kant's practical philosophy that describe the categorical imperative and the moral laws in general as obligation [Nötigung]. That is to say, these laws do indeed possess the character of a third thing, the form of necessity,[6] since, according to Kant, they confront us in such a way that, as rational actors, we cannot but comply with them. To that extent their character as laws is strictly preserved. But, as Kant repeatedly reminds us, they are not natural laws, not laws about existing phenomena, but propositions about what ought to exist. It remains quite unclear whether or not we really act in accordance with these laws. Thus no decision has been made in advance, and whether or not we comply with these laws depends on a third factor, on something not reducible to the laws of nature. Purely descriptively, that, if you like, is the situation that actually underlies the Kantian concept of freedom. I believe that it is only in this light that you can gain a true understanding of the role of the doctrine of freedom and of the relations between freedom and law in Kant.

Thus when we talk of the prescriptive character of reason, its nature as an imperative, what you need to understand is that there has been a crucial change from the concept of reason in antiquity that I reminded you of in connection with Plato. Reason has now ceased to be merely the ability to form the correct concepts and to articulate concepts in accordance with the nature of the matter to be analysed in the manner you find illustrated in the Platonic dialectic itself. Instead, reason in Kant is what we might call a productive faculty, a kind of activity. And the entire argument about the autonomy of its laws is based on this idea of reason as an activity in the sense that my reason does not simply lead me to acquiesce passively in these laws, but rather, these laws are laws that I am to produce from within myself. In this respect, too, the doctrine of the moral law is a kind of neutral concept, since the moral law is – as I have already told you – a given, although not in the primitive sense that you find in the theory of sense perceptions, of 'sensations' or 'perceptions',[7] but 'given' in the sense that it is something necessarily created or produced by me. And this stands in complete contrast to the concept of knowledge in Plato which really amounts to no more than the consciousness of something objectively pre-existing, namely the ideas. This existence in themselves of the ideas, which then are comprehended quasi-passively by reason, is not to be found in Kant. In Kant, even though these ideas are given, they are simultaneously something created by me, they are also, as it were, the product of this active reason. This highlights the affinity of Kant's concept of reason with practice. Thus it is no longer simply the case that I arrive at the knowledge of right action on the basis of a purely rational process, of a more or less logical procedure operating within pre-existing parameters. Instead, this knowledge must – in other words, I must – create the principles on which it is founded. Moreover, if in Kant the concept of the will – about which we shall say something in a moment – occupies such a central position, then you must be aware that we are not speaking here of a different force, a third, additional, factor. By will we mean simply a factor that, metaphysically, is identical with reason, in the sense that reason is itself a force, an activity, a productive power, as indeed had already been argued in the *Critique of Pure Reason* in the theory of original apperception as an original process of creation.[8] To that extent we can say that at its very heart Kantian philosophy did in fact anticipate Fichte's subsequent doctrine in which the practical and the theoretical are directly equated. It follows that reason in Kant means something quite different now from its meaning for the Greeks. It means, and this is the legacy of Rousseau in Kant's practical philosophy, the possibility of a moral organization of the world of a kind that never appeared in antiquity, so far as I have been able to establish, apart perhaps from certain speculations on the part of leftist strands in Socratic thinking. The reason why the Greeks failed to develop along these lines was that from the outset their concept of reason was far too preoccupied with arranging pre-given material. Furthermore, the idea that reality in its entirety might be produced purely by reason was quite alien to them, since they still conceived of the shaping of reality far too much in terms of a secularized natural religion, rather than as something predetermined by the nature of given structures.[9] In the light of the argument I have just outlined to you even the conception of a universal state which was envisaged by the middle Stoics, Panaetius above all, would be separated by an abyss from Kant's tract *On Eternal Peace*.[10] The fact is that in all such matters – and I think this is something that has to be said – Christianity, or the entire Judaeo-Christian tradition with its concept of discipleship with all that entails, has transformed fundamentally, to their very core, all the ideas that have been handed down to us from antiquity, even those that seem to have come down to us more or less literally. Even terms like λόγος or εἶδος λογιστικόν, the faculty of thought, with all their implications, have been so transformed in the Christian world that they mean something utterly different from their original meaning. This remains true even where – as is the case with Kant – traditional Christian ideas on moral philosophy are explicitly excluded. It would be a rewarding task to examine how modern philosophies have decisively transformed Classical ideas at the very points where they take up Classical motifs that had a crucial influence on Christianity as a whole. For example, there is the ancient idea of the *summum bonum*, which was an objective, quasi-passive ideal, external to us. In Kant this yielded to the absolute internalization of the good, the moral, and this internalization really presupposes implicitly the existence of the entire Christian teaching as the medium of internalization. These too are matters that need to be pointed out lest you are left with the idea that speculations about moral philosophy all take place in a sort of vacuum, and in order that you should see how even the subtlest conceptual distinctions bear the marks of particular religious and metaphysical beliefs that have gradually found their way into modern concepts in the course of thousands of years.[11]

Having said this, my next statement may sound heretical to you, but the fact is that Kant is not entirely serious about the idea of the rational nature of the moral. And it is precisely at this juncture that the negative, narrow-minded and dogmatic side of the idea that morality is self-evident comes to the surface. For I believe, and every human being who is reasonably alive to such matters and who has some self-knowledge will discover through experience, that morality is by no means self-evident. It is rather the case that within the complexities of modern life – and in this sense Kant's situation was not a whit less complex than our own – there are countless situations in which it is far from self-evident how we should act, and that we constantly find ourselves in situations where we need to think as hard as we are able, not, I must say, in order to satisfy the requirements of the categorical imperative – far be it from me to venture to aspire to such heights – but where you need all your wits about you simply to behave like a reasonably decent human being. This entire line of thought just goes by the board in Kant, and in the process it always seems as if we were bowing more or less willingly to the moral values of our own day. That is to say, the problem of the distinction between culturally approved norms of the day and norms that flow from the categorical imperative is one that Kant would self-evidently have accepted in theory, but it is a distinction that remains utterly without consequence for him. There is an explanation for this and I do not know whether I have already pointed it out to you. The entire Kantian ethics is, as Lukács observed at a time when he was still allowed to think independently about such matters, a private ethics.[12] This means that it is an ethics in which the problem of possible conflicts between the values imposed on individuals and the objective norms that either hold sway in a given society, or arise from the desire to change society, simply does not arise.[13] When it comes down to it, the world to which this extraordinarily sublimated ethics has been tailored is not so very different from the agrarian society, let us say, of Johann Peter Hebel or Jeremias Gotthelf.[14] Such a society is one in which every individual finds himself in a traditional, solidly built and unproblematical world, and so he really does know at any given moment what he is supposed to do. If you consider the examples that Kant gives by way of illustrating his ethical principles, you will see that these are always taken from the life of the honest merchant who needs, naturally enough, to look out for his own interests, but who must abstain from what we might call pre-bourgeois methods, traditional methods in the bad sense. I am thinking here of fraud and other tricks to get the better of others. It is without doubt one of the concrete sides of the rationality of Kantian ethics – by which I mean the requirement implicit in Kant's ethics to behave in a strictly rational way – that we should act strictly in accordance with the model of bourgeois rationality, that is, with the rules of exchange. According to this model you should give each man what he deserves and you should press for what is due to you without cheating him or allowing yourself to be cheated. Since in fact this principle of sums that come out right is really very close to the original model of rational action, since – to put it slightly differently – such a calculation is the model of rational action, it was natural for Kant to equate what might be termed the commercial values of what was essentially still an agrarian society with action that is truly ethical. The same thing might be said of the civil-service ethics of duty – punctuality, incorruptibility and similar virtues – all of which stood in particular esteem in the age when the Kantian philosophy was conceived because that was an age that stood at the divide between the cameralist, bureaucratic state of mercantilism and a fully developed bourgeois society whose values Kant makes normative for a society that is still organized in a largely irrational way. But as I have said, at this point Kant's argument is inconsistent because he teaches that in order to be good, you have no need of philosophy. This is a claim that Socrates or Plato for whom the radical breach between theory and the practical organization of reality did not yet exist, would never have advanced. Instead, Socrates, if we construe his philosophy correctly, would probably have told his students in the agora in Athens in all innocence that they could only act morally if they had learned how to philosophize. At this juncture he would have taken the idea of reason much more seriously than Kant, who represents the transition to an ethics of 'Dwell in the land and lead an upright life'.[15]

All this notwithstanding, Kant's belief that we have no need of philosophy because the moral is an immediate given also contains an element of truth – and this is something I should like to make clear to you now. The Greek sense of identity, which I have already mentioned, presupposes a relatively homogeneous society. It assumes a society in which at least among those who are free and equal – and Greek philosophers generally did not think about anyone else – differences of consciousness were not so great that the insistence that you had to philosophize in order to be good would have led to a situation in which goodness was a matter of a privileged education,

as is unquestionably true of our own age and was no less true in
Kant's day two hundred years ago. There is, then, something of
a bourgeois revolutionary element here, we might call it a
Rousseauesque element. It opposes an unmediated goodness to the
conventionally stratified hierarchical world, and asserts that goodness should not be made to depend on the privilege of education or
on 'what fashion had sternly separated', to use Schiller's phrase.[16]
Whereas, on the other hand, as early as Kant himself, we find a
strange restriction placed on reason – a restriction that then becomes
standard for the whole of idealism, which is curiously ambivalent on
this question, one which ought to be analysed thoroughly at some
point. This restriction consists in the fact that the greater the emotional investment in reason, that is, the more philosophers strive to
derive everything that exists, even the most concrete specifics, from
reason itself, the greater the tendency to circumscribe reason and
defame it. Precisely because the given ends up as the product of
reason, it then becomes a simple matter to ask people to take
the given as their guide on the grounds that the given is essentially
rational. Thus the later diatribes – I can find no better word – that
you find in Hegel against reasoning, against people who want to
set the world to rights, against mere reflection, against all these
categories – and such invective pervades the whole of the later Hegel
in particular – are all prefigured in Kant right down to the terminology he uses. After all, 'vernünfteln' [quibbling, pseudo-rationality] is
a term of abuse in Kant.[17] The reason we find such diatribes in Kant
is that he does not experience the contradictions in which reason in
its particular employment becomes entangled as necessary, but only
as a kind of aberration, an abuse of reason, whereas reason itself is
seen as exempt from contradiction because it is supposed to have the
character of pure conformity to law.

The fundamental problem of Kantian ethics is autonomy, and its
opposite is heteronomy. I do not believe that you will now require
any lengthy explanation of these terms. Autonomy is the law that I
give myself. However, by 'law' I do not mean the experience we all
have when we emancipate ourselves from universally valid ideas of
law taken from traditional ethics, but at the same time desire to act
morally by promulgating our own code to guide our actions – I
believe that this is a stage we all pass through. This is not what is
meant by autonomy, for in Kant the idea of autonomy contains from
the outset the idea of universality. However, this concept of universality is heavily loaded in the sense that the law I give myself is not
concerned simply with my own personal needs or inclinations or the
chance nature of my individuality. Instead the law must be universal

and this means for Kant that the law I give myself must be of such a kind that I can imagine it as the foundation of a universal legislation, that is, a legislation that does not violate the freedom and the autonomy of other individuals. The opposing concept, and this is the epitome of what Kant rejects as the juridical source of ethics, is heteronomy. Heteronomy is the law that is imposed on me by others, that I receive without its being a law given by my own reason. Freedom – to underscore its place in Kant's philosophy as emphatically as possible – means to give laws to oneself. If I do not give myself laws, if I do not act in accordance with the laws of my own reason, I make myself dependent on heteronomy, on laws that hold good outside myself, and I thereby become unfree. This concept of heteronomy in Kant does not refer merely to unfreedom in a political sense, in other words, to the need to adjust blindly to norms imposed on me by others. It refers also to restrictions on my reason of whatever kind. Thus it includes my own instincts and my own needs, as well as any constraints on my civic freedom by external factors of every kind whatever their source. It is precisely at this point, Ladies and Gentlemen, that Kant finds himself in full accord with the Classical tradition. As early as Aristotle's ethics we find that the concept of ἐλευθερία, of freedom, is understood in the twofold form of freedom from tutelage. What Aristotle, as an early Greek philosopher, means by this is of course tutelage at the hands of the τυραννίς, the tyranny of his own pupil, Alexander the Great, as well as of our dependence on our own emotions.[18] The task of freeing ourselves from these formed part of the teaching of the Cynics in the earlier phase of Greek philosophy, and of the first generation of Stoics in the Classical period. Hence we can say that this twofold meaning of the concept of freedom, of outer freedom and inner freedom, can be said to be a prominent, even dominant theme of the history of philosophy as a whole, and one about which philosophers have agreed, even though in other respects their philosophies are violently opposed to one another. If you read the Excursus on 'Juliette' in the *Dialectic of Enlightenment* you will discover that we have collected examples of this from writers who really do have nothing in common except for the idea that freedom consists in the suppression of the emotions. At the same time, you also find that this view contains the potential for an extraordinarily damaging dialectic. This is that in the name of freedom, that is, in the name of control over the emotions by consciousness, the gratification of the instincts and, in general, happiness of every kind falls victim to a kind of taboo and is banished from philosophy. God knows that such an intention is anything but alien to Kant, for Kant – and here he is not without predecessors, Spinoza does exactly the same thing – banishes sympathy, compassion and the direct expression of pity from his ethics because all impulses of this sort are merely natural impulses, and are purely instinctual. As such they are said to be incompatible with pure reason, with the principle of reason. Therefore, because this extreme view of the concept of freedom is based on its absolute independence from all existing beings, from nature as such, it threatens to become transformed into unfreedom. Human beings have denial imposed upon them and above all they are not able to recover those things they have been forced by this imperative to renounce. But this is a theme I shall return to next time.

Transcript of
LECTURE TWELVE

9 July 1963[1]

On autonomy and heteronomy as central concepts of Kant's ethics. In the concept of autonomy freedom and law are merged directly in a syncopated organization. αὐτός, I myself as subject, freely determine myself. This act of determination shall at the same time be νόμος, the law. Heteronomy: the law stems from others, and as in antiquity, this does not just refer to other people.

The concept of value has no place in Kant. It is no accident that the most celebrated critique of Kant's ethics, that of Max Scheler, believed there should be values, while in Kant's view values are heteronomous and therefore lacking in authority.[2] The cult of values is reactive in nature. It should be regarded as something that arises from the disorientation and the loss of structure in a society. In such a situation traditional norms cease to exist, but individuals do not determine themselves and instead snatch at something to cling to. This cult arises then essentially from the yearning for guidance; its norms are justified not by reason but are themselves the product of yearning. This is expressed in the values themselves. On the one hand, they are arbitrary; on the other, they express the weakness of human beings who are unable truly to determine themselves and to obey their own law, but who instead go in search of something that 'might come by and take them along'. They pride themselves on the result which they refer to as 'solid' and 'down to earth'.

Back to the concept of autonomy. It could be said that even the small amount of freedom that finally emerges in Kant is cancelled out again when freedom is defined as the ability to give oneself the law. But the idea has to be taken more seriously than that. The abstract protestation that the law is the negation of freedom does not do the matter justice. For a condition in which there was no law at all would also be absolutely unfree, since everyone would be exposed to oppression at the hands of everyone else. This would be the *bellum omnium contra omnes* of Hobbes's political theory. The postulated absolute state of lawlessness and freedom is identical with unfreedom. The same thing applies to inner freedom. If people pander to their own needs without reference to reality and with no control over their own egos, they become dependent on themselves and therefore unfree. The addict is the extreme case; he cannot stop himself from satisfying his own needs even when they are incompatible with self-preservation. The idea that an absolute freedom that is not also an intrinsically determined freedom amounts to the negation of freedom is not the invention of puritanical schoolmasters. It has an element of truth. Kant's interlocking of freedom and law is to be taken seriously; it is no mere ideology. On the other hand, the idea of law always contains a potential threat to freedom. The law as an all-embracing regulation that tolerates no exceptions contains a totalitarian element and acts as a constraint on people even when that constraint lacks the justification of reason. Where freedom is restricted it stands on a knife's edge, ready to vanish entirely. The sphere of law, even when it formally subserves the idea of protecting freedom and guaranteeing it, contains the tendency to abolish freedom. The relationship between freedom and the law is not a well-balanced, rational compromise, but possesses dynamic elements on both sides. What the law encompasses is the instinctual energies of human beings; these energies doubtless need to be contained, but should not be sublimated out of existence. On the other hand, a psychological authority that is nurtured by sources of energy that have been separated off – the super-ego, for example – tends to turn into an absolute and to abolish freedom. There, too, there is no balance. Since the law tends to assert itself more effectively than freedom, we have to stay on our guard and be constantly vigilant in the face of a fetishization of law, for example, of juridical norms that claim that decisions once taken are irrevocable. We cannot remain satisfied with any so-called order since no sooner is an order established than it is all up with freedom. We cannot rely on a stable balance between the two.

Kant discovered a highly original framework with which to stabilize the *a priori* balance in the relationship between freedom and law. The freedom of each individual should only be restricted to a certain extent, and should be restricted by law *only* to the extent to which it restricts the freedom of another individual.[3] That is indeed a matter of form, but it does amount to a canon which can serve as a guide. Social function and the principle of moral philosophy are linked. The

individual who exists absolutely for himself is nevertheless a function. In order to be able to exist human beings have been brought
together through the process of socialization. Freedom is not given
to an individual in isolation, but with regard to the social totality in
which human beings live. The concrete specificity of the moral law
can only be made a reality within a concept of social function, not
on the model of a Robinson Crusoe.

The difference between the *Critique of Practical Reason* and the
Groundwork of the Metaphysic of Morals is not easy to grasp. The
Groundwork of the Metaphysic of Morals takes so-called natural
consciousness as its starting-point.[4] The *Critique of Practical Reason*
is held to be more difficult. But you should be warned against such
value judgements, since the simpler writings tend to dispense with the
cogent argumentation. Hegel's *Propaedeutic* is the most egregious
example of this. The *Critique of Practical Reason* was written in
analogy to the *Critique of Pure Reason* in the sense that it attempts
to dissect the *faculty* of practical reason. In the process certain contradictions, the antinomies of practical reason, come to light and are
then resolved. This is followed by a doctrine of method. In contrast,
the *Groundwork of the Metaphysic of Morals* is an original attempt
to advance from natural consciousness to the categories of moral philosophy. It moves from what might be called a pre-critical position
to the standpoint of moral philosophy. In their essential content the
two works are largely in agreement.

The fact that Kant can take natural consciousness as his starting-
point, that he can begin with the moral intuitions that we all have,
is less offensive than might be thought at first sight. This is because
he can take the moral law as a given, one that is even present in our
ordinary consciousness; our task is to lay it bare. However that may
be and whether or not the moral law is a given – this approach contains an element of truth. We cannot simply invent an ethics, we
cannot simply decide to adopt a code that goes against the morals of
one's own age. To do that would mean giving oneself a dispensation
from many otherwise prevailing norms, but it also tends to assume
the existence of norms in others from which you hold yourself to be
exempt. These norms contain an element of universal validity and
this explains why it is always vain and futile to pretend to ignore the
universal. On the other hand, a so-called responsible human being
cannot simply declare himself satisfied with the norms that prevail in
a particular society. Our task rather – and this is what is so valuable
about grounding ethics in natural consciousness – is to confront
prevailing norms with our own consciousness and to measure each
against the other. This cannot be done by imagining that we can

simply invent new norms. For the most part, to set aside existing values without taking into account the reality that underlies them leads to a regression to an even more primitive state of affairs. Ignorance is not the medium of freedom. You can only liberate yourself from prevailing values if you can reflect them within yourself. Kant's method is to advance towards the categorical imperative by means of an increasingly abstract process of thought. His premise is that in general we act in accordance with principles. Kant can scarcely conceive of a life not based on principles. The forethought and concern for the future that are part and parcel of a bourgeois existence are in need of principles. Nowadays, the self-evident need for principles of action is not as powerful as in former times. Who still has the confidence to proclaim such principles? Reality today is so overpowering that it calls for agility, flexibility and conformity – qualities that rule out action in accordance with principles. Kant's principles are predicated on a strong, stable self, something that no longer exists in that form. Anyone who were to act in accordance with principles today would seem to us to be indescribably pedantic. As in antiquity, at the time of the early Hellenic period, there is a crisis of individuality. Aristotle who is to Plato as, say, an Anglo-Saxon is to Kant, takes this into account: the concept of law, which in Kant is absolutely unrestricted, is limited in Aristotle by what he calls 'fairness'.[5] This ideal has faded today. Aristotelian 'fairness' requires that we should not just act in accordance with the law, but that we should also take account of the person we are dealing with and his particular circumstances. In Kant's eyes this would be heteronomy. At one point he represents consistency as alone worthy of philosophy. 'Fairness' would always be inconsistent. The postulate that we should act in accordance with rules, laws and maxims represents the translation of the primacy of reason into the practical sphere, whereby reason is the embodiment of universal principles. So much for the postulation of principles, a curious fact, given that Kant otherwise criticizes heteronomy. Kant does not consider the possibility that someone might not act in accordance with principles, even though it would be far from contemptible freely to confront a situation, rather than to measure it against fixed principles.

> Since I have robbed the will of every inducement that might arise for it as a consequence of obeying any particular law, nothing is left but the conformity of actions to universal law as such, and this alone must serve the will as its principle. That is to say, I ought never to act except in such a way *that I can also will that my maxim should become a universal law*.[6]

The concept of will here is extraordinarily formal in nature. My faculty of desire, from which my actions flow, is supposed to be directed by my reason towards particular ends; the will is restricted to a faculty of desire orientated towards ends and is guided by ends. This definition is important because this concept of will deviates so hugely from normal linguistic usage and is by and large inappropriate to the actual phenomenon of the will. 'I should act so that the maxim of my will can become the foundation of a universal law.'[7] Elucidation of the concept of 'maxim': every citizen acts in accordance with principles. 'Maxim' is derived from the superlative of *magnus*, the highest, the greatest. It is the supreme rule, for example, 'Always be true and honest'.[8] Where such a supreme rule is no more than a law of prudence that ultimately serves my own advancement, it is only empirical. On the other hand, such a principle is the form on which my action bases itself as if it had the force of a norm. The problem implicit in the categorical imperative is this: how does the norm I have given myself come to have absolute and supreme authority? Only when this rule coincides with an absolutely universal and necessary rule can the imperative be called categorical. However, the laws that obtain in reality are not that; they reflect power relations and are just as empirical as my own laws. Hence a third factor is required, a court of reason to which I can submit the rules governing my life for approval. This is how Kant arrives at the categorical imperative. 'Categorical' means absolutely valid, in contrast to 'hypothetical', only conditionally valid. But we are not dealing with laws of nature, for in that case there would be no freedom. The categorical imperative is only a postulate; nevertheless, as a rational being, I cannot resist its claims. Through abstraction Kant effects the transition from the individual to the human subject in the universal sense, the subject that appears as the transcendental subject in the *Critique of Pure Reason* and as consciousness in general in the *Prolegomena*.[9] Because the supreme principle of pure practical reason is simply a given, it cannot be deduced in the same way as the transcendental unity of apperception. We can leave to one side the question whether that deduction is genuine and not rather the unfolding of the elements of a unity.[10]

LECTURE THIRTEEN

11 July 1963

Ladies and Gentlemen,

I should like to follow up what I was saying last time about the problem of the non-deducibility of the categorical imperative. In this problem we can hear the echo of a theme that is not the least important among the more latent impulses of modern philosophy, in particular of phenomenology. Even before phenomenology proper began to exert an influence in philosophy its theme was formulated by Georg Simmel in the statement 'that everything that can be proved, can also be disproved; only what cannot be disproved is irrefutable'.[1] We encounter here the phenomenon of fatigue in the face of argument. This fatigue too has a dialectical structure. It has something of the cumulative experience of problems that cannot be resolved, the so-called Scholastic disputes in philosophy, and of the need to leave them behind with the aid of a kind of philosophy that flees from argument and puts a stop to constant refutation and renewed discourse. Philosophy's impulse to transform itself into teaching, that is, to avoid the relativity of 'That is so – Yes, but . . .' undoubtedly has its legitimate side, but it also has two dangers. On the one hand, there is the danger of bringing philosophy down to the mere acceptance of so-called givens, that is, of banishing genuine thought and transforming philosophy into the investigation of positive facts – just as for its part Positivism has attempted to transform such research into philosophy. On the other hand, there is the danger of setting up arbitrary commandments, of exhorting people to do something or other. Both dangers can be detected in the categorical imperative, although it must be said that there is an element of truth in all this. For if the truth does not also have the power to escape from the cut and thrust of argument, if it does not contain something that transcends that bad infinity, then it will be no more its own master than it is when it abides by a decree or by something merely given.

We had started to discuss the first version of the categorical imperative as it is formulated in the *Groundwork of the Metaphysic of Morals,* and I should now like to consider it in somewhat greater detail. In accordance with my custom I shall take a close look at the actual text. Kant writes, 'I ought never to act except in such a way *that I can also will that my maxim should become a universal law.'*[2] It is interesting to note that the limiting word 'also' is included here. We might almost interpret it to mean that he only wants to say that this maxim does not conflict with a universal law, but without demanding, positively demanding, that every single action should flow directly from that universal law. In this there is perhaps a concession to the conditional nature of action which consists in the realization that it is wrong to expect an absolutely smooth transition between it and the most universal laws. Such considerations may play a certain role here since Kant is concerned to ensure that the categorical imperative should not be left suspended in mid-air, but should retain its validity for real human subjects, even though these subjects should not be reducible to it. But in fact that role is of greater relevance to the concept of volition that he has here, to his concept of will. I should like to emphasize to you once again that the concept of the will has a very specific meaning that is generally overlooked when we refer to the moral faculty, or whatever we choose to call it, as the will. There is a passage in the *Critique of Practical Reason,* in chapter II of the Analytic, 'Of the concept of an object of pure practical reason', where Kant writes 'Reason alone is capable of discerning the connection of means with their ends so that' – and here comes the definition – 'the will might even be defined as the faculty of ends, since these are always determining principles of the desires . . .', etc., etc.[3] According to this, the will is the faculty of desire; its determining principles lie in its ends. This formulation is very striking because it represents one of those countless acts of self-correction that, I would even go as far as to say, go to make up the Kantian system. To put it another way, in its essential motifs, Kantian philosophy objectively presses on towards dialectics, but it is presented in accordance with the rules of traditional logic. Instead of a dialectical treatment of concepts, that is, instead of introducing contradiction directly into the concept, Kant adjusts to this situation by a continuous process of revision and self-correction. If I may offer you a tip on how to read Kant in general, I would say that you will probably only be able to understand him fully, particularly the

Critique of Pure Reason and the *Critique of Judgement,* if you
yourselves learn to distinguish his consistent overall intentions, what
we might call his official intentions, and the innumerable corrections
which constitute his attempt to do justice to the dialectical relations
he encounters. It is important not to misunderstand me here, however,
and to accept that he does this without adopting a concept of dialectics of his own. What I have to say about this passage, however,
is simply that following the old Platonic division of the εἴδη, of the
human faculties, the faculty of desire is directed at the senses and
belongs therefore in principle in the realm of heteronomy. But if the
will is now defined as the faculty of desire determined by ends – and
ends are to be understood as rational ends – what we are confronted
with is a faculty defined in principle as belonging in the realm of the
senses, but because it is conceived in these very formal terms, it is
nevertheless given a mediating link to reason as soon as it is organized in terms of rational ends and is subordinated to them. And, like
all mediating categories, this act of mediation is of vital importance
in Kant because it is only with its aid that the original sensuous
faculty of desire, intention – which is normally the very thing that
moral behaviour is distinguished from – can be given the opportunity to be determined by reason. It is the only way in which the moral
law, the categorical imperative and our behaviour as empirical beings
can all be reconciled. This, then, is the reason for this peculiar
intermediate link, this intermediate determination of the will as a
faculty of desire, but as one that is simultaneously guided by reason.
Moreover, this theory is not so utterly remote from psychology
as might appear at first glance. The mediating category of the will
is not, as it is in Aristotle, a mediation between internal and external, but is purely internal. This means that it is the force by which
the moral is able to realize itself without regard to empirical reality.
If you will allow me to make a concession to the language of
psychology: reason in the shape of the will takes possession of the
instinctual drive, or in the language of psychology, the ego takes
possession of the id. This means that the will is the element of available instinctual energy that is diverted and subjected to the conscious
will; and the concept of the will does in fact always contain
something of this.[4] It is not the least testimony to Kant's greatness
that even when he provides such verbal definitions as this one of the
will – and this is why you should always scrutinize such definitions
very carefully – they do not have that arbitrary quality that you find
so often in instrumental definitions nowadays. Instead, you could
say that they also correspond to a phenomenological reality; in
other words, they satisfy as far as possible Plato's old demand

that they should strive to resemble the nature of the phenomenon being defined.

Thus what characterizes the moral is that the will should be quite free of any consideration of intentions of any kind. Hence what Kant is concerned with is that I should behave in accordance with the moral law and that the question of the effects of my actions, if I may put it like that, should not play an essential role in this. According to the *Groundwork*,

> An action done from duty has its moral worth, *not in the purpose* to be attained by it, but in the maxim in accordance with which it is decided upon; it depends therefore, not on the realization of the object of the action, but solely on the *principle of volition*, in accordance with which, irrespective of all objects of the faculty of desire, the action has been performed.[5]

And this converges with what I have just said, namely that the will is the faculty of desire, but subordinated to the primacy of reason, the primacy of the moral law itself.

Now that we are talking about the will, I should like to note that the concept of will, even in Kant, is rudimentary. That is to say, he consistently resists the claims of psychology, but in order to be able to say anything at all, and to give some kind of underpinning to his laws, his principles and his postulates, he is compelled ultimately to include some elements of psychology – and this too is a basic structural feature of the *Critique of Pure Reason*. Thus we find creeping into his own philosophy something that really ought not to be there, namely the idea of fixed faculties of the soul that ultimately amount to an ontological interpretation of the soul, according to which the soul is said to consist of various essences. In the same way the theory of desiring or logical faculties in Plato, the so-called Platonic psychology – which is the source of this entire way of thinking – is tied to his ontology and his theory of ideas. That is to say, in Plato's philosophy the soul of man has migrated into the faculties which are objective essences in their own right along the lines of the Idea, and it is explicitly stated at one point in the *Phaedo* that 'the soul is related to the Idea by its lack of corporality'.[6] Kant could not say this because, given his critique of the so-called rational theory of the soul, the objectification or reification of the capacities, forces or faculties of the soul was to be repudiated from the outset – such faculties were not to be regarded as things existing in their own right, but rather as functional attributes of the experiential content to which these categories of the soul were applied. But by his very use of such a concept as 'the will' – and it is interesting to see that he cannot quite dispense with it, that he cannot really eliminate it – he talks as if the soul were an existing thing that broke down into faculties such as understanding, desire, will, and the like. We should add that of course the concept of the will in particular includes an infinite number of things, and should not be hypostatized into a single autonomous thing. It is a fact – and since the will is a psychological category, I must inevitably have recourse once again to psychology – that we see again and again that this hypostasis of the will has something arbitrary and feeble about it when compared with the realities of mental life in general and the ways in which people actually behave. We often see this in connection with talk about someone being especially strong-willed or weak-willed. We may think in this connection of Marcel Proust's novel, a work from which we can all learn how to make indescribably subtle distinctions about all such matters, and from which philosophers in particular could profit a great deal. Not the least of the points made there is that there is a deep irony in the fact that his father ceaselessly reproaches him with being weak-willed, and that he lacks will-power while the entire work testifies to the presence of an immensely powerful will, even though not a word is wasted on it. However, there are circumstances in which a strong will can only express itself as a weak will, in terms of the conventions accepted by his father. For his will is directed at completely different ends from those of self-preservation, which is supposed to be the proper concern of the will according to the traditional view. At any rate, I should like to repeat that in his theory of the will Kant very rightly perceived that this concept of the will is not a matter of being obstinate and primitive, but that in it instinctual energy, the instinctual impulse and its rational control, all belong together. And in implementing this process of mediation – and I think it is important to insist on this – the will appears in Kant as something good. At the beginning of the *Groundwork*, in the celebrated first sentence, we read that 'It is impossible to conceive anything at all in the world, or even out of it, which can be taken as good without qualification, except a *good will*.'[7] If we read Kant's overtones here correctly, this means that the will is good as long as it is the faculty of desire guided solely by reason; and that evil is whatever has no will at all: the will-less, the diffuse, everything that drifts in the face of that centralizing, organizing authority. For this reason we can say that in Kant's ethics the bourgeois principle of dominion over nature is reflected, at the very pinnacle of philosophical achievement, in the focusing of instinctual energies on the self that directs them. We might almost say that something like ill will is not really conceivable in Kant because the will as self-consistent rational desire is in fact the good; reason and good-ness coincide. If you read the Excursus on 'Juliette' in the *Dialectic of Enlightenment*, you will find this idea developed further in great detail.[8] We could express the same idea by saying that if the will is in fact the mediating category between desire and reason, then reason itself has an affinity with the will, that it is related to the will. If we look closely at Kantian philosophy and Kantian epistemology, we shall find this confirmed. We shall discover that the central concept of the theory of knowledge and hence the true definition of reason in Kant is in fact something very like the will. This is the idea of origi-nal apperception, that is, of pure productive power. Reason for Kant – and this is one of the most crucial innovations of his philosophy – is not really measured against the objectivities of logic and objective logical laws, but is conceived from the outset as an activity, as productivity, from which logical laws are then supposed to arise. In that sense we could say that the theory of the primacy of practical over theoretical reason that I first explained to you in connection with the relevant chapter from the *Critique of Pure Reason*, could be taken a lot further. For in effect reason is nothing other than the will, except that it is pure will, that is, a kind of activity, of primal activity that has wholly purified itself of all dependency upon pre-existing objects. To that extent you can see how Kantian philosophy, especially his practical philosophy, his moral philosophy, contains within it the seeds of the entire subsequent philosophical tradition. This includes Fichte's philosophy, and in particular we can see that in the light of Kant's own position Fichte's famous or notorious claim that he could interpret Kant's philosophy better than Kant himself is not really as outrageous as it might have first appeared. If we were to express what I have just said in social terms – and that, too, is a way to concretize the abstract or formal Kantian ethic – we might say that what Kant has done is to have taken the work ethic of bour-geois society, that is, the standard governing the process of produc-tion of goods that presides over bourgeois society as a whole, and to have adopted it as his own supreme philosophical standard. In other words, the necessity of social labour as the supreme, binding norm has become an abstract principle in his thought, and we would almost have to say that what he really means by radical evil is nothing other than laziness, the failure to satisfy this requirement of bourgeois society.

Let me now say a few words about Kant's concept of duty, and in particular, the way in which this concept is introduced in its basic form in the *Groundwork of the Metaphysic of Morals*. He writes there: '*Duty is the necessity to act out of reverence for the law.*'[9] Reading once again with a microscope, as it were, I would draw your attention to the two terms for 'lawfulness' in this sentence, namely 'necessity' and 'law'. We could say that two kinds of necessity are predicated here. First, there is the idea that the law must be objectively valid – and as I have pointed out a number of times, this objective validity in Kant is identical with universality and necessity. Second, however, it possesses the meaning that I am compelled to act in this manner rather than any other, that I shall not be let off, and hence must bow subjectively too to this law, this necessity. The mediating term in this necessity, in this postulate, in this imperative gesture 'You must act thus and not otherwise' – is reverence. Reverence [*Achtung*] is a major category in Kant, and he took immense pains to develop the concept. He did so in a highly ingenious manner, one appropriate to his argument. As he remarks in a footnote shortly after the passage I have just read to you, reverence is indeed a feeling, and as a feeling in the sense of the usual psychological doctrine of faculties, it would fall outside the purview of the primacy of reason. But it would still be a feeling that relates to reason in an essential way. Here is what he says about it. I shall read the relevant passage:

> Yet although reverence is a feeling, it is not a feeling *received* through outside influence, but one self-produced by a *rational* concept, and therefore specifically distinct from feelings of the first kind, all of which can be reduced to inclination or fear.[10]

Thus he attempts here, and once again we find him in very close proximity to the phenomenon under scrutiny, to define the distinguishing feature of this feeling. And he defines it as a rational feeling – if you will permit me this paradox – that is, a feeling that is only aroused when I am confronted by reason, by rationality. We may think of it as being an emotional reflection, a mirroring of the principle of reason itself. In this sense reverence can be regarded as a mediating link between my freedom and the law, both the law in itself, its own rationality, and also the imperative gesture that proceeds from it to me, that prevails on me by virtue of this reverence.

Now you may well ask, and you will be right to do so, as one might of a picture puzzle: 'All right, you have now told us for hours on end that the central concept of the *Critique of Practical Reason* and Kantian moral philosophy in general is freedom. But what is left of this freedom now?' You are very much in the right to aim both your question and your criticism at me. You have noticed that the imperative we have been discussing is characterized by necessity, that it appears to me in the guise of a necessary commandment, and, finally, the fact that I should feel reverence towards it only reinforces this possibility once again. In reality the only opening left here for freedom would be for me to extricate myself from this reverence, this conformity to law, this commandment. This would be very strange. For it would mean that if you take his definition seriously the only scope for freedom in Kantian philosophy would be restricted to this negativity. In that event I would be free if I really were to behave in a free manner and set aside the idea that the moral law in its universality is supposed to harmonize with the principle of freedom. If I reflect on how to implement this, and on how I should behave in specific instances, what emerges is that nothing remains of this freedom apart from the opportunity I have to behave like an utter swine. There is an additional factor here, namely that thanks to this entire battery of objective rationalities, of imperatives, of the reverence I have to display, I am so hemmed in that my own genuine freedom, even this miserable freedom to do the wrong thing and behave like an utter swine, is reduced to an absolute minimum, to the point where there is really nothing left of it. And this, Ladies and Gentlemen, has one very crucial implication that we have to include in any critique of Kantian ethics and that cannot be suppressed. This is that his philosophy starts off by postulating freedom and extracts an immense pathos from it, but in the process of developing its meaning, this freedom dwindles to the point of extinction and his philosophy ends up by dispensing with freedom entirely – even though this is done in a purely formal manner, without deferring in any obvious way to authoritarian or hierarchical ideas. Of the two factors that are held in suspension here, that of necessity or law *and* that of freedom, the element of necessity actually devours that of freedom. It is much as in the sphere of economics where every individual economic subject also has the freedom to act irrationally. Thus, the businessman can squander his money and the worker can oversleep instead of going to work – this is a freedom he does possess. But the businessman will go bankrupt and the worker will be sacked – let him just try and make use of his freedom! Thus, the coercive nature of reality, of the social reality in which we live, prevails over freedom, while for its part freedom is exiled to the distant horizon to 'Some far-off war, in Turkey, let's suppose, / Some place where nations come to blows.'[11] This, then, is the repressive element that is implicit in the structure of practical reason. Moreover, thanks to its formal character it proves to be stronger by far than the element of freedom. This in turn has led to the vulgar misconception of Kantian ethics that has reduced the imperative to the point where someone bangs the drum and shouts, 'You shall, you must, you must!' in a way that is unsurpassed in the depiction in [Thomas Mann's] *Buddenbrooks* of Wulicke, the Headmaster, who talks incessantly about the categorical imperative while never ceasing to plague and torment his pupils. There is also the parody of Kantian philosophy in the idealism of after-dinner speakers, a parody which is not without its justification when you compare Kant's own magnificently sober formulations with the ghastly clichés that were produced in the age of German Imperialism.

I believe that we have to admit that this is the position with Kant. The reverence we have spoken of refers back to the validity of the law and is therefore grounded in the law itself. Of course, Kant perceives the problem of heteronomy that enters along with this reverence, and this is why he attempts a phenomenology of reverence as a rational feeling – in analogy to the will as a rational faculty of desire. I can summarize all this by saying that there is a tendency in Kant's elaboration of the practical philosophy to end up by reducing the element of freedom as far as possible. It stands there so imposingly at the start that the situation resembles that of God in deist philosophy. He too appears at the very beginning and He has created the world and is immensely honoured for it, but He ends up being kicked upstairs, as we would say today. In other words, because freedom plays such a glorious part in the origins of the law, it finds itself pushed to one side when it comes to elaborating the law more fully. Potentially, freedom is eliminated; and in the process we see that when Kant tends to stipulate something like an ultimate unity of the natural and the moral, the unity of the natural and the spiritual world, what he basically imagines is that the ideal law of nature is also the model of ethics, and that the world in itself, the thing in itself, is really and truly the law, a belief that recurs also in his theory of intelligible character. This concept of law had only referred to the phenomenal world in the *Critique of Pure Reason* and had specifically excluded the thing in itself. By extending its reach to include the totality, Kantian ethics ensures that the coercive character of nature from which this idea of law has been borrowed is given the last word. That is to say, by declaring itself to have absolute dominion over nature, by proclaiming that its fundamental principle is to suppress nature and ensure control over it, Kantian ethics itself remains subservient to nature. This means that the blind, coercive nature of the laws to which non-human nature remains subject is extended to include the Kantian ethic itself. Roughly speaking, we may legitimately say that the society in which we live, the apparent world of freedom in which we live, is in reality nothing but a continuation of natural history. This is because we are dependent upon blind, organic necessities of the kind that we project onto non-human nature.

Ladies and Gentlemen, I believe that I have now explained to you the most important issues that I wanted to tell you about concerning Kantian ethics. I shall now move on to talk above all about an ethics of conviction in its relationship to an ethics of goods and an ethics of responsibility, a problem that follows on directly from Kant's assertion that ethics must be free of every intention. I would like only to add, and I shall perhaps say more about this next time, that in its rigorous form Kantian ethics aims to make itself independent of the well-being of the species as a whole. This means that even the creation of a happy society is explicitly excluded in crucial passages of Kant's moral philosophy, although the concept of humanity is reintroduced at the conclusion of the *Critique of Practical Reason*. We might therefore formulate the principle of Kantian ethics by saying that it is concerned simply with an objective reason, entirely independent of a rationality extending to subjective, human ends and human goals. This objectivity of reason extends to the final end and includes the reason for the existence of reason in the first place. But this brings me to an extraordinarily complex problem, full of contradictions, and I shall be forced to say a few things at least about this next time, before going on to what I have to say about ethics of responsibility, of goods and of conviction.

LECTURE FOURTEEN

16 July 1963

I should like[1] to add a few comments on the issues raised by Kant's moral philosophy that we have discussed up to now, and shall move on from there to a number of the so-called main problems of moral philosophy in general which we have not yet broached, but which have a meaningful relation to the Kantian problems we have been chiefly concerned with. These will be dealt with in terms of philosophical models. I may remind you that we had defined the moral law or rational principle as the pure principle of the domination of nature, and by this we meant the domination of our inner nature as well as nature outside us. And I established there that Kant stood in a long tradition on this matter, one that can be traced back to Aristotle, on the one hand, and the Stoics, on the other. One of the most astonishing facts that we encounter when we study the history of philosophy is to see how philosophers agree with one another on this point – namely, that the instincts are things that have to be controlled and suppressed – even though their philosophies otherwise differ widely and may even be diametrically opposed. Whether we are dealing with Descartes or Bacon, Kant or Nietzsche, that is, with philosophers who usually figure as mortal enemies in the histories of philosophy, their views on this point turn out to be curiously alike. And in general it is remarkable that the majority of the philosophical disputes which are reflected in the division of the history of philosophy into schools, generally end up being reduced in number once you examine the texts. That is to say, the so-called basic positions and starting-points of philosophers are relatively unimportant for the conclusions that they draw. They all preach more or less the same thing, in so far as they preach at all, that is, in so far as they set out to establish norms. This not only makes us a little sceptical about their initial positions; we also start to question their general stance since this tends to make them the spokesmen of the more powerful tendencies in the development of civilization. The idea of the renunciation of instinct that has been formulated in recent years by psychoanalysis, goes hand in hand, or so I have been arguing, with the direction of civilization, and we could also say with the basic tendency of an urban civilization that is bourgeois in the broadest sense, that is to say, orientated towards work. If I may briefly say something here about psychoanalysis, its separation from moral philosophy is not without its risks, since the very people who are expected to behave well and lead moral lives are also psychological beings and their behaviour depends on their psychological make-up. It is worthy of note that Freud, who started out as a critic of the so-called process of repression, that is, as the critic of this renunciation of instinct, subsequently became its advocate. I cannot go into this in detail here, but he committed this volte-face because he came to the view that without a certain measure of instinctual renunciation, that is, without any restrictions on the pure gratification of instinct – he was thinking here above all of sex – something like civilization, an orderly community of human beings, was simply inconceivable. The distinction that he made was between two kinds of renunciation of instinct. On the one hand there is repression – this is a behaviour that refuses to look this renunciation in the eye, but instead shifts the instincts into the unconscious and produces in their place some kind of surrogate gratification of a precarious and problematic sort. Alternatively, there is the conscious renunciation of instinct, so that even man's instinctual behaviour is placed under the supervision of reason. This is very similar to what happens in Kant's ethics, so that you can see from this example that in a crucial area, that of the rational control of our instincts, the extreme anti-psychological ethics of Kant and the extreme psychological, or, if you like, psychologistical doctrine of Freud are in agreement.[2]

Where should we look for the rational underpinning of this renunciation of instinct? Let us give this concept of reason the same meaning Kant gave it in a pivotal passage in the *Critique of Judgement*, in the Critique of Teleological Judgement, where he states that organisms are constructed for the purpose of self-preservation.[3] If we give it this meaning, it becomes evident that the rational behaviour of human beings is rational in so far as it serves the principle that had been regarded as far back as Spinoza as the true fundamental principle of every existent being: *esse conservare*, self-preservation.[4] Thus reason is defined, in Kant as in Spinoza, as a self-preserving rationality, and for all Kant's rigorism this motif is so powerful that

Kant includes this law of self-preservation among the duties towards ourselves in his detailed doctrine of ethics, the *Metaphysics of Morals*, where he lays down a system of the duties incumbent upon us.[5] Moreover, in the *Groundwork* he explicitly states that we have the right and even the duty to pursue our own happiness.[6] It is this that must be renounced if we follow all these moral philosophers. But there is one reservation about this renunciation in the formulation it is given in the Kantian or Schopenhauerian distinction between a character conceived as a totality and the particular actions of an individual. In other words, the renunciation of instinct that is demanded of individuals is said to be rational because, if you will pardon the vulgar phrase, there is a pay-off for the individual conceived as a whole. Looked at in quantitative terms, the individual may renounce momentarily a certain amount of happiness or pleasure, but he gets it back with interest in terms of the rational organization of his life. So happiness is seen in terms of a kind of economy of thrift that underlies all these moral teachings – though, naturally, Kant does not state this in so many words. But when he finally comes to talk about the happiness of the entire human species as the ultimate purpose, something of this sort is involved, and at this point, Ladies and Gentlemen, you encounter one of the profoundest sources of error in moral philosophy, and I am speaking about social errors here. You may observe in this context that the usual distinction between social science and pure philosophy cannot be sustained because social categories enter into the very fibre of those of moral philosophy. Put simply, the sums do not add up. In social terms, the compensation promised by civilization and by our education in return for our acts of renunciation is not forthcoming. Freud himself made this entire doctrine of the renunciation of instinct his own with his principle of the domination of the id by the ego. He was aware of this state of affairs and said so, not indeed in his theoretical and philosophical writings, his metapsychological writings, as they are usually called, but in the so-called technical writings on psychoanalysis. I should like to commend these to your close attention in this context because they contain an extraordinary amount of crucial material that Freud passes over in silence in the great theoretical essays.[7] In these technical writings he notes the precarious nature of the renunciation of instinct and draws attention to something that constantly renders this renunciation problematic and irrelevant – incidentally exposing the precarious nature of psychoanalysis itself. The problem is that the quantum of pleasure, if I may be permitted to speak in such bluntly rationalistic terms, that individuals are required to sacrifice is not subsequently returned to them in a different form, as ought to be the case according to the underlying rational principle. Instead, this entire process of admonition only exists in order to preserve society as a whole. With very few exceptions individual human beings do not in fact profit from their acts of renunciation – and even where they appear to do so we may enquire whether they truly profited. In Book IV of *The World as Will and Idea*, Schopenhauer remarks that 'the balance sheet of life is negative' and you can grasp the meaning of this profoundly bourgeois metaphor of the balance sheet almost literally by noting that there is no real equivalence between the renunciation of instincts in the present and compensation in the future.[8] In other words, society is organized irrationally. The equivalent reward it always promises never arrives, and so in a very profound and radical sense the interest of the individual and of all individual human beings diverges from that of humanity as a whole.

This casts a curious light on Kant's widening of the renunciation of instinct into an absolute in the shape of the categorical imperative. It is from this angle that you will perhaps be able best to understand that strange separation of the imperative from every possible fulfilment, its so-called rigorism and formalism in one. The situation seems to be that civilization in general demands that we exercise rational control over ourselves and over external nature in the world in which we live, but that it is not able to discover any appropriate reward, while the demand is sustained so that civilization should be preserved. But if that is the case, because civilization cannot prove that such control has benefits for others or is rational in a prudential sense, there is nothing for it but for this demand to become an absolute and to be inflated into something existing in its own right. In fact an inflation of this sort is precisely what we see in Kant's categorical imperative. You can see quite clearly that it really is a matter of such an act of inflation if you realize that the imperative owes its purity to the fact that morally good acts are now separated from every conceivable gratification, however remote. The balance sheet which forms the foundation of this entire calculus of the renunciation of instinct and the dominion over nature can never be presented because if it were presented, the irrational aspect of that rationality would become inescapably visible. We might say – and this appears to me to be the decisive criticism to be made of Kant's moral philosophy – that we are faced here with a model case of fetishism. That is to say, the doctrine of the categorical imperative makes a fetish of renunciation. This means that this doctrine makes renunciation independent of its reward, its *terminus ad quem*, and turns it into something that exists in itself and is a good in itself. This is how the dull and naive consciousness – a consciousness that is particularly deceptive when it is called moral – dangles before us the illusory belief that to renounce something is good in itself, even though we are quite unable to perceive the benefits of this renunciation. This applies with particular force in situations where people tend to regard renunciation as a good even though non-renunciation does not involve anything wicked or evil or destructive. Philosophy has been aware of this from a very early stage – particularly in schools of thought that have been deemed heretical. Thus we find it in the genuine, radical version of hedonism, in Aristippus's theory with its rejection of postponement and its insistence on the immediate gratification of desire, on happiness here and now. A moderate, restrained hedonism is not worthy of the name. The moment a thinker does indeed acknowledge happiness or pleasure – Epicurus is a case in point – but then defers it or sublimates it in favour of the pleasure to be found in knowledge or the like, we know that moral philosophy has drifted into the great, and I am tempted to say murky mainstream of official philosophy. The heretical tendencies I have mentioned have always opposed this, albeit feebly since as forces of civilization they were relatively impotent. Fetishism of the sort I have been speaking of can be seen in Kant – the crucial statements are to be found in the *Groundwork of the Metaphysic of Morals* – when he insists at least in principle that moral behaviour is purely rational and when he makes it independent not just of the happiness of the individual, but equally of the well-being of the human species as such. Through his insistence that not even the happiness of mankind as a whole can be taken into account, he makes reason independent of every possible application to the real world, although on the other hand – and this contradiction enables you to see how intractable the problem is – he regards humanity as the final end of reason. It is easier to mock this contradiction and to find fault with it than to grasp its real significance. For, on the other hand, Kant is perfectly right. In the light of his pure principle of reason, for him to identify reason with a global condition of mankind, however distant, would amount to the identification with some good or other, something empirical. This would make the moral law as dependent on a merely existing phenomenon as any theory of virtue that is fixated on momentary behaviour. But if every such idea of realizing reason is eliminated entirely, then the concept of reason in the strict sense I have tried to expound to you is reduced to a fetish. This means that because of the mistaken nature of its intrinsic calculus, reason itself turns out to be irrational. And this objectively self-contradictory condition is clearly articulated by Kant – and the greatness of Kant is that such contradictions are not fudged, but are clearly expressed. For he asserts both that the moral law should be adhered to purely for its own sake, and also that something like mankind as such should be regarded as the ultimate end of the moral law. The contradictory nature of his position is even indicated by the fact that he sought somehow to mediate between these two things. If in the process, humanity appears as the ultimate end of reason, you should not confuse this concept of mankind in Kant with the empirical mankind that inhabits time and space, and think that this is what he meant by the embodiment of humanity. What he means is nothing but what he frequently refers to in his writings as a being endowed with reason.

This idea that the final end of moral behaviour can be equated with reason, which should both subserve this end and at the same time be the absolute, opens up a vista in which such a substantive end, such a substantive goal of the good life might converge with the formal determinants of reason that Kant has given. And I must expound this possibility to you since to a commonsense view it is the most plausible solution to the difficulty that confronts us. We might say that the particular faculty for self-preservation, in other words, that self-preserving rationality of the individual which Kant with some slight disdain calls prudence, would be identical with the objective rationality of the moral law, once it is made real in such a way that it relates to the entire human species. In short, the two would be the same thing. If you wish, you can also discern this motif in the formulation of the categorical imperative, when Kant states that in my actions I must also be able to will that my maxim, that is, the summation of my subjective prudence, should be capable of becoming a universal law. In other words, it should be capable of being expanded so that it ceases to pertain merely to my particular purposes and interests, and the particular purposes and interests of all individuals, but should instead comprehend in equal measure the interests of all mankind. Furthermore, this inclusion of the particular interests of all and the objectivity of the moral law itself should amount to the mediation between subjective and objective reason. The Kantian principle I recently mentioned to you belongs here. This is that the freedom of each individual should only be restricted at the point where it restricts the freedom of another individual.[9] This, then, would be the idea unifying the empirical realm and empirical mankind and its purposes, on the one hand, with the purely formal, purely *a priori* principle of the moral law on the other. As is well known, this law is indeed so pure that he thinks it superfluous to apply the concept of pure reason to practical reason because a practical reason that was not *pure* practical reason could not exist. Kant then repudiates this unity explicitly as far as the individual is

concerned, and he does so on the basis of his theologically inspired
doctrine according to which individual human beings are characterized by radical evil. However, he seeks out that unity for humanity
as a species. The same thing can be said of his philosophy of history
as it is recorded in his little essay, 'Idea towards a Universal History
from a Cosmopolitan Point of View'. Here he explicitly makes mediation between subjective and objective reason his goal. He does so
by arguing that ultimately the conflicts between the interests of individuals work towards the creation of a global situation in which
something like reason and freedom have been realized. But this is a
purely hypothetical possibility. I think this is an important point and
one that Kant has correctly perceived. Such a hypothetical possibility cannot be taken directly as a norm by which to govern my
behaviour. In other words, I cannot directly take ideas that apply to
the creation of a just society as a whole, a just world, and deduce
from them a guide to my own behaviour here and now. Especially,
since that just society is, to use Kant's own language, not given, but
presented as a task. I may not treat it as a given, unless I am
prepared to treat something infinite as finite, to fetishize it, in short.
Such fetishistic procedures are not without consequences, since they
mean that people come along and say that the good is what benefits
their nation, or good is what a party decrees, what a party orders
them to do, because the party or the nation is, so to speak, the organ
of the World Spirit – something that it can never be in that direct,
transparent way. Moral action, right action here and now is not
immediately identical with what is good for the species as a whole.
And if Kant refused to bring these two things together – something
which is both plausible and tempting, as I have suggested – he was
inspired to do so by a profound and correct instinct that can be found
at work throughout his philosophy. This is the instinct to make distinctions, rather than to create false identities and to bring together
by a *coup de main* things that are quite separate in reality. In this
context I may perhaps remind you of a modern writer, a writer who
because of his political affiliations may lead you to expect something
quite different. I am thinking here of Brecht, for Brecht was acutely
aware of this problem and was unusually sensitive towards it. He saw
perhaps more sharply than anyone the parting of the ways between
the personal or subjective morality and objective morality. The way
in which he hypostatized the objective interest and in the process
ignored human freedom, above all in such plays as *The Measures
Taken*, which are horrifying in that respect, is not something that
need concern us here. I would only bring to your attention here that
he saw this problem as the central, burning problem of moral phi-

losophy today. He treated it, contrapuntally, as it were, in two different plays, both of which I recommend you to read. The first is *St Joan of the Stockyards* in which we are shown a person who has an absolutely pure will in the Kantian sense, that is, who practises a pure ethics of conviction and who literally and truly behaves as the categorical imperative requires. What we then see is that thanks to this she becomes the agent of the very worst and most dangerous interests, and that what Johanna does turns into the very opposite of what she wants. And finally, her martyr's death redounds to the advantage of those dominant and exploitative forces that she had set out subjectively to oppose. The other play inverts the same problem. This is *The Good Person of Szechwan* which deals with a woman who, like Johanna, wants to do good, but discovers that in a society that is felt to be deeply questionable she can only succeed in doing good by making herself evil, by donning the 'Mask of Evil' as Brecht calls it in a poem with that title.[10] However, this brings us to a problem that we shall not really have time to discuss today, but with which we shall have to concern ourselves with in detail. I am speaking of the difference between a so-called ethics of conviction and a so-called ethics of responsibility. This can be seen as the decisive problem of Kantian moral philosophy and of the debates that followed on from it.

But a further point has to be made about this problem of the convergence of the subjective and objective elements in moral philosophy. This represents a great danger of the gravest kind, and one that even Brecht was unable to master. I would like to describe it here as the problem of Jesuitism, without wishing at all to refer to the historical order of that name, but simply because it sums up a principle that, rightly or wrongly, has been associated with the Jesuits. This is the principle that the end justifies the means. This theory may be said to acknowledge the divergence between a present good and the good that is required, total goodness; but it imagines it can solve the problem by giving the totality, the ultimate end, priority over the particular and the individual. Plausible though the idea may seem to be at first, we have been able to see it tested out with the most catastrophic consequences in our own age. We now know what it really means to commit crimes in the name of such a primacy of the ultimate end or the social totality. We now know that what it leads to is to strip the concept of the good of every tangible substance, and that it amounts to nothing more than abstract domination on the part of whoever happens to have the greater power. Such rulers barricade themselves behind the idea of the objectively greater good and claim that merely subjective interests and rights are safe in their hands.

Looked at in the context of moral philosophy we have to say that it is important to protest against all such claims. This includes Brecht's *The Measures Taken* which I have just mentioned and which can be said to have furnished such terrible acts with an ideological justification.[11] We can object to such claims by saying that the relationship between the universal that is being advocated and the victims or the objects of what is being done here and now, must be transparent. It will not do to accept abstract assurances that things are as they are said to be. Instead, the relationship must be transparent in the sense that the particular interests of individual human beings must be made to prevail here and now, just as much as that global interest – a synthesis that will hardly ever be encountered. At any rate, the ultimate end must not be postulated dogmatically or be conceived as a fixed, objective thing opposed to human beings because, if it were, it would necessarily conflict with the concept of human reason, which of course includes the preservation of self, of the individual person. In this sense – and I believe this can really be maintained – Kantian moral philosophy is incompatible with totalitarian morality, with the totalitarian reversal of morality in which the rather playful principle that the end justifies the means is turned into one that is deadly serious. This remains true for all the vaunted formalism of the Kantian system, by which is meant that it must be independent of a specific moral code. The reason for this can be said to lie in the facts of the matter, namely in the fact that in every single case individual and society point in opposite directions. Moreover, since moral philosophy, as we see in those models, directly and consistently joins the side of society, it necessarily does a wrong to the individual. For the individual could only become free in a just society, but hitherto he has constantly experienced the social constitution as something opposed, antagonistic to himself; he has experienced it as heteronomous. And a moral philosophy and a moral practice that ignore this antagonism between the highly justifiable interests of the whole and those of the individual, between the conflicting interests of the universal and the particular, must inevitably regress to barbarism and heteronomy. Moral philosophy must give expression to this antinomy, just as Kant gave expression to it, magisterially. It is not the task of moral philosophy to strive to reduce conflict to harmony.

Finally, something should be said about the idea of reason as an ultimate end of mankind. If you take this literally, that is, if you take the idea of reason as it has been established historically and do not use it to reflect on itself, you will be left with the concept of reason as that which exercises dominion over nature; it is the oppressive principle and itself particular in essence. However, it is highly questionable whether this oppressive, particular principle, concerned as it is with the self-preservation of man, can be equated with an objective moral rationality as such. In his day Schopenhauer held it to be the particular merit of his own moral philosophy that it also included a view of our treatment of animals, compassion for animals, and this has often been regarded as the cranky idea of a private individual of independent means. My own view is that a tremendous amount can be learnt from such crankiness. I believe that Schopenhauer probably suspected that the establishment of total rationality as the supreme objective principle of mankind might well spell the continuation of that blind domination of nature whose most obvious and tangible expression was to be found in the exploitation and maltreatment of animals. He thereby pointed to the weak point in the transition from subjective reason concerned with self-preservation to the supreme moral principle, which has no room for animals and our treatment of animals. If this is true, we can see Schopenhauer's eccentricity as the sign of great insight. If we picture to ourselves what an institutionalized reason as the supreme principle of mankind might actually look like, we should surely think of it as something from which this dominant principle has been eradicated. Its eternal chorus of 'This is how things have to be, this is how they should be forced into line, monitored and organized' should be heard no more. Certainly, it would be better to eliminate it than to install it in perpetuity, in order, finally, in the name of morality to establish society itself as a vast joint-stock company for the exploitation of nature. This appears to me to be the most powerful objection to the attempt to equate the subjective prudence needed for self-preservation with the supreme universal principle of morality. Perhaps this was one of the reasons that led Kant to separate the two. If, on the other hand, reason becomes purely objective, that is, independent of the interests of human subjects and their self-preservation, as is implied in the Kantian principle of morality, that would be no less problematic. For in that event human beings would be excluded from the creation of what Hegel called an ethical world, and instead this world would be transformed into heteronomy pure and simple.

LECTURE FIFTEEN

18 July 1963

Ladies and Gentlemen,

The question we had reached last time was whether moral philosophy in Kant, and moral philosophy in general, should be orientated towards mankind, its continued existence and its happiness, in the light of the fact that the concept of reason, which is the concept of humanity, already contains these elements within it. This leads to a fundamental problem of moral philosophy in general that I would like to discuss with you more or less independently of the Kant text, because it is one of those questions that are treated in a dismissive way in Kant and is therefore not susceptible to textual analysis. For I would have the feeling that I would be leaving you in the dark if I failed to go into the main issues surrounding this problem. This problem is that of the so-called ethics of conviction as represented in Kant, not simply in its relation to the so-called ethics of goods [*Güterethik*] a notion that may strike you as mythological and *a priori* archaic, but rather in relation to what has been called the ethics of responsibility to distinguish it from Kant as well as from the dogma of the *summum bonum*.[1] For to think about mankind in terms of the contents of people's lives would essentially be a question of responsibility, responsibility towards empirical existence, self-preservation and the fulfilment of the species to which we belong for good or ill. This idea of responsibility is the very thing that Kant rejects fundamentally as a principle of ethics; there is no real place for it in his moral philosophy. You are aware that Kant inherited the concept of freedom from Greek ethics, but that he radicalized it to an extraordinary degree. The fact that without freedom, without the idea of freedom, moral philosophy would make no sense at all will be clear to you, because given the situation of complete, unrelieved determinism every criterion of good and evil would be absolutely meaningless; it would not even be possible to raise the issue. But the concept of freedom was modified by Kant in a very crucial way. I may remind you that even in Aristotle it was not simply defined as freedom from external compulsion, but also as freedom from emotions, that is, from instinctual drives, and ethical behaviour was equated, as by the Stoics, with mastery of the feelings. As I have already had occasion to mention, this is a motif characteristic of the entire tradition of moral philosophy with the exception of the very few radical hedonists. In Kant this trend is taken to an extreme in which the concept of freedom is taken to refer exclusively to something that cannot be said to possess an ulterior cause. This means that Kant's moral philosophy can be said to be essentially an ethics of conviction. In it this definition of freedom is made so formal, or if you like, so much a matter of epistemology, that not only is every dependence on concrete realities eliminated, but also every relation to any matter of substance that might be brought to bear on the ethics itself. For it is self-evident that if a free action is an action that is not to be reducible to any cause of whatever kind, this would rule out any action that is caused, for example, by the failings of a given situation, or even by factors governing any given situation on which I must base my action in order to achieve anything at all. Any such action would be regarded as heteronomous, as an action that reintroduced the element of causality into freedom. Thanks to this Kant's philosophy became an extreme ethics of conviction, and Kant was well aware of the particular nature of his own achievement in moral philosophy when he placed the moral, the locus of morality, squarely in the interior of the human subject. When I use the term 'interiority' you should not think of interiority in the psychological sense that will be familiar to you from talk about the internalization of external commandments, the internalization of the super-ego or other principles of that sort. But since we are speaking here simply of a universal ego determined solely by reason, the site of this interiority must be described, if you will allow the problematic epithet, as a complete blank. That is to say, this interiority is nothing but the abstract reference point of reason itself, but defined negatively as something radically distinct from everything external of whatever kind. Thus moral philosophy is to be based on a pure reason existing only in itself, and to the extent that it does not externalize itself and remains independent of every factor external to it. Such external elements would include, above all, the happiness of the individual. But strictly speaking – and I have already made this point earlier on – any course of action would also have to be pursued independently of the happiness of human beings in general,[2] as is the case with a later, very radical philosopher of interiority. The thinker I have in mind here is Kierkegaard, who goes so far as to say that acts of compassion, for example – and here he differs from Kant, who gives compassion a bad press[3] – should only be performed out of compassion, and not in order to remedy any situation that had provoked pity in the first place. Here, then, the standpoint of radical interiority is combined with the idea that we should not meddle with the nature of reality and that we should not take the nature of external reality into account in our own behaviour.[4] This motif also appears in a certain sense in Plato, with an objectivizing tendency, namely in the sense that the absolute nature of ideas means that they only become accessible to purely logical behaviour, to a purely logical faculty. But Kant would have dismissed even this as heteronomous, and in fact he criticized the whole of the ethics of antiquity as heteronomous on the grounds that justice in Plato – and justice is Plato's highest value – is not the product of pure reason, but should be regarded by us as something that exists in itself. To that extent, as something external that confronts us from outside there is something opaque about it, something irrational or, as Kant would say, heteronomous. The decisive distinction between Kant's ethics of conviction and Plato's ethics of ideas lies in the fact that the only defining factor of moral action Kant will allow is the universal principle of subjectivity itself, without regard to anything objective, apart from the most universal fact that there must be something objective, some thing or other must exist, if action is to be possible at all. In this respect, then, Kant's ethics is in fact in agreement with the philosophy of Fichte.

Kant's thinking has two targets here. He is opposed not just to the heteronomy of sensual desire in the broadest sense, but also to theology. I believe that you must be clear in your minds that Kant was a metaphysicist and that he faced in two directions. On the one hand, against empiricism, and thus also against the senses wherever he encountered them; and on the other hand, against heteronomy in the shape of theology. The moral law may not be conceived as coming from God, and it is nothing but a purely conceptualized subjectivity. If God has any role in this morality, then only as the guarantor of the moral law that emanates from pure reason, as the being to which the moral law is attached – to use an analogous formulation to one that occurs in this context in the *Critique of Pure Reason*.[5] In Kant's view this means that in the absence of God and the hope of immortality, the world would be a hell. But this must not be, thinks Kant.

There is a profound connection between this definition of the world as negativity and his rejection of the empirical. That is to say, Kant's rejection of empirical motifs corresponds to his belief that – and this is a highly theological matter – evil rules in the world, that this world is the realm of evil.[6] And if we can say that Kant's rigorism is more critical, that is, it is more intransigent towards existing circumstances than the seemingly more humane and appealing account of ethics in Hegel's philosophy, this is precisely the point at which his radicalism appears. This really does bring us to the crucial question of the distinction between, on the one hand, the so-called ethics of conviction and on the other, the ethics of goods, and more particularly the ethics of responsibility about which we should say something now. An ethics of conviction is an ethics that seeks refuge in the pure will, that is, it recognizes the interiority of the moral subject as its only authority. In contrast to that, the ethics of goods and the ethics of responsibility take as their starting-point an existing reality, though under certain conditions this may be a mental reality, as perceived by this subject to which it is then counterpoised. Thus these conceptions of ethics start from an existing reality in *intentio recta*, just as old-style theory of knowledge was *intentione recta*, but without any reflection on the constitutive subject. And because of this objectivizing tendency of the *intentio recta*, the highest moral good at any given time is also objectivized, we might even say reified, and this thing-like thing is when compared to pure action, the *actus purus* [of Kant], always heteronomous, a good for us – and in so far as it exists for us, it is subject to the critique levelled at hedonism.

Ladies and Gentlemen, many of you will be thinking, these are the cares of the philosophers. If they do not have anything more important to worry their heads about, they ought just to shut up shop, since all this seems at first sight to be no more than an empty scholastic dispute. It might be thought that it is only necessary to pitch the concept of the greatest good high enough, as Plato had already done with his concept of justice, and something would emerge of its own accord that would be free from ephemeral, empirical motifs. This procedure would at a stroke bridge the gap between an objective ethics of goods and a purely formal ethics of conviction. In fact many thinkers, right down to the writings of the Marburg neo-Kantians, have pointed again and again to the agreement of the ethics of Kant and Plato. I recollect in particular Paul Natorp's book on Plato.[7] Schopenhauer, too, who followed Kant's ethics to an extraordinary degree, also tends to take the view that the two conceptions of morality are identical.[8] However, it is typical of Kant's insistence on precise distinctions between concepts that he is not satisfied with this. Instead he maintains that even this highest good, however it may be defined, stands opposed to me as an alien, external thing. As such, it would render null and void the identity of my moral will with the principle of subjectivity, with the principle of the pure self. As an idealist, he is quite unconcerned about the possible consequences of this moral philosophy; whether, for example, his own moral philosophy coincides with Plato's because of his rejection of sensuous reality in the broadest sense. Such considerations are a matter of indifference to him. What interests him – and this is the true sign of his idealism – is purely the question of principle, that is, the question of how such a theory can prove itself. In other words, does it prove itself in terms of rationality, or does it treat reason as something alien? I might add that having done this, he was not too concerned about content. Kant does not share Plato's disapproval of sensuality, a disapproval we can see from Plato's statement that 'the body is the grave of the soul'.[9] Instead, by incorporating the duty to procure one's own happiness in the definition of duty he even showed a certain tolerance at the level of ethical content. Only as far as the principle itself was concerned did he prove quite unwilling to make concessions. It should be pointed out here that in this respect he showed himself to be heir to the tradition that interiority, like the soul, should be the object of desire because it is immortal, the highest good. The idea that the principle of subjectivity should be what is normally thought of as the highest good is Christian in origin, not just in a superficial historical manner, but in a profound sense. Underlying it is the idea of the absolute substantiality of the soul, which is linked in turn to the idea of the immortality of the soul, of the soul that was redeemed by Christ – and this idea is then secularized and made abstract until it becomes the moral law existing in its own right. The same idea also contains the bourgeois ethos of unlimited striving, which goes back to a particular strand of Christianity – that of predestination, which became increasingly influential in Lutheranism and above all in Calvinism. This is the idea that no one knows whether he is one of the elect and that the very greatest efforts are required if one is to have any hope at all. The fact that this hope only appears distantly on the horizon, that it is very faint and barely more than a memory, is something Kant shared with Protestantism. The Pietist representatives of Protestantism took offence at this aspect of the general Protestant faith; it was they who criticized Kant on the grounds that his philosophy lacked hope.[10] Heinrich von Kleist's celebrated reaction on reading Kant belongs in the same context.[11] This reaction contains a momentous truth, namely the uncertainty that is actually implied in the concept of hope. But Kant responds to this in a manner reminiscent of Beethoven: this hell, which we must acknowledge our life on earth to be, cannot be the last word. Man's nature itself contains something like a promise that this is not all, and that there must be something further. In this sense I would say that the ontological proof of the existence of God, which Kant himself subjected to withering criticism, continues to live on. The mediating link between unlimited effort and pure conviction [*Gesinnung*] is created in Kantian ethics by including it in the constellation of supreme concepts, above all the concept of duty, which merges in a completely abstract way with the concept of unlimited effort. For, as an absolute concept, duty knows no bounds, since it is an absolute which is not located in any given order, and, thanks to its own infinite or unbounded nature, it possesses this quality of never coming to rest. A philosophy like Kant's, I would like to say, never simply repeats what goes on in society, but has the tendency to criticize existing society and to hold up to it an alternative image of the possible, or an imageless image of the possible. We find this here, combined in a quite inspired manner with the principle of formalism. The corrective function of reality is sought here in the relation between means and ends. In the emerging high-capitalist society – and Kant's age does indeed coincide with the first stage of the Industrial Revolution in England – Kant has recognized the trend towards total functionality. That is to say, everything in the social realm has only a functional value for other things for which it acts as a means. Now the pathos of Kantian philosophy lies in the fact that it seeks an end which is in conflict with the tendency for everything to become merely a means. This is already implied in his criticism of intention of which I have already spoken. But from this vantage-point you will be able to give the antithesis to this a very real meaning, one that I have not mentioned before, but one that is of cardinal importance in Kant's moral philosophy. It is that of price and worth. This is the idea that everything is functional, that exists for the sake of something else and that is exchangeable, has its price – just as of course the concept of price is based on the process of exchange. In contrast whatever exists strictly for its own sake, or happens for its own sake, as is the case with moral action, according to the Kantian moral law – and nothing else – possesses what he calls 'dignity' [*Würde*]. The concept of dignity has a very different resonance from its later manifestations in the nineteenth century, when the idea degenerated into the shabby pretentiousness that some person or other might claim dignity for himself merely because he set himself up as important or weighty. This might be called the empirical concept of dignity and you can occasionally encounter it still today, but it is nothing but a mockery and the complete inversion of what it originally meant in Kant.

I do not go into these social issues in order to devalue Kant's philosophy. Criticism of a philosophy is only ever possible as a criticism of its truth. The mere indication that it is positively or negatively related to some social condition or other has no critical force. On the other hand, even the most abstract distinguishing features of the kind we have encountered in Kant have their place in the real social matrix from which they have arisen. And it is possible to assign to the abstract concepts of Kant's moral philosophy something of the concrete specificity that is not immediately perceptible in them, but which does lie hidden in their underlying substance. There are two aspects to this. First, Kantian moral philosophy may call itself bourgeois – in the very positive sense of an indescribably strengthened self-confidence. The idea that the human subject should freely give himself a law, that his pure conviction is the law of the world, is a principle that is at the opposite pole to traditionalism of every sort and to any corporatist, feudal or absolutist order. Indeed, we might say that the abstract nature of Kant's moral philosophy is social when contrasted with the limited positivism of given conditions, what might be called scientific conditions. We might add that the transition to the abstractness we have observed in Kant is itself concrete in the sense that it may be seen to express the increasing rationalization and emancipation of society from the blind, organic elements which serve mankind as a guide to its behaviour. This particular insight that abstraction is not a basic phenomenon common to all epochs, but a historical and, if you like, a social category, is one that was articulated with the greatest possible force by Marx, and the Kantian philosophy is one of the best tests, one of the most magnificent examples of this thesis that can be conceived. In Kant we can clearly feel something of the pathos, the self-confidence of the youthful bourgeois class that wishes to extricate itself from tutelage of every kind. This pathos comes to the fore with particular force whenever he criticizes theology as the foundation of moral philosophy and where in consequence this moral philosophy echoes the meaning of his statement about 'mankind's emergence from his self-incurred immaturity'.[12] If you do not sense the echoes of this motif even in the repressive aspects of the Kantian concept of law, you will have failed to understand the infinitely complex and subtle distinctions at work in his moral philosophy as a whole. Furthermore, however, his moral philosophy is bourgeois in the specific sense that it reveals the extensive influence of Rousseau. This is generally known, but it is less well known that it gives an interesting and highly original twist to Rousseau's belief that human reason has been unable to bring about a progressive increase in happiness in the world. I think it more interesting to see *what* Kant made of these Rousseauesque ideas than simply to keep pointing to them in the manner you can see in every history of philosophy. For Kant teaches that in fact the human disposition to reason is not the appropriate instrument with which to procure that progressive growth in happiness for the benefit of mankind; only it leads him to the opposite conclusion. He maintains that we should not attempt to harmonize these two things, reason and happiness. Instead, at least as far as individual behaviour, or rather the ethics of private life, is concerned, the destination of reason should be sought elsewhere than in a constantly improving well-being. You will perhaps recollect that I tried to explain to you last time about the difficulties to which the absolutized concept of reason would lead, even if we were successful in distinguishing the sphere of subjective interest and the sphere of objective morality. The chief difficulty was that a moral society would lead to the universal suppression of nature. That will show you perhaps where the element of truth is to be found in Kant. We may add that this streak of scepticism about the principle of oppression, about the principle of reason with its hostility to nature and its desire to suppress it, points to the very positive influence of Rousseauian ideas on Kant. The inference he draws from this is that mankind, or at least the single individual – the situation with mankind as a whole is a little different and more complicated in Kant – has no other ultimate end than to live in accordance with the concept of the law, and that this in turn represents the supreme union of all the determining features of reason.

I have decided to concentrate today on this aspect of the ethics of conviction, that is, on the interconnections between private life, interiority and bourgeois society. Having made this decision, I should like to add that concepts like 'bourgeois' are commonly used in far too vague a manner. The first point to be made is that within bourgeois society itself interiority should be regarded as a reactive stance, that is, it should be seen dialectically, and not as something quintessentially bourgeois. I have already said something about universal functionalism, and its corollary, the tendency for human beings to withdraw into themselves, as a kind of protest against the overpowering machinery of external reality in which we are all caught up. Interiority becomes a refuge to which the individual retreats as a response to the overwhelming might of the external world. Only in this sense can we say that interiority is a function of the functional world. This naturally goes hand in hand with the fact that it was the disintegration of the theological cosmos – an

unmediated rupture that was not alleviated by any mediating transition – that was actually the tacit premise for the emergence of interiority in the first place. In so-called closed cultures, cultures that
would be called 'substantial' in Hegel's terminology, the way human
beings act is more or less unproblematic, their course of action is self-
evident. In such cultures there is no room for interiority, and I believe
that I do not go too far if I say that the concept is unknown in antiquity, even though I expect that there will be amongst you a classical philologist who will doubtless be able to point to some passage
or other in a classical author that could be interpreted in such a way
as to show the presence of interiority. Nor would I wish to deny this
possibility. I would only make the methodological point that of
course all such motifs occur in antiquity, but the air they breathe, the
climate in which they exist is so utterly different from the climate of
the Christian world that even terms that are identical in meaning
come to have a completely different meaning in a climate in which
subject–object problems, for example, are quite unknown. Thus if
you read writers like Homer and Tacitus, or Boccaccio or Chaucer,
or *Don Quixote* or the early English seventeenth-century novels, you
will come across the same common nucleus of what today we call
bourgeois, namely the direct relation to an organized urban market
economy. On the other hand, however, it is particularly important
not to forget that in Kant's day bourgeois conditions were not developed to the same degree in Germany as in other Western nations. It
is true that in the realm of thought all the bourgeois categories and
ideas had been created, or were at least intimated and alive, but there
can be no doubt that economic reality had not kept pace with the
self-confidence of the bourgeoisie, and that the latter had not yet
attained the positions of power which it had gained in England and
France. The concept of the bourgeoisie was in advance of developments in the actual world – and that is very characteristic of the
German situation in general. This made it more radical than in the
Western nations where a more advanced reality could always act as
a brake on the more advanced ideas. But it also made it more limited
because the sense of reality had not entered into it to the same degree,
and in this sense we may well say that morality is 'an utterly German
object', as Morgenstern says of the moon in his poem.[13] That is to
say, morality, or rather duty in this narrower sense, really only exists
in the realm of German thought. If you read Hume, to name just one
contemporary of Kant's, if you read Hume's moral philosophy, you
will see that the climate is so very different that you will scarcely have
the feeling that they are talking about the same thing. At any rate,
the idea that the moral behaviour of the individual might decisively

impinge on external reality is entirely absent from Kant. And this element of the genuine impotence of the individual in the face of external reality is undoubtedly one of the crucial internal preconditions for the pure construction of interiority in Kant. From the very outset the moral subject plays no part in the construction of the world; he has no influence on the world, aside from some extremely abstract meditations on the shaping of history – in which, however, the relation of the moral subject to concrete historical forces plays no role. Because of this lack of influence morality is necessarily turned into a matter of conviction, basically, into the form of action of people who are firmly convinced that their action is quite unable to change the course of the world in the here and now. This impotence can be discerned throughout the entire corpus of moral philosophy in German idealism. Conviction is something that simply exists for itself; it finds fulfilment in itself and remains without influence on the organization of society. In return, there is a sense in which it remains relatively unthreatened by society. Its pathos is to criticize a society in which everything becomes a means and in which nothing remains an end. But on the other hand, this idea should be supplemented by its dialectical opposite. This is the idea that reason, the faculty that gives a law to itself, thereby becomes an end in itself, and hence, as I asserted last time, becomes a fetish because it despairs of being able to realize any goals in the world outside itself. The immense pathos of the emancipated citizen becomes fused with the feeling of impotence, and these twin themes are deeply embedded in Kant's ethics. I believe, Ladies and Gentlemen, that I have now given you a preliminary introduction to the problems underlying both an ethics of conviction and an ethics of responsibility. In particular, this feeling of impotence justifies us in criticizing the ethics of conviction because it fails to offer us anything concrete, in other words, it fails to provide us with a casuistic method, one that would enable us to apply a general moral principle to a particular case. And on the other hand – I hardly need to spell this out – it has been shown again and again that moral casuistry has surrendered to relativism by following the principle of justifying the means by the end, and that it can therefore lead to negativity and evil. Kant would resist casuistry by maintaining that it is enough to reflect on the universal character of the maxim. That is to say, if I truly reflect at every moment on whether my principle can be made into a principle of universal legislation, then the problem would be solved. But I believe – and it is perhaps as well that I should use the few remaining seconds of this lecture to say this to you – just reflect for a moment whether it is at all possible to act in accordance with the categorical imperative, or indeed whether you can even imagine anyone doing so at every moment and with regard to every action. Consider, first, whether you are following a maxim – and God knows, just suppose you could do this, even though a person who acted in that way would be more of a monster than a human being, but just suppose you could do it. And second, try and become clear in your own mind whether your maxim can serve as the basis of a universal law. If I may apply a Kantian scheme for once, that really would be to assume that the infinite ramifications of social possibilities, an infinite choice then, is actually at my disposal so that I really would be in a position to establish the connection between my maxim and this universal law. In other words, the categorical imperative does indeed exist on paper, but it is not really valid in the strict, internal Kantian sense. This is because it is tacitly assumed that I can verify my judgement, that I can establish whether my maxim is an appropriate basis for such a universal law, whereas in reality my judgement presupposes innumerable reflections, reflections which are beyond the capacities of individual human beings. For a vast amount of knowledge would be called for, something which cannot be claimed to exist as a self-evident moral fact.

LECTURE SIXTEEN

23 July 1963

Ladies and Gentlemen,

I explained to you last time that there is a problem with the categorical imperative. We can describe it in simple terms by saying that the path from the supreme universality of the moral law to the specific case is not as unproblematic as it appears in Kant's moral philosophy. It is quite remarkable that Kant himself does not address this question explicitly, even though it looms large in his theory of cognition. It appears there by the name of 'judgement' – in the strict sense of the word – as the faculty to think of the particular as subsumed under the universal. Kant conceives of two alternatives here. The first is to advance from the general to the particular: this is the so-called determinate judgement, which he does not find unproblematic, and second, there is the reflective judgement. The latter sees itself confronted by the question of how to rise from what might be called unclassified experience, experience not yet subsumed under a universal, to that universal itself – and Kant's entire third major work is devoted to that question.[1] By analogy, we would be concerned in the *Critique of Practical Reason* with the first alternative, that is, with determinant judgement, but there is not even a hint of a reference to that. I hope that I shall not be guilty of any disrespect, if I venture the suspicion that Kant was wary of broaching the problem of a link, the problem of the relation between universal and particular, because he himself felt uncomfortable with it and because he realized that it would plunge him into all sorts of difficulties. Of course, if we could summon him to appear here as a witness he would refuse to admit this, and would probably appeal to the immediate moral consciousness of every individual which, as you know, he had introduced in a certain opposition to the deducibility of the moral law. But, Ladies and Gentlemen, precisely at this point there is a very serious and difficult problem. This is that the moral is not self-evident, but instead a pure moral demand can by virtue of its own purity be transformed into evil. It may do this, to put it briefly, by destroying the object, or more accurately, the subject, on whom this moral demand is imposed.

We have now reached the last lectures of this course and it is only due to that fact that we ourselves have felt obliged to accede to our own categorical imperative and hence to refrain from cancelling these classes because of the heat. We have thus deprived ourselves of an old childhood pleasure.[2] That being the case, I thought I would take the liberty of spending some time on a literary example. I should perhaps preface my comments by saying that I am fully conscious of the problematic nature of using literary works to illustrate moral problems. The question is: how far is it proper to apply moral categories to people who necessarily are metaphorical in nature? I shall content myself with saying that the work I wish to tell you about is explicitly concerned with the exploration of a moral problem, and in fact the moral problem we have just been discussing. I am referring to a play by Ibsen, *The Wild Duck*. When I was young it was one of Ibsen's most famous plays, and it is one of the less than pleasing signs of the passage of time that today this play – like most of Ibsen's works – cannot be assumed to be familiar to you. And if I may ask you to do something it would be to read this play during the vacation, perhaps along with some of his earlier plays such as *Ghosts* or *An Enemy of the People*. I believe that if you would like to learn something about the dialectics of morality – and that, after all, is the subject of this course of lectures – you will not find any more concrete examples and more logically worked-out instances than these works by Ibsen. *The Wild Duck* deals with the question of how a man becomes immoral simply by defending the moral law – or, as he puts it in an almost Kantian way, by defending the ethical commandments in their purity. To be specific, he brings about the destruction of – if you will forgive the crude expression – the most valuable human being of the entire group, or at any rate, the only person who is not ensnared in the web of guilt that is gradually revealed in the course of the action. The victim is a fourteen-year old girl, an adolescent and it is precisely this character who is not implicated in the general guilt who becomes caught up in events and led to her doom. Here is the story. An important businessman once had an associate – this all happens before the play begins. As always in Ibsen, the central events are put into the past, and the play itself, the present, is in a sense no more than an epilogue. Aesthetically, this has a profound meaning and is connected with the metaphysics of this type of drama. But that is not something I can go into now. However that may be, before the play opens there are two men who are business associates; their names are Werle and Ekdal. Ekdal had been a dashing officer. The two of them were involved in some very shady financial dealings of the sort that are very prominent in Ibsen's later plays, and their misdeeds came to light. Werle escaped scot-free and became immensely wealthy, while his associate was caught and sent to gaol. This old Ekdal appears in the play as a former prisoner who has served his time, and who is now a ruined man and a semi-vegetating drunkard. He has a son, Hjalmar Ekdal, a photographer. Hjalmar is really the principal character in the play, we could call him the passive hero, or the focal point around which the whole drama revolves. Old Werle has provided this Hjalmar Ekdal with a modest living. He has enabled him to train as a photographer – Hjalmar does not follow this profession himself, but he has induced his wife, whom he exploits, to do the work for him. In addition Werle has married him off to his own discarded mistress, Gina, who was already pregnant with his (Werle's) child. The rather pompous, self-important and hypocritical Hjalmar Ekdal is led to believe the child is his. Something of an idyllic life is then built up by Hjalmar, this Gina – who is by no means unsympathetically portrayed – and her child Hedwig. It is an idyllic, petty bourgeois life, though the shadows of the past and of present deprivation weigh on it heavily. Nevertheless, it is a life in which all three feel quite contented and Hedwig is very attached to her supposed father Hjalmar, perhaps by bonds of adolescent love. Now Old Werle also had a son, Gregers Werle, and in the play it is he who represents the categorical imperative. He wants to rebel violently against his father, and to show that the life the Ekdals are living is intolerable, not because he is particularly indignant about them, but because he is the closest and indeed the only friend of Hjalmar Ekdal. He cannot bear to see – or at any rate believes he cannot bear to see – his friend living in a life-lie, that is to say, in a world in which the real situation gives the lie to everything the participants believe about themselves and their lives. I shall not recount to you the entire, highly complicated plot. The crux of it is that Gregers Werle falls out with his own father out of what might be called respect for abstract moral principles; he turns down the offer of a partnership in the large firm, and prefers to eke out a life in poverty. In short, he is fully prepared to take the consequences of his actions. After quarrelling with his father, he tells the young Ekdal family, Hjalmar and Gina, about everything that has happened

earlier on, and little Hedwig hears about it too. The only consequence
is that Hjalmar treats Hedwig as if he no longer trusted her now that
he knows she is not his child. He acts as if he can no longer believe
that she loves him and overwhelms her with moralizing reproaches,
whereupon the young girl takes her own life. That is the content of
the action. It is a story in which – and I have to add this – the Ekdal
family seem to be completely at home in their life-lie. The term, life-
lie, incidentally, comes from this play. Today, it is probably forgot-
ten, though it is no more irrelevant now than it was at the time it
was written. And as is suggested by a cynical character in the play,
a dissolute doctor called Relling, once the grass has grown over
Hedwig's grave, the family will settle down once again in the squalor
of their mediocre existence and live as happily and contentedly as
they had done before.

Ladies and Gentlemen, I should like to pass over one problematic
point in the play. This is connected with the fact that Gina has
brought an illegitimate child into the marriage – something, incidentally, that Hjalmar had presumably half-guessed for himself. This
motif reflects the attitudes of the 1880s, but was taken very seriously
at the time, whereas we are less inclined to find it so terribly shock-
ing. What is really at stake in the play is the campaign of moral
purification, that is, the attempt of a man of integrity, of Gregers
Werle, in short, to introduce some order or, as is so admirably said
nowadays, to clear matters up. This attempt leads straight to disaster. As someone remarks in another of Ibsen's plays, in *Ghosts* in fact,
'Yes, conscience – that can be very hard on us sometimes.'[3] If you
follow the tug of your conscience, you may end up doing something
very unconscionable, in the present case, it means actually killing a
human being full of gentleness and grace. Now Ibsen shows himself
to be a very important writer in his refusal to identify with, for
example, the cynical reasoning of Relling. Instead he demonstrates
that the conflict between an ethics of conviction and an ethics of
responsibility can be insoluble. In this case, the people and the situation that Gregers Werle confronts are in fact horribly hypocritical
conformists and intolerable in every respect. On the other hand, his
attempt to give morality a helping hand is not only doomed to fail,
but is even transformed into an act of injustice.

Behind this play there is a further feature that appears much more
prominently in some of Ibsen's other plays. This is the idea that
morality is equated with a certain kind of puritanical, Protestant narrowness, as contrasted with the more expansive nature of the emancipated bourgeois forces of production of industry and finance capital
with which Ibsen evidently sympathizes, simply as the more advanced

historical force. In his youth, incidentally, he was not untouched by Hegel's philosophy, which was very influential in the Nordic countries, and we may justifiably regard this aspect of his work as echoing the impact of Hegel. To explain what he achieves in *The Wild Duck* I would like to cite a very perceptive comment by Paul Schlenther, whose writing about Ibsen is exceptionally intelligent and sympathetic: '*The Wild Duck* does not solve the contradiction, but instead articulates its insoluble nature.'[4] Now, the situation is that Gregers Werle, the man with ethical principles, is depicted very much as a man full of resentments. Nowadays, we would call him a man with an unresolved Oedipus complex who feels nothing but rancour for his corrupt, but experienced and, in a sense, very mature father. At the same time, he is an unusually ugly, unco-ordinated and clumsy man who feels himself to be 'the thirteenth at table',[5] and thus the very type of the misfits Nietzsche wrote about at around the same time *The Wild Duck* was written.

Nietzsche claimed that their resentment-driven morality would poison the world. However – and this is where Ibsen's greatness shows itself – he does not stop at this negative characterization. Gregers is also shown to have an extraordinary sense of justice. Despite his resentful nature and in general what might be felt to be unsympathetic features in his nature or his character, he is a man of true integrity. The demands he makes on others he also makes on himself, and he is prepared to accept all their consequences. So we might say that the contradiction I have been at pains to point out to you, the contradiction between the conditional nature of moral action and the categories of the moral itself, the objectivity and authority of moral concepts themselves – all that is encapsulated in this very concrete figure. The ideal he stands for – and this can really be seen as very Kantian – is simply that of truth, or we might call it the ideal of abstract reason. Incidentally, we might note that this is an ideal that as early as Ibsen anticipates the moral ideas of contemporary Existentialism, since this rigorous insistence on abstract truth means nothing more in reality than that human beings should be identical with themselves. To be true for Ibsen means as much as saying: no life-lies. Declare your beliefs and stand up for them. Be identical with yourself. And in this identity, in what we might call this reduction of moral demands to being true to oneself and nothing more, it is natural for every specific principle about how we should behave to begin to evaporate, to the point where according to this ethics you could end up being a true man if you are a true, that is, a conscious and transparent, rogue. Thanks to the reduction of the pure principle of reason to a mere matter of identity with itself, the ideal of

reason receives its comeuppance by being reduced to a kind of relativism. But that is not really what concerns us here in this context.
What concerns us is the relation between an ethics of conviction and
an ethics of responsibility. It is easy to claim that Gregers acted irresponsibly. Similarly, it could be said that his pig-headed, conceited
insistence on principle is itself psychologically conditioned; that in
truth, as Kant would say, he is motivated more by an intention than
by the rational ideal by which he believes himself to be guided.
In consequence, it looks as if what Ibsen defends against Kant and
against the ethics of conviction – and here he is absolutely Hegel's
heir – is the ethics of responsibility. What is meant by this is an ethics
in which at every step you take – at every step you imagine yourself
to be satisfying a demand for what is good and right – you simultaneously reflect on the effect of your action, and whether the goal
envisaged will be achieved. In other words, you are not just acting
out of pure conviction, but you include the end, the intention and
even the resulting shaping of the world as positive factors in your
considerations. In the play this is the position embraced by the cynic,
Relling, who also expresses it very intelligently. But dramatic justice
and, you may also think, the really dialectical element lies in the fact
that even in this play the ethics of responsibility and the world for
which it acts as a sort of apologia are also depicted as so problematic, so bad, and above all so much in collusion with the existing
order, that Gregers Werle, who is in the wrong as the advocate of
abstract morality, is seen also as being in the right. In short, when I
told you that Ibsen reveals the insolubility of the contradiction, this
means that he has not only perceived, but also succeeded in repre-
senting on stage, the fact that 'there can be no good life within the
bad one', if you do not mind my repeating this old quote of mine.[6] I
have already drawn your attention to this element of criticism of
Gregers Werle in his moment of defeat – he says, and these are his
last words, that his destiny is 'to be the thirteenth at table'. This
critique is identical with the kind of critique levelled at Kant's ethical
philosophy by Hegel. According to this, an ethics of responsibility
would be one which takes consequences into consideration, and
refuses to concern itself exclusively with the pure will. Indeed, both
Hegel and Ibsen in their different ways unmask the pure will as a
delusion, as something on which we cannot rely. In the pure interiority thrown back on itself that is embodied in this eccentric, Gregers
Werle, who lives on his own somewhere up in the far north and
broods, we see a kind of benighted reality. This reality comes to life
in his character. Because of the neurotic guilt he feels for being the
son of a wealthy man, he becomes entangled in the world of cause

and effect, while at the same time he confuses these neurotic guilt-feelings with absolute goodness. Ibsen is very well aware that when we imagine that we are impelled by the good, our motives are very frequently nothing more than a hidden egoism – a problem, incidentally, that can already be seen in Kant, in his distinction between the empirical character and the intelligible character. For Kant had a sharp eye for the fact that the motives that we think of as pure, and hence in conformity with the categorical imperative, are in truth only motives whose source lies in the empirical world. They are ultimately linked to our faculty of desire and therefore with the gratification of what I would term our moral narcissism. We may say in general – and this is what is valid about this critique – that it is right to feel a certain wariness towards people who are said to be of pure will, and who take every opportunity to refer to their own purity of will. The reality is that this so-called pure will is almost always twinned with the willingness to denounce others, with the need to punish and persecute others, in short, with the entire problematic nature of what will be all too familiar to you from the various purges that have taken place in totalitarian states. The failure to include reality perverts the consequences that the pure will is so proud of, and the criticism that would be in place here – and it is remarkable that it has no place in Kant's own moral philosophy – is that if I identify the moral law with the principle of abstract reason, this implies the obligation to follow through the implications of my ideas as far as any individual possibly can. I can perhaps express it by saying that the requirement that moral behaviour should be purely rational behaviour in conformity with the categorical imperative amounts to saying that in all our actions we should be ruled by reason, and that means that we should include within reason everything that it can possibly encompass. Because of the internal contradictions inherent in Kantian moral philosophy, of which I have now told you more than enough, Kant utterly fails to draw this conclusion. Instead he regards this logical consistency on the part of reason, the fact that it is capable of rationally thinking the consequences through to the end, as a kind of lapse, and he thereby manages to eliminate[7] entirely – I am thinking here in philosophical rather than psychological terms – the problem that is raised by the character of Gregers Werle. But by the same token, by taking consequences into account, there is a sense in which moral philosophy does make itself dependent on external reality. And the cynicism of Old Werle, as well as of Dr Relling, and the moral depravity and hypocrisy of Hjalmar Ekdal imply an accommodation with the world just as it happens to be. Everything that these cynics represent means simply that the world as it has become, existing circumstances, – even if only at the level of family relationships – are put in the right as compared with abstract reason. At the end of Act I, Old Werle dismisses his son as a 'neurotic' and a 'poor fellow' because he is unable to gain control over this reality. As someone who enjoys a certain power, albeit limited, he gives vent to his utter contempt, feeling himself vastly superior to impotence of every sort.

Philosophy has attempted after its own fashion to get to grips with the problem that I have tried to explain to you by producing a sort of model derived from literature. Hegel's doctrine of the objective nature of reason, that is, the idea that the real is also rational, is his attempt to solve this dilemma, if we make due allowance for the rather narrow and specialized standpoint from which we are considering the matter. It is easy to see this. Let us suppose that the philosophy Hegel championed was in fact able to demonstrate that a kind of reason is at work in actual situations in the world, right down to the concrete level of the individual family. And since there is only one reason, it is the same reason that I vainly and fraudulently delude myself into thinking can represent the moral in opposition to the way of the world. But by submitting to this world and adjusting to it, I would not be committing an offence against reason and the categorical imperative, but would instead transcend the abstract dualism of the moral subject and the unqualified world of objects. And by coming to revere reason in the object as sincerely as, according to Kant, I must revere it in myself, I shall do greater justice in a higher sense to reason than Kant did in the *Critique of Practical Reason*. Naturally, I do not have time here to discuss the problems raised by this entire Hegelian theory of the rationality of the real. Let me just say that of course this theory does contain an element of truth. You will perhaps find that easiest to understand if you reflect on the idea that things themselves may be said to have their own logic. In other words, in the course of necessary historical development a kind of logic is at work that makes itself felt even in the smallest events and is in no way identical with the logic of cause and effect. Instead, this logic is of such a kind that *post festum*, after the fact, and very significantly in every chain of events, whether political and historical or in the private sphere, it is possible to perceive the kind of rationality, the triumph of a self-sustaining and, we might say, abstract principle which subsequent apologias can base themselves on. Take, for example, the case of Franz von Sickingen as he lay on his deathbed – having been fatally wounded during a siege. His last words were 'Nothing without cause'.[8] These words do not just amount to a generalized statement of the law of causality; they also point to the reasons underlying that chain of events. In the same way, an analysis of all the characters in *The Wild Duck* would entitle us to claim that all the characteristics of all these people have come together to create the meaningful constellation that was then attacked so violently by the young Gregers Werle – who, incidentally, is not so very young; we should think of him as being in his late thirties. And we might well conclude that no other pattern was possible. But that would be to convert the principle of morality into a principle of conformity. We are accustomed in the German tradition – and it is perhaps a good idea for you to bear this in mind – to identify the moral principle almost automatically with the categorical imperative, abstract interiority and the moral law. But in the whole of the Western world, particularly in the Anglo-Saxon world, I should really say throughout the Anglo-Saxon world, it is almost as self-evident for the moral norm to be equated with social conformity as it is for us to equate it with the categorical imperative. So here, in what might be termed the difference between two moral cultures, you can see the philosophical contradiction that I have been attempting to explain to you by laying bare its theoretical roots. In consequence, what the ethics of responsibility amounts to is that existing reality – or what Hegel calls the way of the world [*der Weltlauf*], which he defends against the vanity of protesting interiority – is always in the right over against the human subject. And this theory of morality is in fact the predominant theory in Hegel, one which he defends in his *Philosophy of Right* with extreme consistency and indeed with an obviously repressive and politically ultra-conservative rigour along the lines I have described to you. This leads to the very paradoxical consequence that Kant's seemingly formalistic ethics ends up being far more radically critical than the content-based ethics of Hegel, even though Hegel does engage with society and is critical of particular social phenomena. This is because Kant's principle of universality elevates his ethics above every determinate configuration of the world that confronts it, above society and existing conditions, and it also makes him more critical of limited and finite moral categories. Roland Pelzer has written a very fine dissertation under my supervision in which he shows in detail that the apparent advance that Hegel represents when compared to Kant, together with his critique of Kant and Kant's moral philosophy, in reality redounds to the benefit of repression, of 'the powers that be'.[9] Pelzer goes on to conduct a metacritique of Hegel's criticism of Kant's moral philosophy and, if we may say so, of moral philosophy in general. In the course of a dialectical analysis he undertakes something like a rehabilitation of moral norms as opposed to the social reality that is not identical with such norms and is even incompatible with them. His work is due to appear in

Kempski's *Archiv für Philosophie* and I should like to draw your attention to it.[10] Its main thrust enters at precisely the point where we shall be forced to break off our discussion. Now this line of thought has one very radical consequence. For if we suppose that the object really does possess reason, this means that there is a kind of conflict of reason with itself in a far more serious sense than the relatively harmless 'antinomy of practical reason' that Kant examined in the *Critique of Practical Reason*. In other words, the reason that makes itself objective and gives shape to itself in the world, on the one hand, and critical reason, on the other, are not only not one and the same thing, as Hegel would like us to believe, but they are utterly incompatible with each other. Therefore, in this distinction between a reason that objectifies itself and a reason that thinks subjectively we see the questionable nature of the total reason embodied in a single moral principle, or what might be termed *the* moral principle. To act in accordance with reason would be abstract self-preservation freed from the self, and it would degenerate into the evil that is the way of the world in which the stronger emerges as the victor. For this reason, then, there is no good life in the bad one, for a formal ethics cannot underwrite it, and the ethics of responsibility that surrenders to otherness cannot underwrite it either. The question that moral philosophy confronts today is how it should react to this dilemma, and I should like to say something about that next time.

LECTURE SEVENTEEN

25 July 1963

Ladies and Gentlemen,

I wanted to use this last hour to say something about the nature of moral philosophy today. This is to assume that it is possible to say anything at all on the subject in the light of the statement I tried to make sound persuasive to you in my discussion of the ethics of conviction and the ethics of responsibility, namely that in the bad life a good life is not possible. Incidentally, long after I formulated this sentence I discovered a similar statement in Nietzsche, although it is very differently phrased.[1] On the question of whether moral philosophy is possible today, the only thing I would be able to say is that essentially it would consist in the attempt to make conscious the critique of moral philosophy, the critique of its options and an awareness of its antinomies. In these lectures I have tried to provide you with something like a model with which to do this. More than this, I believe, cannot in all decency be promised. Above all, no one can promise that the reflections that can be entertained in the realm of moral philosophy can be used to establish a canonical plan for the good life because life itself is so deformed and distorted that no one is able to live the good life in it or to fulfil his destiny as a human being. Indeed, I would almost go so far as to say that, given the way the world is organized, even the simplest demand for integrity and decency must necessarily lead almost everyone to protest. I believe that only by making this situation a matter of consciousness – rather than covering it up with sticking plaster – will it be possible to create the conditions in which we can properly formulate questions about how we should lead our lives today. The only thing that can perhaps be said is that the good life today would consist in resistance to the forms of the bad life that have been seen through and critically dissected by the most progressive minds. Other than this negative prescription no guidance can really be envisaged. I may add that, negative though this assertion is, it can hardly be much more formal than the Kantian injunction that we have been discussing during this semester. So what I have in mind is the determinate negation of everything that has been seen through, and thus the ability to focus upon the power of resistance to all the things imposed on us, to everything the world has made of us, and intends to make of us to a vastly greater degree. Little else remains to us, other than the power to reflect on these matters and to oppose them from the outset, notwithstanding our consciousness of our impotence. This resistance to what the world has made of us does not at all imply merely an opposition to the external world on the grounds that we would be fully entitled to resist it – all such attempts would merely fortify the principle of the 'way of the world' that is anyway at work in us, and would only benefit the bad. In addition we ought also to mobilize our own powers of resistance in order to resist those parts of us that are tempted to join in. I would almost go so far as to say that even the apparently harmless visit to the cinema to which we condemn ourselves should really be accompanied by the realization that such visits are actually a betrayal of the insights we have acquired and that they will probably entangle us – admittedly only to an infinitesimal degree, but assuredly with a cumulative effect – in the processes that will transform us into what we are supposed to become and what we are making of ourselves in order to enable us to survive, and to ensure that we conform. What I mean is that this temptation to join in is something that cannot be avoided entirely by anyone who is not a saint. But even a saint's existence is precarious today. We are incessantly urged to join in, and for goodness' sake do not imagine that I am being even the least bit pharisaical in proclaiming that you should refrain from joining in. Perhaps the situation is that if we start to reflect on what is involved in joining in, and if we are conscious of its consequences, then everything we do – everything that goes on in our minds to contribute to what is wrong – will be just a little different from what it otherwise would have been. But even that contains too much vanity for us to say it – and if I do say it to you, then I really say it so as not to give you the notorious stones instead of bread, rather than with the intention of making exaggerated claims about the benefits of such a process of reflection. This resistance, then, if I may apply it to the problem we have been considering, should be extended to include resistance to the abstract rigorism that we have seen through; that is, an integral part of this process of reflection, which I would

describe as a precondition of what might be meant by the good
life nowadays, is that we should not behave like Gregers Werle. Hence
the idea of resistance contains an element that is as critical of abstract
morality as it is of the cynicism of those adversaries Old Werle and
Dr Relling that I have told you about. On the other hand, it is
clear that something like the good life is not conceivable unless you
hold fast to both conscience and responsibility. At this point then we
find ourselves really and truly in a contradictory situation. We need
to hold fast to moral norms, to self-criticism, to the question of
right and wrong, and at the same time to a sense of the fallibility
of the authority that has the confidence to undertake such self-
criticism. I am reluctant to use the term 'humanity' at this juncture
since it is one of the expressions that reify and hence falsify crucial
issues merely by speaking of them. When the founders of the Humanist Union invited me to become a member, I replied that 'I might
possibly be willing to join if your club had been called an inhuman
union, but I could not join one that calls itself "humanist".' So if
I am to use the term here then an indispensable part of a humanity
that reflects on itself is that we should not allow ourselves to be
diverted. There has to be an element of unswerving persistence, of
holding fast to what we think we have learnt from experience, and
on the other hand, we need an element not just of self-criticism, but
of criticism of that unyielding, inexorable something that sets itself
up in us. In other words, what is needed above all is that consciousness of our own fallibility, and in that respect I would say that
the element of self-reflection has today become the true heir to what
used to be called moral categories. This means that if today we can
at all say that subjectively there is something like a threshold, a distinction between a right life and a wrong one, we are likely to find
it soonest in asking whether a person is just hitting out blindly
at other people – while claiming that the group to which he belongs
is the only positive one, and other groups should be negated – or
whether by reflecting on our own limitations we can learn to do
justice to those who are different, and to realize that true injustice
is always to be found at the precise point where you put yourself in
the right and other people in the wrong. Hence to abstain from self-
assertiveness – and this goes right up to the metaphysics of death and
the defiant self such as can still be found in Heidegger's 'resoluteness'
[*Entschlossenheit*][2] – seems to me to be the crucial thing to ask from
individuals today. In other words, if you were to press me to follow
the example of the Ancients and make a list of the cardinal virtues,
I would probably respond cryptically by saying that I could think of
nothing except for modesty. Or to put it another way, we must have

a conscience, but may not insist on our own conscience. For example, if you find yourself on a committee – just assume you belong on a committee, and nowadays all of you will be a member of some committee or other, that is the name of the game – and hear someone saying 'My conscience forbids me to do this or that', you should make up your minds to treat such a person with the greatest possible distrust. Above all, when we ourselves feel tempted to say that we 'are making our stand and can do no other',[3] we too deserve to be distrusted in precisely the same way, because this gesture contains exactly the same positing of self, the same self-assertion as positivity, which really just camouflages the principle of self-preservation, while simultaneously pretending to be the moral with which – as I hope I have demonstrated in the course of my critical analysis – it also coincides.

On the other hand, resistance also means resistance to heteronomy in its concrete forms. Today this means the countless forms of morality that are imposed from outside. The form positive morality assumes today has escaped from its transparent theoretical underpinning, much as the link with religion has been cut. Moral imperatives used to be embedded in philosophy in a transparent rational way, but this is no longer the case. Because of these developments the forms of morality generally prevailing in society have assumed the evil and repressive complexion that always makes its appearance when concepts have been undermined. Their substance has evaporated, but people still cling to them, turning them into fetishes. I believe that the most drastic instances of this are to be found in the realm of sexual morality, and I have attempted to analyse them in a study in *Eingriffe*.[4] In this sphere of human experience the religious ideas that used to act as a prop for conventional sexual morality have been severely shaken, as far as the majority of people are concerned. I am thinking here above all of the belief in the sacramental character of marriage. On the other hand, it can no longer be said to be self-evident that the erotic demeans the human dignity of others, as Kant still claimed. This has been exposed as narrow-minded prejudice. Notwithstanding this, a sexual morality that has ceased to have anything to offer is running riot, feasting on the moral indignation that you can see in the articles on Christine Keeler and her friends,[5] but also in the codes of conduct such as the one recently imposed on the ZDF [the second television channel] by its supervisory body and which you can read in the latest issue of *Der Spiegel*.[6] Such codes are a disaster because they literally recodify the objective spirit, that is, the embodiment of the opaque and for that reason inexorable and repressive norms to which people today are exposed. If the moral does have a proper point of departure today it must be the resolute and wholly uncompromising stand against all the manifestations of this spirit that you can find today. I may remind you in this context of slogans disseminated in the current wave of moral indignation, slogans that my friend Habermas has subjected to a measured, but penetrating critical scrutiny in *Merkur*,[7] an article I would like to bring to your attention. The positive religions have now largely lost their power over people's minds, but what Nietzsche once said about them, all too innocently, has now become universal and has been extended to include objective spirit, cultural consciousness in general. As the religions have declined, their restrictive and repressive power has simply been transferred to the silent, wordless, groundless form of mind that pervades life in our society. We might say that wherever people strike moral poses nowadays and appeal to an idea of the good, this good, wherever it is not resistance to evil, turns out to be nothing but a cover for it. And what I have in mind is not just individuals, but above all everything that is written, publicized and that echoes through the mass media. Strindberg's statement 'How can I love the good unless I hate the evil?'[8] has doubly proved its validity, but in catastrophic fashion. On the one hand, the hatred of evil in the name of the good has turned into a destructive force; on the other, the good, instead of regarding evil as a foil to itself, has become evil in its own right. And that is in effect the shape of ideology everywhere today, just as everywhere where moral ideologies are at work – I may remind you of the dominant ideology in the East – the idea of so-called positive, good, heroic models prevails. Incidentally, the term 'models' [*Leitbild*] tells you everything about the reality. It is not for nothing that for the National Socialists such terms as 'purification' [*Reinigung*], 'restoration' [*Wiederherstellung*], 'renewal' [*Erneuerung*] and 'ties' [*Bindungen*] played such a decisive role. While it is true that this ideology has been decapitated politically speaking, and that it is no longer able to attack minorities directly, it can be ready to pounce at any moment, to oppose any deviation and to smash it. Its legacy can be seen above all in the countless forms of anti-intellectualism. One that is by no means amongst the most harmless is the habit of blocking thought by ceaselessly confronting people with demands, without leaving them time to reflect: All right, so what are you going to do about it? What is happening then? Of what use is that to me? Who do you think will be interested in that idea? The elements of Kant's critique of reason that are still alive today probably amount to the critique of all such phenomena.

The transition to such a critique was in fact accomplished by Nietzsche. Nietzsche is uniquely important because he denounced the presence of the bad in the good and thereby also criticized the way in which the bad has assumed concrete form within the positive institutions of society and, above all, in the different ideologies. That in my view far transcends the way in which every possible obscurantist and reactionary trend has based itself on certain propositions of his. And the critique he has provided has been far more subtle and specific than, for example, Marxist theory, which has condemned ideologies *en bloc*, but has never succeeded in entering into their inner workings, their lies, as deeply as Nietzsche. The difficulty underlying all this is of course the difficulty of a private ethics, that is, the behaviour of the individual has long since ceased to link up with objective good and evil. However, it is very important that you should not misunderstand me here. It is not at all my intention to score points off Nietzsche since, to tell the truth, of all the so-called great philosophers I owe him by far the greatest debt – more even than to Hegel. Despite this I believe that particularly in a dialectical course of lectures on moral philosophy I do owe it to you to say a few dialectical words on Nietzsche's criticism of morality. At all events, I would criticize Nietzsche for having failed to go beyond the abstract negation of bourgeois morality, or, to put it differently, of a morality that had degenerated into ideology, into a mask which concealed a dirty business. I would add that his analysis of the individual moral problems he faced did not lead him to construct a statement of the good life. Instead, having proceeded in a summary fashion, he came up with a positive morality that is really nothing more than the negative mirror-image of the morality he had repudiated. Even when we have understood what is wrong with a repressive ideology that has been intensified to the point of absurdity, it is not possible nowadays, in the age of the Culture Industry, simply to read off a true morality from it. A positive morality – he would not have called it morality – cannot possibly exist in Nietzsche because of the absence of a substantive, objective spirit. In other words, given the state of society and the actual state reached by mind in that society, the norms Nietzsche opposed to it were not available in concrete terms and so had simply to be imposed from outside. It is not for nothing that in *Zarathustra*, his most positive work in terms of actual teachings, the language he employs breathes the spirit of *Jugendstil*; it is a kind of biblical imitation, a biblical affectation complete with allusions to the Ten Commandments. This is the language in which he speaks of the new values, the new tablets he proposes to erect. Whereas in reality this very attempt on the part of a lone individual to set up new norms and new commandments based simply on his own subjective whim implies their impotence, their arbitrary and adventitious nature from the very outset. The ideals he has in mind – nobility [*Vornehmheit*], real freedom, the virtue of generosity, distance – all these are wonderful values in themselves, but in an unfree society they are not capable of fulfilment, or at best can only be realized on Sunday afternoons, that is, in private life. Just let all those at the bottom of the pile try and be 'noble' for a change! Well, Nietzsche would have said 'Quite so!' and would have brushed this objection aside. But because they control the labour of others, even those who rule are too implicated in the general catastrophe to be able to afford this nobility. If a prominent businessman were seriously to attempt to be as noble as Nietzsche postulates – and not merely as an aesthetic gesture – he would undoubtedly go bankrupt. His business actually pressures him into the opposite of nobility. Nietzsche had sharp ears and they should have told him that the concept of nobility contains within itself the stigma of non-nobility since the nobleman is the person who is noble in his own eyes and wishes to appear as such to others. Thus in reality these norms are all feudal values that cannot be directly realized in a bourgeois society. They are attempts to recapture lost values, would-be revivals, a Romantic ideal that is completely powerless under the rule of profit. But they also benefit this rule of profit. For what Nietzsche means by man, and what he celebrates as the Superman – and it is not for nothing that the latter is based on the model of the appalling and barbaric condottiere Cesare Borgia – would be the go-getter[9] or captain of industry today. In other words, while Nietzsche intended these new values as a counter to the Wilheminian empire of the years following 1870, they remained objectively – against their own intentions – the ideology of an expanding imperialism. For example, Nietzsche's hostility to compassion is a purely abstract negation of Schopenhauer's ethics of compassion, and it was put to the test by the Third Reich and in general by the totalitarian states in a way that would have horrified Nietzsche more than anyone. On the other hand, we must admit that Nietzsche's criticism of the morality of compassion has an element of truth. This is because the concept of compassion tacitly maintains and gives its sanction to the negative condition of powerlessness in which the object of our pity finds himself. The idea of compassion contains nothing about changing the circumstances that give rise to the need for it, but instead, as in Schopenhauer, these circumstances are absorbed into the moral doctrine and interpreted as its main foundation. In short, they are hypostatized and treated as if they were immutable. We may conclude from this that the pity you express for someone always contains an element of injustice towards that person; he experiences not just our pity but also the impotence and the specious character of the compassionate act. I believe that if you reflect on your own simple experience and think about how you feel when you give twenty pence to a beggar, you will understand perfectly what I mean and what I find to object to in Nietzsche. This too shows that there is no right behaviour within the wrong world; and certainly none today that is not saturated with Nietzschean disgust with the petty bourgeoisie. I have absolutely no wish to defend the brutalities of Nietzsche's moral philosophy and, after what I have said, I do not think anyone will suppose that I want to. Nevertheless, they do contain an element of truth. This is contained in the perception that in a society that is based on force and exploitation, a violence that is unrationalized, frank and open and, if you like, an 'expiatory violence'[10] is more innocent than one that rationalizes itself as the good. Force only really becomes evil the moment it misunderstands itself as the *gladius dei*, the sword of God. I should like to draw your attention here to Max Horkheimer's 'Egoism and Freedom Movements' that appeared, I believe, in 1936 or 1937, in the *Zeitschrift für Sozialforschung*, and in which you can find this entire dialectic very clearly set out.[11] Nietzsche failed to recognize that the so-called slave morality that he excoriates is in truth always a master morality, namely the morality imposed on the oppressed by the rulers. If his critique had been as consistent as it ought to have been, but isn't – because he too was in thrall to existing social conditions, because he was able to get to the bottom of what people had become, but was not able to get to the bottom of the society that made them what they were – it should have turned its gaze to the conditions that determine human beings and make them and each of us into what we are. For example, Nietzsche coined the phrase 'No herdsman and one herd'.[12] He may have succeeded in discovering a formula to describe what the ghastly slogan now calls 'mass society', but that is not, as he imagined, the denunciation of the 'Ultimate Man'. It is a description of a completely functionalized and anonymous form of domination, that nevertheless rules over this herd with incomparably greater brutality than if there were a visible bell-wether for them to follow. Even today there is no lack of bleating in this shepherdless flock or fatherless society or community. Nietzsche had imagined that by calling for such values he would 'transcend' [*überwinden*], to use the appalling term that has become so fashionable, the so-called relativism that he had himself advocated in the ethics of his middle period. We should note the following: the concept of value in the abstract, that is, values that are postulated in isolation from their own dialectical development, is highly problematic, just like that concept of 'transcending' that plays such an appalling role whenever people are confronted with radical theories of whatever kind. As soon as they catch sight of such theories, they feel themselves impelled to say, 'Yes, but that is something we have to transcend.' And I can give you an example of moral dialectics here. Whenever anyone expects you to deal with something intellectually uncomfortable by asking you to 'transcend' it, just pause and ask by what authority you should do so. If you were to do that, I think that would be an instance of a right action in a wrong world.

But I would like to say a few words at least on the subject of relativism. You will perhaps have noticed that I have not concerned myself overmuch in these lectures with the famous problem of moral relativism. I have omitted to do so because I truly believe that it is in great measure a pseudo-problem – to use another much-abused term. For the positive nature of beliefs, of ideologies, that prevail here and now is not relative at all. They confront us at every moment as binding and absolute. And the criticism of these false absolutes – or what Hegel, the young Hegel, called 'the positive nature of prevailing moral beliefs'[13] – is much more urgent than the quest for some absolute values or other, fixed in eternity and hanging from the ceiling like herrings, which would enable us to transcend this relativism with which, as real living people who are attempting to live decent lives, we have absolutely nothing to do. On the other hand, however, the postulates and values that surface wherever people imagine that they have to overcome relativism, are the products of arbitrary acts, things that are freely posited, that are created and not natural, and thus they necessarily always succumb to the relativism they denounce. In that sense we can say, as indeed I attempted to show in another theoretical piece, in the *Metakritik*, that the concept of relativism is the correlative of absolutism. Dialectical thinking, on the other hand – if I understand properly what that is supposed to be – is a kind of thinking that, to express it in Nietzschean terms, would persist beyond that alternative.[14] In contrast to this, the concept of determinate negation as you find it enshrined, for example – and I should like after all to mention his name in the last minutes of this course of lectures – in the stupendous *œuvre* of Karl Kraus, really does lead beyond this so-called relativism. We may not know what absolute good is or the absolute norm, we may not even know what man is or the human or humanity – but what the inhuman is we know very well indeed. I would say that the place of moral philosophy today lies more in the concrete denunciation of the inhuman, than in vague and abstract attempts to situate man in his existence. In short, all the problems of moral philosophy come under the general rubric of private ethics, that is, they refer in reality to a society that is still individualistic, a

society of the sort that has been overtaken by history. This individualistic society has its limitations and its particular features; they can
be read off from the so-called basic problem of moral philosophy,
namely that of free will. That is why for a moral philosophy which
is necessarily a theory of private ethics, the highest point it can rise
to is that of the antinomy of causality and freedom which figures in
Kant's philosophy in an unresolved and for that reason exemplary
fashion. But what appears in Kant as the intertwining of man and
nature is also the intertwining of man and society. For in that second
nature, in our universal state of dependency, there is no freedom. And
for that reason there is no ethics either in the administered world. It
follows that the premise of ethics is the critique of the administered
world. This is why the authority of conscience withers away in
individual human beings. It atrophies, just as the psychologists have
observed – most recently my friend Mitscherlich in his book on
society without fathers.[15] In the same spirit I have shown how the
exteriority of the super-ego has come to confront the interiority of
the moral principle that had been the achievement of philosophy at
its zenith. Freedom, Kant thought, is literally and truly an idea. It
necessarily presupposes the freedom of all, and cannot even be
conceived as an isolated thing, that is, in the absence of social
freedom. Existentialist ethics appears to many of you to be advanced.
Motivated by its protest against the administered world, it made an
absolute of spontaneity and of the human subject in so far as it has
not been co-opted. That is the error of this ethics since precisely
because this spontaneity lacks reflexivity and is separated from objective reality, objectivity re-enters it, just as Sartre has ended up placing
himself at the service of Communist ideology. This means that either
this spontaneity will be eliminated, if it is seriously intended, and
buried beneath the great ideology, or it lapses into administration. In
short, anything that we can call morality today merges into the question of the organization of the world. We might even say that the
quest for the good life is the quest for the right form of politics, if
indeed such a right form of politics lay within the realm of what can
be achieved today. – I should like to thank you for your attentiveness
and to wish you an enjoyable vacation.

Editor's Notes

BIBLIOGRAPHICAL REFERENCES

Translator's Note

References to standard English translations have been provided wherever possible. The most commonly used are given here, along with the German editions referred to where no suitable English translations are available. Material added by the translator is enclosed within square brackets, both in the body of the text and in the notes. Except where indicated all notes are those of the editor.

The following translations of Adorno's writings have been used:

[with Max Horkheimer], *Dialectic of Enlightenment*, trans. John Cumming, Allen Lane, London, 1973.
The Jargon of Authenticity, trans. Knut Tarnowski and Frederic Will, Routledge and Kegan Paul, London, 1973.
Minima Moralia, trans. E.F.N. Jephcott, NLB, London, 1974.
Notes to Literature, vol. 2, trans. Shierry Weber Nicholsen, Columbia University Press, New York, 1992.

In the absence of translations references are to the following:

GS   *Gesammelte Schriften*, ed. Rolf Tiedemann, with the assistance of Gretel Adorno, Susan Buck-Morss and Klaus Schultz, Suhrkamp, Frankfurt am Main, 1973
NaS *Nachgelassene Schriften*, the posthumously published writings, which have appeared in six sections. They include 16 vols of previously published courses of lectures
Ts   Unpublished typescripts
Vo   Unpublished single lectures

The following works of Kant have been used:

'M. Immanuel Kant's Announcement of the Programme of his Lectures for
the Winter Semester 1765–1766', in Immanuel Kant, *Theoretical Philosophy, 1755–1770*, trans. and ed. David Walford in collaboration with Ralf
Meerbote, Cambridge University Press, Cambridge, 1992.
Critique of Pure Reason, trans. Norman Kemp Smith, Macmillan, London,
1928 [subsequent editions retain the original pagination]. In accordance
with common practice, references to the first and second German editions
are given as A and B.
Critique of Practical Reason and other works on the Theory of Ethics, trans.
Thomas Kingsmill Abbott, Longman, London, 1959 [reprint of 6th edn
1909; 1st edn 1873].
Critique of Judgement, trans. James Creed Meredith, Clarendon Press,
Oxford, 1973.
Kant: Political Writings, ed. Hans Reiss, trans. H. B. Nisbet, Cambridge University Press, Cambridge, 1970.
The Metaphysics of Morals, trans. Mary Gregor, Cambridge University
Press, Cambridge, 1991.
Observations on the Feeling of the Beautiful and Sublime, trans. John T.
Goldthwait, University of California Press, Berkeley and London, 1973.
Prolegomena to Any Future Metaphysics, the Paul Carus translation extensively revised by James W. Ellington, Hackett Publishing, Indianapolis,
1977.
The Moral Law: Groundwork of the Metaphysic of Morals, trans. and
analysed by H. J. Paton, Routledge, London and New York, 1991. [Cited
as *Groundwork*]
Religion and Rational Theology, trans. and ed. Allen W. Wood and George
Di Giovanni, Cambridge University Press, Cambridge, 1996.

Where no translations were available, reference is to Immanuel Kant, *Werke
in sechs Bänden*, ed. Wilhelm Weischedel, Wissenschaftliche Buchgesellschaft, Darmstadt, 1964, reprinted 1983.

References to Nietzsche's works are as follows:

The Genealogy of Morals, ed. Keith Ansell-Pearson, trans. Carol Diethe,
Cambridge University Press, Cambridge, 1996.
Daybreak, ed. Maudemarie Clark and Brian Leiter, trans. R. J. Hollingdale,
Cambridge University Press, Cambridge, 1997.
The Gay Science, trans. Walter Kaufmann, Vintage Books, New York, 1974.
Thus Spake Zarathustra, trans. R. J. Hollingdale, Penguin Books, Harmondsworth, 1969.
Twilight of the Idols, in Walter Kaufmann (ed. and trans.), *The Portable
Nietzsche*, Penguin Books, Harmondsworth, 1978.

References to Freud's works are generally to:

The Pelican Freud Library, ed. Angela Richards, Penguin Books, Harmondsworth, 1973– .

Essays not available there are to be found in:

The Standard Edition of the Complete Psychological Works of Sigmund Freud, translated under the editorship of James Strachey in collaboration with Anna Freud, The Hogarth Press, London, 1966– . [*The Standard Edition*]

Hegel is quoted in the following translations:

Philosophy of Right, trans. T.M. Knox, Oxford University Press, London, Oxford and New York, 1981; *Elements of the Philosophy of Right*, ed. Alan W. Wood, trans. H.B. Nisbet, Cambridge University Press, Cambridge, 1991.
Science of Logic, trans. A.V. Miller, George Allen and Unwin, New York, 1976.
Phenomenology of Spirit, trans. A.V. Miller, Oxford University Press, Oxford, 1977.

References to Schopenhauer's works are as follows:

On the Basis of Morality, trans. E.E.J. Payne, Berghahn Books, Providence, RI, and Oxford, 1995.
The World as Will and Idea, trans. R.B. Haldane and J. Kemp, Kegan Paul, Trench, Trübner and Co., London, 1909.

References to Heidegger are to *Being and Time*, trans. John Macquarie and Edward Robinson, Oxford University Press, Oxford and Cambridge, Mass., 1995.

NOTES

Lecture One

1 Adorno is referring to *Minima Moralia*. In the dedication to Max Horkheimer he writes: 'The melancholy science from which I make this offering to my friend relates to a region that from time immemorial was regarded as the true field of philosophy, but which, since the latter's conversion into method, has lapsed into intellectual neglect, sententious whimsy and finally oblivion: the teaching of the good life. What the philosophers once knew as life has become the sphere of private existence and now of mere consumption, dragged along as an appendage of the process of material production, without autonomy or substance of its own' (*Minima Moralia*, p. 15).

2 Conjectured substitute for 'possible' in the original.

3 *Minima Moralia*, p. 39. [Jephcott's translation reads: 'Wrong life cannot be lived rightly.' *Trans.*]

4 A comparable statement in Nietzsche could not be found. In Lecture 17 on 25 July 1963 Adorno again refers to this parallel, but adds 'although it is phrased very differently'. Adorno presumably has in mind *Human, All Too Human*, I, nos 33 and 34.

5 See the *Groundwork*: 'It would be easy to show here how human reason, with this compass in hand, is well able to distinguish, in all cases that present themselves, what is good or evil, right or wrong – provided that, without the least attempt to teach it anything new, we merely make reason attend, as Socrates did, to its own principle; and how in consequence there is no need of science or philosophy for knowing what man has to do in order to be honest and good, and indeed to be wise and virtuous' (p. 69).

6 Scheler says: 'A sharp distinction must be made [. . .] in the whole field of ethics: between an ethics "practised and applied" by ethical subjects [. . .] and groups of ethical principles that can only be derived from a

methodical, logical procedure for which that "applied ethics" provides the material. That is to say, between the ethics of a natural, practical world view expressed in natural language (to which the proverbial wisdom of all times and places belongs, as well as all traditional maxims and the like) – and the more or less scientific, philosophical and theological *ethics* that is accustomed to "justify" that applied ethics and "ground" them in the highest principles, even though these "principles" do not need to be *known* by the subject of the applied ethics.' Max Scheler, *Der Formalismus in der Ethik und die materiale Wertethik. Neuer Versuch der Grundlegung eines ethischen Personalismus.* Now in *Gesammelte Werke*, vol. 2, 4th edn, Berne, 1954, p. 321. [Translated by Manfred S. Frings and Roger L. Funk as *Formalism and Non-Formal Ethics of Values*, Northwestern University Press, Evanston, Ill., 1973. Trans.]

7 See *Critique of Pure Reason*, p. 635, A 805/B 833, where Kant asks this question, albeit in the singular: 'What ought I to do?'

8 Adorno goes further into the relation of theoretical and practical reason in Lecture 3 on 14 May 1963 (see pp. 25–8).

9 Adorno fluctuates in his view of Fichte's contribution to moral philosophy. The earlier course of lectures entitled *Problems of Moral Philosophy* of 1956/7 proceeds from Fichte's attempt 'to synthesize [Kant's] theoretical and practical reasons. In the process practical reason is given precedence. 'It can be recognized today that Fichte's development of Kant's line of thought contains an important kernel of truth: Today conduct worthy of human beings is one that is not blindly dependent upon external factors, that is not beholden to the concrete, that does not look to things for the fulfilment of its existential needs and that is inspired by the consciousness of what is human even while inhabiting a world overwhelmed by things' (Lecture of 20 November 1956, Vo 1310; cf. also Lecture 11 of 4 July 1963, p. 115).

10 See Adorno's lecture to the Berlin Congress of German Sociological Society in May 1959, now in *GS*, vol. 8, pp. 93–121.

11 Adorno is referring to the essay 'Dubious Knowledge' in which Golo Mann replied to a lecture by René König that the latter had given in Munich in 1960 with the title 'The Sociology of the 1920s'. 'Mere knowledge, the striving for knowledge for its own sake, would never satisfy me. We find this even today among those whom Mr König calls *revenants* because their ideas of education stem from that period. Let us take Theodor W. Adorno, whose name he mentions, with his analyses that go no further than asking what things are, what is half-education, what is the theory of half-education today? I would say in reply that such an approach takes us nowhere. What I want to know is, how can we overcome ourselves, how can we help others?' (Golo Mann, 'Fragwürdige Erkenntnis', in *Wissen und Leben*, the in-house journal of W. Kohlhammer Verlag, Stuttgart, 1960, no. 15, p. 13). Adorno also commented on Mann in a letter to

Franz Böhm of 15 July 1963 in which he enclosed excerpts from an essay by Mann 'On Anti-Semitism' (from *Geschichte und Geschichten*, [History and Histories], Frankfurt am Main, 1961, pp. 169–201): 'Here, as agreed, are the passages from the works of Golo Mann. Needless to say, the comments on the Jew-free Bonn Republic reflect worse on him than the abuse he flings at me and which amounts to the assertion that a theorist is a theorist. I should like to emphasize that what concerns me in all this is not so much my own sensibilities as the unspeakable anti-intellectualism that is being proclaimed.'

12   Adorno used the English word. In his handwritten notes he remarked 'The *more uncertain* the practice, the more frantically it is sought after. The constantly recurring complaint: What shall we do? The joiner with a cause.'

13   This statement as formulated could not be found in Fichte. It is possibly a conflation of Fichte's position on ethics with that of Friedrich Theodor Vischer's assertion 'The moral is self-evident', from *Auch Einer. Eine Reisebekanntschaft*, Stuttgart, 1879, now available with an afterword by Otto Borst, Frankfurt am Main, 1987, p. 25.

14   Adorno alludes here to Freud's formula of cultural work: 'Where id was, there ego shall be'. Sigmund Freud, *New Introductory Lectures on Psychoanalysis*, trans. James Strachey, in *The Pelican Freud Library*, vol. 2, Harmondsworth, 1973, Lecture 31, p. 112. For Freud's conception of morality see also 'The Ego and the Id': 'From the point of view of instinctual control, of morality, it may be said of the id that it is totally non-moral, of the ego that it strives to be moral, and of the superego that it can be supermoral and then become as cruel as only the id can be.' In *The Pelican Freud Library*, vol. 11, Harmondsworth, 1984, p. 395.

15   These considerations underpinned Adorno's subsequent criticism of the student movement. Cf. 'Marginalien zu Theorie und Praxis', in *GS*, vol. 10.2, pp. 759–82, and also *Resignation*, ibid., pp. 794–9.

16   See Lecture 15 of 18 July 1963 and Lecture 16 of 23 July 1963. [This distinction goes back to Max Weber's early essay 'Politics as a Vocation'. For an ethics of conviction what matters is remaining true to principle, 'keeping the flame of pure intention undampened', even where this might lead to harmful results. An ethics of responsibility, on the other hand, demands that the individual take full responsibility for the total consequences of his actions. Although Max Weber believed that the 'genuine' man would combine the two, he thought that only the ethics of responsibility was appropriate to the field of politics, regarding the man of conviction as 'otherworldly'. H.H. Gerth and C.W. Mills, *From Max Weber: Essays in Sociology*, Routledge and Kegan Paul, London, 1947, pp. 77–128. *Trans.*]

17   [This was the plot of 20 July 1944 under the leadership of Claus Graf Schenk von Stauffenberg and Carl Goerdeler. Although Stauffenberg managed to set off a bomb in Hitler's bunker in East Prussia, the plot

failed, the leading conspirators were brutally executed and a wider circle of associates were ruthlessly hunted down. *Trans.*]

18 In the course of lectures entitled *Problems of Moral Philosophy* which he gave in the Winter Semester of 1956/7, Adorno did reveal the name (cf. Vo 1307), and he also noted it in the manuscript of the first lecture of the present series (cf. Vo 8799). He was talking about Fabian von Schlabrendorff (1907–80), a lawyer and, later, a judge in the Federal Constitutional Court. He had been an aide-de-camp to the Chief of the General Staff. He was arrested on the grounds of belonging to the circle responsible for the coup of 20 July 1944, but was acquitted in March 1945. [It may be added that he was tortured, but did not break down, and he refused to reveal the names of any fellow-conspirators. In his memoirs he claims that Roland Freisler, the leading Nazi judge, was holding his (Schlabrendorff's) file in his hand when the building in which the case was set down for hearing suffered a direct hit in an air raid, killing Freisler at once. *Trans.*]

19 Adorno probably has in mind a laconic aphorism handed down by Gustav Schwab. It is to be found in the Große Stuttgarter edition of Hölderlin's works, ed. Friedrich Beißner, vol. 4.1, Stuttgart, 1961, p. 293: 'That man has a higher moral calling in the world can be learnt from the assertions of morality and is evident in many things.' For the development of Hölderlin's critique of morality see especially his letter of 1 January 1799 to his half-brother Karl Gock (ibid., vol. 6.1, pp. 326–32), and also his *Entwürfe zur Poetik* [Sketches on Poetics] (Frankfurter Hölderlin edition, ed. Wolfram Groddeck and Dietrich E. Sattler, Frankfurt, 1979, vol. 14, p. 48).

20 [German has three terms – *Moral*, *Ethik*, and *Sitte/Sittlichkeit* – to cover the meanings given by ethics and morality in English. There is no fully satisfactory English equivalent for *Sitte*, whose meanings range from custom, through (good) manners, to morality (for example, the *Sittenpolizei* are the vice squad). The overlap with *Moral* (morals, morality) compounds the problems created by the overlap between 'morals' and 'ethics' in English. Often no distinction need be made: Kant's *Metaphysik der Sitten* is regularly translated as 'The Metaphysics of Morals'. On the other hand, Hegel emphasized the social roots of *Sitten* as the customs of a people, thus establishing the tendency to distinguish between (personal) morality (*Moral*) and (social) ethics (*Sitte*). In the light of Adorno's discussion of 'ethics' that distinction is ruled out here. *Trans.*]

21 In the earlier course of lectures entitled *The Problems of Moral Philosophy* Adorno had said: 'The concept of ethics is much more popular than moral philosophy. It does not sound so inflexible, it appears to have loftier, more human connotations; it does not simply abandon human actions to the realm of chance, but contains the promise of something like a specific sphere of universality against which human behaviour can be measured. Ethics is bad conscience, conscience about oneself. It is the attempt to talk about conscience without appealing to the

element of compulsion it contains' (Lecture of 8 November 1956, Vo 1295).

Lecture Two

1 Adorno deviates from Büchner's text, although not in such a way as to weaken his thesis about the tautological nature of the Captain's morality. The starting-point for the Captain's moral rebuke to Woyzeck is the haste with which he performs his duties as a barber: 'You always look so worked-up. A good man doesn't look like that.' When the Captain suggests to him that the wind 'is a north-southerly' this is made the occasion of a second reproach: 'God, but the man's dense, horribly dense.' And this gives rise to the self-contradictory idea that 'You're a good man, Woyzeck, but (*Solemnly*) you've no morals. Morals are . . . well, observing morality, you understand. That's the way of it. You've got a child without the church's blessing [. . .].' Georg Büchner, *Woyzeck*, trans. George Mackendrick, Methuen, London, 1979, p. 11 [translation slightly adjusted].

2 See 'Third Essay: What Do Ascetic Ideals Mean?' of Nietzsche's *The Genealogy of Morals* for a discussion of 'ascetic ideals'. [In Friedrich Nietzsche, *The Genealogy of Morals*, pp. 72–128. *Trans.*]

3 In *The Jargon of Authenticity* Adorno criticizes this identification of 'Being' and 'personality' as the core of Heidegger's philosophy (pp. 113–16).

4 The essay 'Religion within the Boundaries of Mere Reason' defines 'personality' as 'an element of the determination of the human being [. . .] as a rational and at the same time *responsible* being' (*Religion and Rational Theology*, p. 74).

5 This is Nietzsche's epithet for Schiller as one of his 'impossible ones'. See his 'Skirmishes of an Untimely Man', in *Twilight of the Idols*, in Kaufmann, *The Portable Nietzsche*, p. 513. [Nietzsche's jibe at what he saw as Schiller's excessive moralizing involves a pun on the title of a famous epic, *The Trumpeter of Säckingen*, by Joseph Viktor von Scheffel (1826–86). This tells the rather sentimental story of a trumpet player, a wandering minstrel in the Romantic style, who falls in love with a nobleman's daughter, defends the former's castle during a peasants' revolt, but is rejected as a suitor because of his lower station in life. Having served as a musician in the service of the Pope, he meets his beloved once again, and this time the Pope ennobles him and enables the lovers to marry. *Trans.*]

6 See Hegel, *Philosophy of Right*, p. 13. [See also *Elements of the Philosophy of Right*, p. 23. *Trans.*]

7 Adorno's lecture course in the Winter Semester 1956/7 deals in detail with the moral philosophy of Socrates and Plato in the lectures given between 11 December 1956 and 10 January 1957. Following Hegel and Nietzsche, Adorno thinks that Greek thought since the Sophists was

characterized by a 'fundamentally practical tendency' and 'reflection on the subject' (Vo 1345). The Platonic moral theory 'like every other [. . .] arises from the fact that from the standpoint of subjective reason, – however broadly conceived and however closely related to the [human] race – from the standpoint of the fulfilment of the desires and needs of the individual, the equation between momentary failure and future fulfilment does not work out. In this sense the objective rationality of morality is an aporetic concept. This means that the Platonic theory of morality provides the model for all subsequent moral philosophies' (Vo 1373–4). On the question of the 'conservative tendency' and the disputes with the Sophists, see the lecture of 10 January 1957: 'The rigid antithesis between the intelligible and empirical worlds [. . .] always implies a certain resignation and conformism. You turn God into a decent chap, as it were, and leave the ideas suspended in their ideal heaven. For such thinking always raises the question of how – to put it simply – the ideal is to be made real' (Vo 1389–90).

8   See Max Scheler, *Der Formalismus in der Ethik und die materiale Wertethik. Neuer Versuch der Grundlegung eines ethischen Personalismus*. See *Gesammelte Werke*, vol. 2, 4th edn, Berne, 1954, p. 321. On Steinthal, see ibid., n. 2.

9   [The term *Zersetzung* was popular with the Nazis. Unlike the English word 'disintegration' which has been used to translate it here, the verb *zersetzen* can also be used transitively, usually with highly negative connotations: it implies that an active, corrosive process has been at work, undermining otherwise healthy phenomena. In Nazi parlance it was generally Jews or Communists who had caused older values or customs to disintegrate. In the same way, modern art was said to have brought about the disintegration of older representational painting. *Trans.*]

10 See William Graham Sumner, *Folkways: A Study on the Sociological Importance of Usages, Manners, Customs, Mores and Morals*, Boston, 1906. Cf. also Adorno's *Introduction to Sociology*, in *NaS* IV, vol. 15, p. 65.

11 Émile Durkheim's contributions to the theory of morality have been collected in the volume *Soziologie und Philosophie*, Frankfurt am Main, 1967, to which Adorno wrote the introduction. See *GS*, vol. 8, pp. 245–79.

12 Adorno refers specifically here to *Haferfeldtreiben*, courts in Bavaria and the Austrian Tyrol where offenders against local customs or morals were put on trial in the middle of the night and punished by being dressed in a goatskin and chased around. [NB *Haberfell*, 'goatskin', is what is meant here (rather than *Haferfeld*, 'field of oats', as might be supposed). *Trans.*]

13 [Literally, 'racial defilement'. The reference is to the Nazi Nuremberg laws of 1935, which made sexual relations between Jews and Aryans a criminal offence. *Trans.*]

14 See *Groundwork*, p. 106.

Lecture Three

1   In his novel *Nächte in Alexandria. Roman einer Ägyptenreise* [Alexan-
    drian Nights: Novel of a Journey to Egypt], Düsseldorf and Cologne,
    1963, pp. 215–18, Paul Lüth (1921–86), a doctor, tells of his attendance
    at the lecture series on Philosophical Terminology in the Winter Semes-
    ter 1962/3. Lüth wrote to Adorno on the subject on 13 May 1963,
    saying that the novel was an attempt 'to give a picture of the thoughts
    and feelings of contemporary students'. Adorno replied to Lüth on 20
    May 1963, saying: 'After reading your letter, I took the very first oppor-
    tunity to raise this matter in my next lecture, and to talk to the students
    about the difficulty of taking notes, etc. I think it was very well received.
    You can see, then, that what has come via you from the empirical world
    has quickly found its way back into that world.'

2   Cf. Kant, 'Announcement of the Programme of his Lectures for the
    Winter Semester 1765–1766', in *Theoretical Philosophy, 1755–1770*, p.
    292, as well as *Critique of Pure Reason*, p. 657, A 837/B 865.

3   Adorno is alluding once more to Lüth's novel which mentions the 'whis-
    pering' that went on before the lecture (see pp. 215–16), and to which
    he opposed a 'murky' definition of dialectic: 'Obscurity and taciturnity
    at the beginning, then a torrent and mirroring, the dialectic of oppo-
    sites, the unending dissolving of contradictions in a new abyss that
    receives them in darkness and becomes the new beginning' (p. 217).
    Lüth's final statement on the lecture course on Philosophical Terminol-
    ogy can be found in his 'Letter from a Country Practice', in *Theodor
    W. Adorno zum Gedächtnis. Eine Sammlung* [In Memory of Theodor
    W. Adorno: A Collection of Essays], ed. Hermann Schweppenhäuser,
    Suhrkamp, Frankfurt am Main, 1971, pp. 116–23.

4   The literal source has not been found. Adorno must have been think-
    ing of this passage from *Twilight of the Idols*: 'I mistrust all systema-
    tizers and avoid them. The will to a system is a lack of integrity'
    (Aphorism 26, p. 470).

5   See Max Horkheimer, 'Fragen des Hochschulunterrichtes' [Problems of
    University Education], in *Gesammelte Schriften*, vol. 8, *Vorträge und
    Aufzeichnungen* [Lectures and Notes] *1949–1973*, ed. Gunzelin Schmid
    Noerr, Suhrkamp, Frankfurt am Main, 1985, p. 393.

6   See Adorno, *Der getreue Korrepetitor. Lehrschriften zur musikalischen
    Praxis* [The Faithful *Répétiteur*: Essays on Musical Practice], in *GS*, vol.
    15, pp. 192–3.

7   ['If we may compare small things with great', Virgil, *The Georgics*,
    Book IV, line 176. *Trans.*]

8   See Section 1 of the 'Canon of Pure Reason', in *Critique of Pure Reason*,
    pp. 630–4, A 797–804/B 825–32.

9   See ibid., and also the lecture entitled 'Kant's "Critique of Pure Reason"'
    of 14 May 1949, *NaS* IV, vol. 4, pp. 27–9.

10 Hans Cornelius, *Kommentar zu Kants 'Kritik der reinen Vernunft'*,
    Erlangen, 1926, p. 125.

11 See *Critique of Pure Reason*, pp. 393–4, A 421/B 448–9.

12 Ibid., p. 99, A 81/B 86. The necessarily illusory character of dialectic that Adorno is concerned with here is discussed in the introduction to the 'Transcendental Dialectic', where Kant speaks of 'a *natural* and inevitable *illusion*' (*Critique of Pure Reason*, p. 300, A 298/B 354). See also Lecture 5 of 28 May 1963 and n. 3 to that lecture.

13 Adorno's view of Kant's conception of dialectic undergoes a number of changes. In the lecture of 12 February 1957 he characterizes the section on the antinomies as a model of dialectical logic: 'Dialectics is not presupposed here as a model of philosophical method, but is treated phenomenologically, that is, as if it were coextensive with the topic under discussion. This is because the Kantian analysis leads to a situation in which a concept used consistently needs its own opposite in order to become valid' (Vo 1471). The section in *Negative Dialectics* entitled 'Pseudoproblems' gives a critical view of the contradictory conceptions of dialectic in Kant: 'The point would be to reflect on the topics under discussion not by deciding whether or not they exist, but by expanding their definition so as to include both the impossibility of capturing their essence and the obligation to do so. This is what is attempted, with or without any such explicit intention, in the antinomy chapter of the *Critique of Pure Reason* as well as over long stretches of the *Critique of Practical Reason* [. . .]' (*GS*, vol. 6, pp. 211f.). [A new translation of *Negative Dialectics* is being prepared by Robert Hullot-Kentor.]

14 *Critique of Pure Reason*, p. 395, A 424/B 451–2.

Lecture Four

1 Cf. *Critique of Pure Reason*, p. 328, A 340/B 398.

2 See ibid., pp. 393–4, A 421/B448–9.

3 The concept of 'spontaneity' is introduced by Kant as 'the capacity' 'of receiving representations (receptivity for impressions) and the power of knowing an object through these representations in the production of concepts' (*Critique of Pure Reason*, p. 92, A 50/B 74). In the second edition he makes this more precise: 'That representation which can be given prior to all thought is entitled intuition. All the manifold of intuition has, therefore, a necessary relation to the "I think" in the same subject in which this manifold is found. But this representation is an act of *spontaneity*, that is, it cannot be regarded as belonging to sensibility. I call it *pure apperception*, to distinguish it from empirical apperception, or, again, *original apperception*, because it is that self-consciousness which, while generating the representation "*I think*" (a representation which must be capable of accompanying all other representations, and which in all consciousness is one and the same), cannot itself be accompanied by any further representation. The unity of this apperception I likewise entitle the *transcendental* unity of self-consciousness, in order to indicate the possibility of *a priori* knowledge

arising from it' (ibid., p. 153, B 132). The thesis of the third antinomy that Adorno is concerned with here defines 'transcendental freedom' as 'an *absolute spontaneity* of the cause, whereby a series of appearances, which proceeds in accordance with laws of nature, begins *of itself*' (ibid., p. 411, A 446/B 474).

4   *Critique of Pure Reason*, p. 409, A 444/B 472.
5   [Ibid., pp. 120–69. *Trans*.]
6   Ibid., p. 409, A 444/B 472.
7   Ibid., pp. 409–10, A 444/B 472.
8   Ibid., p. 410, A 444/B 472.
9   Ibid., p. 410, A 444–6/B 472–4. [Adorno comments on Kant's use of the word *subaltern* which, like the equivalent English word 'subaltern', has value connotations that are unexpected in this context and may seem irrelevant to Kant's argument. *Trans*.]
10 Ibid., p. 410, A 446/B 474.
11 Cf. the 'Second Analogy of Experience', ibid., pp. 218–33, A 189–211 /B 232–56.
12 Ibid., p. 410, A 446/B 474.
13 Ibid. [Norman Kemp Smith rightly gives 'the proposition that . . .', and this is in line with Adorno's comment. The translation here is more literal (rendering 'der Satz, als wenn . . .' as 'the proposition as if'), since otherwise Adorno's remark about the slight syntactic awkwardness in Kant's sentence would not be comprehensible. A German reader might well stumble over the original. *Trans*.]
14 Ibid., pp. 410–11, A 446/B 474.
15 In a later passage Kant comments further on this question: 'Now this acting subject would not, in its intelligible character, stand under any conditions of time [. . .]. In a word, its causality, so far as it is intelligible, would not have a place in the series of those empirical conditions through which the event is rendered necessary in the world of sense. This intelligible character can never, indeed, be immediately known, for nothing can be perceived except in so far as it appears. It would have to be *thought* in accordance with the empirical character [. . .]' (*Critique of Pure Reason*, p. 468, A 539–40/B 567–8).
16 'Determined empirically' is a conjecture to fill a gap in the text.
17 See *Critique of Pure Reason*, pp. 585–9, A 727–32/B 755–60.
18 See the references in n. 3 to this lecture.
19 *Critique of Pure Reason*, p. 409, A 445/B 473.
20 Ibid., pp. 409–10, A 445/B 473.
21 Ibid., p. 410, A 445/B 473.
22 Ibid.
23 Ibid., p. 410, A 445–7/B 473–5.
24 Cf. Aristotle, *Metaphysica*, XII. 8. 1073a; *De Anima*, III. 10. 433b; *Physica*, VIII. 5. 256b, 13–25.
25 *Critique of Pure Reason*, pp. 410–11, A 447/B 475.
26 Ibid., p. 411, A 447/B 475.

Lecture Five

1   The lectures on 21 and 23 May had been cancelled because Adorno was ill.
2   Adorno is alluding here to Joachim Schumacher, *Die Angst vor dem Chaos. Über die falsche Apokalypse des Bürgertums* [Fear of Chaos: The False Apocalypse of the Bourgeoisie], Paris 1937; 2nd edn, Frankfurt am Main, 1978.
3   Kant's 'Solution of the Cosmological Idea' conceives the necessity of the antinomies as one of appearance and not of objects themselves (see the *Critique of Pure Reason*, pp. 464–79, A 532–58/B 560–86). Adorno goes into this aspect of the question in *Negative Dialectics*: 'Kant called transcendental dialectics a logic of illusion: the logic of the contradictions in which every treatment of transcendent things as positively knowable is bound to become entangled. His verdict is not rendered obsolete by Hegel's efforts to vindicate the logic of illusion as the logic of truth. But this verdict on illusion does not put paid to further reflection. Once made conscious of itself, the illusion is no longer what it was. What finite beings say about transcendence is the illusion of transcendence; but as Kant well knew, it is a necessary illusion. This explains the incomparable metaphysical importance of the salvaging of illusion, which is the object of aesthetics' (*GS*, vol. 6, pp. 385f.).
4   [Psalm 37: 3. The usual English renderings are 'and verily thou shalt be fed' (Authorized Version) or 'and enjoy safe pasture' (New International Version). The Luther version Adorno quotes has more evident moral, and even puritanical, overtones which I have tried to convey here, particularly since in German-speaking countries this verse has acquired proverbial status and is used, for example, to dissuade people from leaving the country or from other non-conformist courses of action. *Trans.*]
5   On the distinction between Positivism and Kant, cf. Adorno's *Logic of the Social Sciences*: 'What he [i.e. Kant] objected to in scientific judgements about God, freedom and immortality, was designed to oppose a condition in which the attempt was made to salvage these ideas for reason by stealth, once they had lost their theological authority. That Kantian term "stealth" [*Erschleichung*] unmasks the apologetic lie at the heart of the fallacy. Criticism was militant enlightenment. A critical attitude, however, that stops short of reality and is content to refine its own being would scarcely have made any progress as a force for enlightenment' (*Zur Logik der Sozialwissenschaften*, *GS*, vol. 8, p. 557). In *Negative Dialectics* he adds: 'Kant's confession that reason cannot but entangle itself in those antinomies which he proceeds to resolve by means of reason was anti-positivistic. Yet he did not spurn the positivistic comfort that a man might make himself at home in the narrow domain left to reason by the critique of the faculty of reason, that he

might be content to have that solid ground under his feet. He acquiesces in the eminently bourgeois affirmation of one's own confinement' (*GS*, vol. 6, p. 375).

6 Adorno is referring here to the chapter 'The Ultimate End of the Pure Employment of our Reason' in the 'Doctrine of Method'. He discusses it in detail in Lecture 6 on 30 May 1963 (*Critique of Pure Reason*, pp. 630–4, A 707–804/B 825–32).

7 Kant's actual words are: 'Logical illusion, which consists in the imitation of the mere form of reason (the illusion of formal fallacies), arises entirely from lack of attention to the logical rule' (*Critique of Pure Reason*, p. 299, A 296/B 353).

8 For Hegel's interpretation of Kant's discussion of the antinomies, see the *Science of Logic*, pp. 190–9 and 234–8.

9 On Kant's view of the principle of contradiction, see *Critique of Pure Reason*, p. 190, A 151/B 190. On the contrasting positions of Kant and Hegel, see Adorno's *Three Studies on Hegel*: 'In Kant philosophy was concerned with the critique of reason. What might be thought of as a naive scientific consciousness, assertion based on the rules of logic, what today would be called "phenomenology" was applied to consciousness as the condition of knowledge. Kant ignored the relation between the two, between the philosophical, criticizing consciousness and the criticized consciousness that obtained direct knowledge of objects in the world. This relation now became the focus of attention in Hegel who made it thematic. In the process consciousness becomes an object that has to be comprehended by philosophy; it becomes the finite, limited and inadequate thing that Kant, in tendency at least, had understood it to be when, in the name of this finitude, he forbade it to stray into the realm of the intelligible' (*Drei Studien zu Hegel*, GS, vol. 5, p. 310).

10 [The editor replaced the phrase 'ein zweites Freien' in the original with 'ein zweites – freies – Element'. *Trans*.]

11 In *Negative Dialectics* Adorno writes, 'The argument for the thesis of the third antinomy, that of the absolutely spontaneous cause – a secularized version of God's free act of creation – is Cartesian in style; it must prevail so that the method may be satisfied. Complete cognition is established as the epistemological criterion; we are told that without freedom "even in the [ordinary] course of nature, the series of appearances on the side of the causes can never be complete"' (*GS*, vol. 6, p. 247). The quotation from Kant is from the *Critique of Pure Reason*, p. 411, A 446/B 474.

12 See the *Critique of Pure Reason*: 'This requirement of reason, that we appeal in the series of natural causes to a first beginning, due to freedom, is amply confirmed when we observe that all the philosophers of antiquity, with the sole exception of the Epicurean School, felt themselves obliged, when explaining cosmical movements, to assume a *prime mover*' (pp. 414–15, A 451/B 478).

13 In the *Three Studies on Hegel* Adorno seizes on this motif as a sign of the failure of Hegel's dialectic to resolve this contradiction: 'Rightly

understood, the choice of a starting-point, of the very first thing, is irrelevant to Hegel's philosophy. It does not acknowledge the existence of any first thing as a firm principle that remains immutable throughout the progress of thought. [. . .] But this does not mean the renunciation of idealism. The absolute rigour and coherence of argument that Hegel, together with Fichte, aspires to over against Kant nevertheless insists on the priority of spirit, even though at every stage the subject defines itself as object, just as, conversely, the object defines itself as subject' (*GS*, vol. 5, p. 261).

14 Ernst Cassirer, in his *Zur Einstein'schen Relativitätstheorie. Erkenntnistheorethische Betrachtungen*, Berlin, 1920, differs from Hermann Cohen, since he does not think of Kant's philosophy as 'the philosophical system of Newton's natural science' (p. 12). Instead he emphasizes its methodological character, its critical concern with 'concept[s] of measure [*Maßbegriff*]' (as opposed to concepts of things), which can also be seen as underlying relativity theory (cf. pp. 7–25). [See Ernst Cassirer, *Substance and Function* and *Einstein's Theory of Relativity*, trans. William Curtis Swabey and Marie Collins Swabey, New York, 1923, p. 355. *Trans.*] Cassirer's *Determinismus und Indeterminismus in der modernen Physik. Historische und systematische Studien zum Kausalproblem*, Göteborg, 1937, develops the significance for moral philosophy of this critical approach to the concept of causality in the spirit of Kant's doctrine of the antinomies: 'If we understand "determinism" in a metaphysical sense, rather than a critical one, [. . .] then causality ceases to be a principle governing our knowledge of the physical world; [. . .] instead it becomes a metaphysical fate' (p. 260). Both essays can now be found in Ernst Cassirer, *Zur modernen Physik*, Darmstadt, 1957.

15 See Lecture 4 of 16 May 1963 and the reference there to *Critique of Pure Reason*, p. 409, A 444/B 472 at n. 6.

16 See *Critique of Pure Reason*, pp. 281–8, A 268–80/B 324–36. [An amphiboly is an ambiguity. *Trans.*]

17 See *Negative Dialectics*, pp. 255–6.

18 In contrast to Hume, for whom the knowing subject 'cannot think in any other way than [causally]' and for whom 'all knowledge attained through the supposed objective validity of our judgements is nothing but mere illusion', Kant insists on the necessity of causal connections (see the *Critique of Pure Reason*, pp. 174–5, B 168). In this sense Adorno differentiates later on between Kant and both the empiricism of Hume and Positivism. See Lecture 10 on 2 July 1963, p. 107.

19 Cf. Schopenhauer, *On the Basis of Morality*, §16, 'Statement and Proof of the Only Genuine Moral Incentive', pp. 140–7.

20 Cf. Adorno's criticism of 'the grounding of causality in the subjective experience of motivation' (*Negative Dialectics*, see *GS*, vol. 6, p. 266).

21 Cf. the observation on the thesis of the third antinomy: 'For the absolutely first beginning of which we are speaking is not a beginning in time, but in causality. If, for instance, I at this moment arise from my chair, in complete freedom, without being necessarily determined hereto

by the influence of natural causes, a new series [. . .] has its absolute beginning in this event [. . .]' (*Critique of Pure Reason*, p. 414, A 450/ B 478).

22 Adorno starts the sentence with the words: 'And the entire problem of freedom in Kant now appears . . .', but fails to complete it.

23 Cf. Kant: 'It follows that all the actions of men in the [field of] appearance are determined in conformity with the order of nature, by their empirical character and by the other causes which cooperate with that character; and if we could exhaustively investigate all the appearances of men's wills, there would not be found a single human action which we could not predict with certainty, and recognize as proceeding necessarily from its antecedent conditions' (*Critique of Pure Reason*, p. 474, A 549–50/B 577–8).

24 Cf. Kant's distinction between the 'empirical' and the 'intelligible' character. ['On the above supposition, we should, therefore, in a subject belonging to the sensible world have, first, an *empirical character*, whereby its actions, as appearances, stand in thoroughgoing connection with other appearances in accordance with the unvarying laws of nature. And since these actions can be derived from the other appearances, they constitute together with them a single series in the order of nature. Secondly, we should also have to allow the subject an *intelligible character*, by which it is indeed the cause of those same actions [in their quality] as appearances, but which does not itself stand under any conditions of sensibility, and it is not itself appearance. We can entitle the former the character of the thing in the [field of] appearance, and the latter its character as thing in itself.' *Trans.*] *Critique of Pure Reason*, p. 468, A 539/B 567.

25 See in this connection *Negative Dialectics* where the chapter entitled 'Freedom', which was originally called 'Determinism' (see Ts 15136), contains the following: 'If in causality we were looking for a definition of things themselves – no matter how subjectively conveyed – such specification would open the perspective of freedom as opposed to the undifferentiated One of pure subjectivity. It would apply to whatever is distinguished from compulsion. In that event compulsion would no longer be extolled as an act of the subject; its totality would no longer evoke an affirmative response. It would be stripped of its *a priori* power that had been extrapolated from its actual power. The more objective the nature of causality, the greater the possibility of freedom; this is not the least of the reasons why he who wants freedom must insist upon necessity' (*GS*, vol. 6, p. 247).

Lecture Six

1 The Europa Symposium in Vienna took place on 11–15 June 1963. The theme was 'The European Big City – Vision and Mirage'. Adorno was a member of a panel discussion on the theme of the conference on 11

June and on 12 June gave a talk with the title 'Amateur Art or Organized Philistinism?', which was followed by discussion. The text of his contributions to the symposium as well as of his improvised lecture can be found in *Wiener Schriften*, edited by the Amt für Kultur, Volksbildung und Schulverwaltung der Stadt Wien, vol. 20: *Europa-Gespräch 1963: Die europäische Großstadt. Licht und Irrlicht*, Vienna, 1964, pp. 39–71 and 88–99.

2   In the face of the dominance of the causality of nature as formulated by the understanding, Adorno regards as too feeble Kant's distinction between a mathematical and dynamical synthesis of appearances (*Critique of Pure Reason*, p. 462, A 529/B 557), according to which 'in the dynamical series, on the other hand, the completely conditioned, which is inseparable from the series considered as appearances, is bound up with a condition which, while indeed empirically unconditioned, is also *non-sensible*. We are thus able to obtain satisfaction for *understanding* on the one hand and for *reason* on the other . . . and the propositions of reason . . . may *both* alike be *true*' (ibid., pp. 463–4, A 531–2 /B 559–60).

3   Cf. *Critique of Pure Reason*, p. 633, A 802/B 830: '[The fact of] practical freedom can be proved through experience.' Cf. also the *Critique of Practical Reason* (p. 88) and §91 of the *Critique of Judgement*: 'But there is this notable point, that one idea of reason, strange to say, is to be found among the matters of fact – an idea which does not of itself admit of any presentation in intuition, or, consequently, of any theoretical proof of its possibility. The idea in question is that of *freedom*. Its reality is the reality of a particular kind of causality [. . .] and as a causality of that kind it admits of verification by means of practical laws of pure reason and in the actual actions that take place in obedience to them, and, consequently, in experience' (*Critique of Judgement*, p. 142).

4   Adorno recapitulates here the fundamental idea of the Second Excursus of *Dialectic of Enlightenment* ['Juliette or Enlightenment and Morality'] about which he states in the introduction: 'They [Kant, Nietzsche and de Sade] show how the subjugation of everything natural by the autocratic subject finally culminates in the rule of blind objectivity and nature' (*Dialectic of Enlightenment*, p. xvi) [translation amended].

5   See Lecture 4 of 16 May 1963 and *Critique of Pure Reason*, p. 411, A 447/B 475.

6   Adorno is alluding here to Hölderlin's conception of 'the one differentiated in itself' (cf. *Hyperion* in the Große Stuttgarter edition of Hölderlin's works, vol. 3, Stuttgart, 1957, p. 81) that has entered into the aphorism 'The Root of All Evil': 'Being at one is god-like and good, but human, too human, the mania / Which insists there is only the One, one country, one truth and one way': trans. Michael Hamburger [freely, but capturing the spirit – *Trans.*] in Friedrich Hölderlin, *Poems and Fragments*, Routledge and Kegan Paul, London, 1967, pp. 70–1. In the

talk he gave on Hölderlin on 7 June 1963 with the title 'Parataxis', at the same time as he was giving these lectures, Adorno wrote: 'The paratactic revolt against synthesis attains its limit in the synthetic function of language as such. What is envisioned is a synthesis of a different kind, language's critical self-reflexion, while language retains synthesis. To destroy the unity of language would constitute an act of violence equivalent to the one that unity perpetrates; but Hölderlin so transmutes the form of unity that not only is multiplicity reflected in it [. . .] but in addition the unity indicates that it knows itself to be inconclusive. Without unity there would be nothing in language but nature in diffuse form; absolute unity was a reflection on this' (*Notes to Literature*, vol. 2, p. 136).

7   Cf. *Critique of Pure Reason*, p. 630, A 797/B 825. The concept of speculation is introduced on p. 527, A 634/B 662.

8   Ibid., p. 630, A 797/B 825.

9   On the concept of the 'Kantian block' see Adorno's seventh Meditation on Metaphysics: Rescuing Urge and Block, in *Negative Dialectics* (*GS*, vol. 6, pp. 377–82).

10   *Critique of Pure Reason*, pp. 630–1, A 797–8/B 825–6.

11   Ibid., p. 631, A 798/B 826.

12   Ibid.

13   See Nietzsche, *Thus spake Zarathustra*, p. 333. The verse is also cited by Adorno in *Negative Dialectics* in a critical comment on populist tendencies in modern philosophy: 'Pleasure – which desires eternity, according to an inspired saying of Nietzsche's – is not the only thing to balk at transitoriness. If death were the absolute thing that philosophy tried in vain to conjure up positively, then everything is nothing at all; our every thought is thinking into a void; none can be thought with truth' (*GS*, vol. 6, p. 364).

14   *Critique of Pure Reason*, p. 631, A 798/B 826.

15   Ibid.

16   The reference is to Goethe: 'There's nothing better, on a holiday, / Than talk and noise of war to while the time away. / Some far-off war, in Turkey, let's suppose, / Some place where nations come to blows. / One watches from the window, sips one's glass, / While down the river all those fine ships pass. / And back home in the evening, we congratulate / Each other on our peaceful, happy state' (*Faust*, Part I, 'Outside the Town Wall', trans. David Luke, Oxford University Press, Oxford and New York, 1987, p. 29).

17   *Critique of Pure Reason*, p. 631, A 798–9/B 826–7. [Since Adorno interrupts the quotation and omits Kant's clause 'either the appearances of this present life or the specific nature of a future state', the translator has partly restored the quotation and followed the editor in omitting Adorno's 'neither' and adding 'from this' in the next sentence. *Trans.*]

18   Ibid., p. 631, A 799/B 827.

19 The precise source of this quotation has not been identified. On the point of substance, see Christian Wolff, *Gesammelte Werke, 1. Abteilung: Deutsche Schriften*, vol. 7, *Vernünftige Gedanken (Deutsche Teleologie)* [Section 1: German Writings, vol. 7. Rational Thoughts (German Teleology)], ed. Hans Werner Arndt, Hildesheim and New York, 1980, §33 (p. 50), §70 (p. 106) and §98 (p. 161).

20 *Critique of Pure Reason*, p. 632, A 799–800/B 827–8.

21 Cf. ibid., p. 650, A 829/B 857: 'belief in a God and in another world is so interwoven with my moral sentiment that as there is little danger of my losing the latter, there is equally little cause for fear that the former can ever be taken away from me'.

Lecture Seven

1 This was the lecture when he had to attend the Europa Symposium. See Lecture 6, n. 1.

2 'Morality, by itself, constitutes a system. Happiness, however, does not do so, save in so far as it is distributed in exact proportion to morality. But this is possible only in the intelligible world, under a wise Author and Ruler. Such a Ruler, together with life in such a world, which we must regard as a future world, reason finds itself constrained to assume; otherwise it would have to regard the moral laws as empty figments of the brain, since without this postulate the necessary consequence which it itself connects with these laws could not follow' (*Critique of Pure Reason*, p. 639, A 811/B 839).

3 For this formulation see Lecture 15 of 18 July 1963 and n. 6 to that lecture.

4 *Critique of Pure Reason*, p. 632, A 800/B 828.

5 See Lecture 5, n. 11.

6 *Critique of Pure Reason*, p. 632, A 799/B 827. Kant writes '[. . .] must concern [. . .]'.

7 Ibid. p. 633, A 802/B 830.

8 On the 'given' nature of the moral law, see ch. 2 of the *Groundwork*, pp. 79–80.

9 See René Descartes, *Meditations on First Philosophy*, especially the Fourth Meditation: Concerning the True and the False, and the Fifth Meditation: Concerning the Essence of Material Things; and again, concerning God, that He exists. *Descartes' Philosophical Writings*, selected and trans. Norman Kemp Smith, Macmillan, London, 1952, pp. 232–47.

10 For the formulation of the categorical imperative see the *Groundwork*, p. 84 ['Act only on that maxim through which you can at the same time will that it should become a universal law' *Trans.*], and the *Critique of Practical Reason*, p. 119 ['Act so that the maxim of thy will can always at the same time hold good as a principle of universal legislation' *Trans.*].

11   Adorno writes in *Negative Dialectics*: 'Irresistible in the young
     Beethoven's music is the expression of the possibility that all might
     be well. However fragile, the reconciliation with objectivity transcends
     eternal sameness. The instants in which an individual frees itself
     without in turn, by its own individuality, confining others – these
     instants are anticipations of the unconfined, and such solace radiates
     from the earlier bourgeoisie until into its late period' (*GS*, vol. 6,
     p. 301).

12   Wilhelm Sturmfels (1887–1967) wrote a dissertation entitled 'Law and
     Ethics in their Mutual Relationship' (Gießen, 1912). After this he taught
     from 1921 to 1933 at the Academy of Labour, a college of further edu-
     cation for workers linked to the University of Frankfurt. He returned
     to Frankfurt in 1946, where he was active at first as an honorary pro-
     fessor and then as an extraordinary professor in philosophy, sociology
     and adult education. He continued to teach until 1967.

13   See Schopenhauer, *On the Basis of Morality*, §4, 'On the Imperative
     Form of the Kantian Ethics', pp. 52–8.

Lecture Eight

1   On this image see also *NaS* IV, vol. 4, pp. 40 and 55.

2   See *Critique of Pure Reason*, pp. 50–1, A 9–10/B 13–14.

3   Cf. Kant's assertion: 'The consciousness of a *free* submission of the
    will to the law, yet combined with an inevitable constraint put upon
    all inclinations, though only by our own reason, is respect for the
    law. [. . .] An action which is objectively practical according to this
    law, to the exclusion of every determining principle of inclination, is
    called *duty*, and this by reason of that exclusion, contains in its concept
    practical *obligation* [*Nötigung*], that is, a determination to actions,
    however *reluctantly* they may be done. The feeling that arises from
    the consciousness of this obligation is not pathological, as would be
    a feeling produced by an object of the senses, but practical only,
    that is, it is made possible by a preceding (objective) determination
    of the will and causality of the reason' (*Critique of Practical Reason*,
    p. 173).

4   See Freud, *The Ego and the Id*, *The Pelican Freud Library*, vol. 11,
    1984, pp. 382 and 390–3.

5   See *The Gay Science*, 'Long live physics!': 'And now don't cite the
    categorical imperative, my friend! – [. . .] It makes me think of the old
    Kant who had obtained the "thing in itself" by *stealth* [. . .] and was
    punished for this when the "categorical imperative" crept stealthily
    into his heart and led him *astray – back* to "God," "soul," "freedom,"
    and "immortality", [. . .]. What? You admire the categorical imperative
    within you? This "firmness" of your so-called moral judgement? This
    "unconditional feeling" that "here everyone must judge as I do"?
    Rather admire your *selfishness* at this point. And the blindness, petti-

ness, and frugality of your selfishness!' (*The Gay Science*, Book IV, no. 335, pp. 264–5).

6   *Critique of Pure Reason*, p. 632, A 800/B 828. See also Lecture 6 of 30 May 1963 and Lecture 7 at n. 4.

7   *Critique of Pure Reason*, p. 632, A 800/B 828. Adorno breaks off the quotation in the middle of the passage with the word 'etc.'. The entire sentence continues: 'in the one single end, *happiness*, and in co-ordinating the means for attaining it. In this field, therefore, reason can supply none but *pragmatic* laws of free action, for the attainment of those ends which are commended to us by the senses; it cannot yield us laws that are pure and determined completely *a priori.*'

8   *Critique of Pure Reason*, p. 632, A 800/B 828.

9   Ibid.

10 Ibid., pp. 632–3, A 800–1/B 828–9.

11 Adorno is referring here to Kant's concept of a 'moral theology' which is 'of immanent use only. It enables us to fulfil our vocation in this present world by showing us how to adapt ourselves to the system of all ends [. . .]' (*Critique of Pure Reason*, p. 644, A 819/B 847). It proceeds from the question 'If I do what I ought to do, what may I then hope?' (ibid., p. 636, A 805/B 833).

12 Exact citation not found. See *Critique of Practical Reason*, pp. 229–30.

13 *Critique of Pure Reason*, p. 633, A 801/B 829.

14 Ibid., p. 633, A 802/B 830.

15 Ibid.

16 Ibid., pp. 633–4, A 802/B 830.

Lecture Nine

1   The reason for the cancellation of the lecture on 25 June 1963 is not known.

2   *Critique of Pure Reason*, p. 633, A 802/B 830.

3   Ibid., p. 634, A 802/B 830.

4   Ibid., p. 634, A 803/B 831.

5   By Kant's first interpretation Adorno means 'the intention of nature to coincide with freedom'. See pp. 91 and 93.

6   Cf. Walter Benjamin: 'For even in its most paradoxical periphrasis, as *intellectus archetypus*, vision [*Schau*] does not enter into the form of existence which is peculiar to truth, which is devoid of all intention, and certainly does not appear as intention. Truth does not enter into relationships, particularly intentional ones. The object of knowledge, determined as it is by the intention inherent in the concept, is not the truth. Truth is an intentionless state of being, made up of ideas. The proper approach to it is not therefore one of intention and knowledge, but rather a total immersion and absorption in it. Truth is the death of intention' (*The Origin of German Tragic Drama*, trans. John Osborne, NLB, London, 1977, pp. 35–6).

7   Kant talks of the 'world concept' (*conceptus cosmicus*) as the intention
    of philosophy, to describe 'the relation of all knowledge to the essential
    ends of human reason' (*Critique of Pure Reason*, p. 657, A 838–9/B
    866–7). In his 'Reply to the Question: What is Enlightenment?' he
    defines the 'public use' of the scholar's reason in these terms. [See *Polit-
    ical Writings*, p. 57. *Trans.*]
8   See 'Religion within the Boundaries of Mere Reason': 'Now if a propen-
    sity to this [inversion] does lie in human nature, then there is in the
    human being a natural propensity to evil; and this propensity itself is
    morally evil, since it must ultimately be sought in a free power of choice,
    and hence is imputable. This evil is *radical*, since it corrupts the ground
    of all maxims [. . .]' (*Religion and Rational Theology*, p. 83).
9   *Critique of Pure Reason*, p. 152, B 131. Max Horkheimer draws atten-
    tion to this quotation: 'Self-preservation is the constitutive principle of
    science, the soul of the table of categories, even when it is deduced ide-
    alistically, as with Kant. Even the ego, the synthetic unity of appercep-
    tion, the authority that Kant calls the supreme point to which the logical
    form of all knowledge must be attached, is in fact both the product of
    material existence and its precondition' (*Dialectic of Enlightenment*, pp.
    86–7 [translation altered]. Cf. the references to Spinoza and Hobbes in
    the same passage.)
10 Kant explains, 'On the other hand, to preserve one's life is a duty, and
    besides this everyone has also an immediate inclination to do so. But
    on account of this the often anxious precautions taken by the greater
    part of mankind for this purpose have no inner worth, and the maxim
    of their action is without moral content' (*Groundwork*, p. 63).
11 See Lecture 1, pp. 8–9.
12 [This is the conclusion of the story of the Good Samaritan in Luke
    10: 37. *Trans.*]
13 [This is the usual translation of the phrase 'Die Furie des Versch-
    windens'. It literally means 'the fury of disappearance' and is used by
    Hegel to describe the Reign of Terror in the French Revolution. See
    Hegel, *Phenomenology of Spirit*, p. 359. *Trans.*]
14 See Paul Valéry, *Rapport sur les prix de vertu* (1934), in Œuvres, vol.
    1, Bibliothèque de la Pléiade, Librairie Gallimard, Paris, 1957, pp.
    936–57.
15 Nietzsche writes: 'In comparison with the mode of life of whole mil-
    lennia of mankind we present-day men live in a very immoral age: the
    power of custom is astonishingly enfeebled and the moral sense so
    rarefied and lofty it may be described as having more or less evaporated
    [. . .]. Morality is nothing other (therefore *no more!*) than obedience to
    customs, of whatever kind they may be; customs, however, are the *tra-
    ditional* way of behaving and evaluating. In things in which no tradi-
    tion commands there is no morality; and the less life is determined by
    tradition, the smaller the circle of morality. The free human being is
    immoral because in all things he is *determined* to depend upon himself
    and not upon a tradition' (*Daybreak*, p. 10).

Lecture Ten

1   In the transcription of the audio tape there is a gap at the very start of the lecture. However, Adorno's handwritten notes for the lecture show that the first sentence that has survived is exactly where he intended to start: 'The paradox of the experience of practical freedom as a natural matter. Paradox admitted by Kant himself: "thus a problem remains", i.e. dualism is as unsatisfactory as its elimination impossible' (Vo 8812). What is missing is presumably the introduction establishing a link with the previous lecture.

2   See *Critique of Pure Reason*, p. 634, A 803/B 831. [This seems to be Adorno's rephrasing rather than a direct quotation. The passage reads: 'While we thus through experience know practical freedom to be one of the causes in nature, namely, to be a causality of reason in the determination of the will, transcendental freedom demands the independence of this reason – in respect of its causality, in beginning a series of appearances – from all determining causes of the sensible world. Transcendental freedom is thus, as it would seem, contrary to the law of nature, and therefore to all possible experience; and so remains a problem.' *Trans.*]

3   Adhémar Gelb (1887–1936) was made Professor of Psychology at Frankfurt University in 1924 and was also Director of the Psychological Institute. In 1931 he was given a Chair in philosophy with a particular reference to psychology at the University of Halle. The Nazis dismissed him from this post in 1934.

4   See Schopenhauer, *The World as Will and Idea*, vol. 3, ch. 48, 'On the Doctrine of the Denial of the Will to Live', pp. 420–59. [In the Upanishads Schopenhauer found the idea that phenomenal reality, or the world of perception, is ultimately 'illusion' (Māyā), that it is 'impermanent' and 'fleeting' and to be contrasted with that which is truly 'eternal'. See Patrick Gardiner, *Schopenhauer*, Harmondsworth, 1963, p. 294. *Trans.*]

5   For Adorno's view of Book IV of Schopenhauer's *The World as Will and Idea* and its relation to Kant and idealism in general [vol. 3, pp. 247–475 – *Trans.*], see *Negative Dialectics*: 'By allowing only reason as the motor of practice, Kant failed to escape from the toils of that faded theory for all his efforts to complement it by devising the primacy of practical reason. His entire moral philosophy is an attempt to shake it off' (*GS*, vol. 6, p. 228). And: 'What the great rationalist philosophers understood by the concept of the will amounts to a denial of it, without accounting for this in so many words. The Schopenhauer of Book Four was not labouring under a delusion when he felt himself to be a Kantian. The fact that without a will there is no consciousness becomes blurred in the minds of the idealists into a pure identity; it is as if the will were nothing but consciousness. [. . .] It is not simply that reason has evolved genetically from the force of human drives by a process of differentiation. Without the kind of willing that is expressed in the arbitrary nature of

every thought-act – the kind that alone gives us a reason to distinguish such an act from the passive, "receptive" aspects of the human subject – there would be no thinking in the proper sense of the word. However, idealism is committed to the opposite idea and cannot admit that on pain of its own destruction. This explains both the distortion and its proximity to the true facts' (*GS*, vol. 6, pp. 229f.).

6   See §§52 and 53 in Heidegger, *Being and Time*. Heidegger distinguishes authentic concern from 'the fetters of a weary "inactive thinking about death"' (p. 302), a 'Being-toward-death as a *Being toward a possibility*' as distinct from a 'brooding over death' that weakens 'its character as a possibility' (p. 305). Understanding does not mean 'just gazing at a meaning, but rather understanding oneself in that potentiality-for-Being which reveals itself in that projection', the structure of 'the anticipation of death' (p. 307).

7   For Adorno's criticism of the relationship between authenticity and subjectivity in Heidegger see *The Jargon of Authenticity*: 'The observing subject prescribes whatever is authentic to the subject as observed: it prescribes its attitude toward death. This displacement robs the subject of freedom and spontaneity: it freezes, like the Heideggerian states of mind, into something like an attribute of the substance "existence" [*Dasein*]' (pp. 126–7). Heidegger's dubious connection with idealism can be seen in the fact that 'what was a necessary element in the experience of consciousness, in Hegelian phenomenology, becomes anathema for Heidegger, since he compresses the experience of self-consciousness into self-experience. However, identity, the hollow kernel of such selfness, thus takes the place of idea' (ibid., pp. 121–2).

8   See Ernst Troeltsch, *Der Historismus und seine Probleme*, *Gesammelte Schriften*, vol. 3, Tübingen, 1922.

9   See Hermann Cohen, *Kants Begründung der Ethik. Nebst ihren Anwendungen auf Recht, Religion und Geschichte* [Kant's Grounding of Ethics: Together with its Application to Law, Religion and History], 2nd, enlarged and improved, edn, Berlin, 1910 (1st edn 1877). Cohen begins by defining the 'content of the formal moral law' as something given in 'the community of autonomous beings' (p. 227) and in the introduction to Part 4 he defines 'the reality of the ethical in historical experience' by taking 'the theory of law' as his starting-point (cf. pp. 381–454).

10   This quotation has not been identified. Adorno may have had in mind a sentence of Kant's from the *Anthropology* in which, however, the function of the Graces was in fact reversed: 'The *cynic's purism* and the *anchorite's mortification of the flesh*, lacking any social well-being, are distorted forms of virtue and not inviting for it; instead, abandoned by the Graces, they can make no claim to humanity' (Kant, *Werke*, VI, p. 622).

11   Cf. Julius Ebbinghaus, *Deutung und Mißdeutung des kategorischen Imperativs* [Interpretation and Misinterpretation of the Categorical Imperative], in *Gesammelte Aufsätze. Vorträge und Reden* [Collected Essays: Talks and Speeches], Darmstadt, 1968, pp. 80–96.

Lecture Eleven

1 Cf. Adorno's lecture of 18 December 1956: 'On Plato. In Socrates reason was posited as the only authoritative guide to right behaviour. The way to achieve this was presumably through conceptual analysis. In Plato this is converted into a principle in a strict and authentic manner. In the early dialogues his actual method is to analyse concepts. With the aid of this conceptual analysis reason emerges as the only authoritative method of defining virtue [. . .]' (Vo 1364). That means: There is no theory of virtue applicable to the individual virtues; that would contradict the concept of virtue. They can only be generated altogether by virtue of their relation to the central principle of the logos. In the process we can see how the central motif of Socratic intellectualism, namely the equation of virtue with knowledge, becomes a critical authority [. . .] (Vo 1365–6). Adorno's account of the non-Platonic elements in Socrates' thought is based on Xenophon's *Memorabilia of Socrates*.

2 For Fichte's own account of his relation to Kant's philosophy, see the Second Introduction to *Die Wissenschaftslehre* [The Theory of Science], in *Johann Gottlieb Fichte's sämmtliche Werke*, Veit und Comp., Berlin, 1845, *Erste Abteilung: Zur theoretischen Philosophie* [Philosophical Theory], vol. 1, pp. 468–71.

3 Cf. *Negative Dialectics*, p. 228.

4 Adorno starts the sentence with the words 'In order to give this Kantian theorem its true significance, you must recollect that Kant's concept of reason . . .'. He then breaks off and starts again.

5 Cf. *Critique of Pure Reason*, pp. 637–8, A 812/B 840, where Kant builds on Leibniz's distinction between the 'kingdom of grace' and the 'kingdom of nature'.

6 'The form of' is a conjectured reading.

7 [Adorno used the English words. *Trans.*]

8 Cf. the first edition of the *Critique of Pure Reason*: 'There must therefore exist in us an active faculty for the synthesis of this manifold. To this faculty I give the title, imagination. Its action, when immediately directed upon perceptions, I entitle, apprehension' (p. 144, A 120). In contrast to this, the second edition ties the faculty 'of the synthetic, original unity of apperception', the consciousness 'that I am' (p. 168, B 157), to the categories of the understanding, 'whose whole power consists in thought, consists, thereby, in the act whereby it brings the synthesis of a manifold, given to it elsewhere in intuition, to the unity of apperception – a faculty, therefore, which by itself knows nothing whatsoever, but merely combines and arranges the material of knowledge, which must be given to it by the object' (p. 161, B 145).

9 Adorno's lecture of 19 December 1956 reconstructs the exceptional position adopted by Socrates: 'The decisive feature of Socrates is his turning towards the individual, something that is expressed in a series of motifs; initially, in contrast to the kind of speculation that preceded

him, it found expression in his blunt rejection of scientific thought and speculation about natural philosophy, something he justifies by pointing to the unreliability and the contradictions implicit in statements about nature' (Vo 1346).

10   See Friedrich Ueberweg, *Grundriß der Geschichte der Philosophie*, Part 1. *Die Philosophie des Altertums* [Outline of the History of Philosophy, Part 1: The Philosophy of Antiquity], ed. Karl Praechter, Berlin, 1926, pp. 476–7.

11   Cf. Adorno, *Philosophische Terminologie*, ed. Rudolf zur Lippe, vol. 1, Suhrkamp, Frankfurt am Main, 1973, pp. 58–60.

12   [The reference is to the Hungarian philosopher and literary critic Georg Lukács (1885–1971), whose early works – *Soul and Form*, *The Theory of the Novel* and *History and Class Consciousness* – Adorno admired. However, Adorno wrote scathingly about his later books which he regarded as the products of a Stalinist hack. *Trans.*]

13   Georg Lukács, *History and Class Consciousness*, trans. R.S. Livingstone, Merlin, London, 1971, pp. 124–5.

14   [Johann Peter Hebel (1760–1826) was a Protestant parson born in Basle who gained a literary reputation for moralistic poems in the local Swabian dialect of south-west Germany as well as for pithy anecdotes, the products of a sincere and unaffected mind. Jeremias Gotthelf, the pseudonym of Albert Bitzius (1797–1854), was likewise a pastor. His most famous writings were his novellas and novels of Swiss country life, characterized by strong moral and social commitment. They are written in a homespun style with a powerful didactic streak. His natural gift for story-telling has won him a permanent place in German literature with stories like *The Black Spider* and his rural *Bildungsromane*. Both writers represent a world in which moral certainties are intact. *Trans.*]

15   In his lecture of 18 December 1956 Adorno writes of Socrates: 'What is magnificent about this theory that morality is grounded in reason is that Socrates, unlike all subsequent philosophers, let the cat out of the bag and spelled out in detail what is meant by the rational grounding of ethical action and where it leads. The very elements that were later separated out in the process of compartmentalization are those that we find disconcerting in this theory. For these prejudices that have been dinned into us for thousands of years are so deeply ingrained in us that everyone who learns of this theory recollects that while his grandmother may have been stupid, she was certainly good. This mechanism that Socrates pilloried from the outset contains *in nuce* the critique of all later morality. But an unconscious goodness cannot exist [. . .]' (Vo 1361).

16   Line 6 of Schiller's 'Ode to Joy', which Beethoven set to music in the last movement of the Ninth Symphony. Adorno's MS had 'frech' (insolently) instead of 'streng' (strictly, sternly).

17   See *Critique of Pure Reason*, p. 327, A 339/B 397.

18   Cf. Aristotle, *Nicomachean Ethics*, Book III, 1–4, 1109b–1112a. [*The*

Ethics of Aristotle, trans. J. A. K. Thomson, rev. Hugh Tredennick, Penguin Books, Harmondsworth, 1981, pp. 111–15. *Trans.*] Adorno gives a more detailed account in his lecture of 10 January 1957: 'The crucial difference from Plato is that Aristotle is the first to expand the concept of reason as the ordering principle by adding to it two qualifications that constitute a serious rupture with the Socratic element in Plato's moral philosophy. First, the concept of freedom – he asserts that a good, meaningful life can only exist if we are free, if we have the opportunity to make real in society whatever we have recognized to be right. He goes a long way down this road and even anticipates a development to be rediscovered in Kant's distinction between the intelligible and empirical character. He says that our freedom can be restricted not just by slavery and the like, but also internally, by certain habits, by a character that is alien to our reason and that compels us to act in conflict with our reason. Such a character is just as much a limitation upon our freedom as restrictions imposed by external political factors. In such apparently empirical limitations upon the idea of reason as the ruling principle the way is prepared for the developments that have proved decisive in all subsequent moral philosophy. – The same may be said of the concept of the will. The will is what has to mediate between what has been perceived to be right and its translation into reality. Right knowledge and right action are not automatically one and the same thing. For them to become so we need the particular sphere of the will.' (Vo 1396–7).

Lecture Twelve

1   For this lecture no transcript of the recording itself was available. These notes were written up by Hilmar Tillack and were integrated into the series during Adorno's lifetime. Their main points contain a recapitulation of the previous lecture and correspond to Adorno's own manuscript outline. This in turn was based on an excerpt from his lecture of 22 January 1957 to which his own page number 'p. 129' refers. (See now Vo 1421.) The page references to Kant are to the text of the *Groundwork of the Metaphysic of Morals* in *Sämtliche Werke in sechs Bänden*, vol. 5, *Moralische Schriften*, ed. F. Gross, Leipzig, 1922. Adorno's headings are as follows:

On the point that absolute lawlessness is in fact the opposite of freedom. *Bellum omnium contra omnes.* An extreme internal example: addiction/abuse. The role of law.

Conversely, the idea of law also contains a potential that is hostile to freedom; a set of restrictions in which it disappears. Always on a knife's edge. Kant's inspired formula about the limitation of freedom only where it jeopardizes the freedom of others. This contains the functional framework of society.

p. 129 of the *Groundwork*
So-called natural consciousness as starting-point, i.e. moral attitudes as empirically given. This contains an element of truth. Ethics cannot simply be conjured out of thin air. Even today it thrives only as critique of widely held ideas that are simply affirmed. Ethics always suffers from the fact that it expects from others what it does not demand from itself.

By dint of abstraction it assumes the form of the categorical imperative. At the same time the procedure in accordance with principles is presupposed.

First definition, Kant, p. 26
Rational. Explain the maxim: transition from individual to the subject. Later in the *Critique of Practical Reason*: the moral law is not 'deducible' like the principles of theoretical reason.

9 July (Vo 8813)

2   Cf. Max Scheler, *Der Formalismus in der Ethik und die materiale Wertethik, Neuer Versuch der Grundlegung eines ethischen Personalismus. Gesammelte Werke*, vol. 2, 4th edn, Berne, 1954, pp. 176–8.

3   Cf. *Groundwork*, pp. 99–100.

4   At this point Adorno returns to his lecture of 22 January 1957: 'In the *Groundwork of the Metaphysic of Morals* it appears that Kant begins in a way that may even have served as a model for Hegel. He begins with "natural" consciousness, with the fact of moral intuitions that I simply have, and proceeds from there by a process of abstract thought to a critical analysis of these intuitions, to the categorical imperative and the pure definition of the moral law' (Vo 1421).

5   See the *Nicomachean Ethics*, Book V, 14, 1137a–1138a. [J. A. K. Thomson's translation gives 'equity': see *The Ethics of Aristotle*, Penguin Books, Harmondsworth, 1981, pp. 198–201. *Trans.*]

6   *Groundwork*, p. 67.

7   See Lecture 7, n. 10 for other definitions of the categorical imperative.

8   ['Üb' immer Treu und Redlichkeit' is a line by the eighteenth-century poet, Ludwig Hölty. *Trans.*]

9   See §36 of the *Prolegomena to Any Future Metaphysics*: 'For we know nature as nothing but the totality of appearances, i.e., of representations in us; and hence we can only derive the law of their connection from the principles of their connection in us, that is, from the conditions of their necessary unification in a consciousness, which constitutes the possibility of experience' (p. 61).

10 In his lecture of 22 January 1957 Adorno goes into this question more fully: 'Later, in a crucial passage in the *Critique of Practical Reason*, Kant comes to the realization that a deduction of the moral law is not possible in the way that the categories had been deduced from the unity of self-consciousness and the principles of pure reason had been deduced from the synthetic unity. The categorical imperative cannot be inferred logically in the same way as the various principles of pure reason which, according to Kant, explain the mathematical natural sciences in terms of the categories and, ultimately, of the unity of self-con-

sciousness. In the last analysis we are forced back in a sense to the moral
law as a fact' (Vo 1421–2).

Lecture Thirteen

1   Cf. Georg Simmel, *Hauptprobleme der Philosophie* [The Principal Prob-
    lems of Philosophy], Berlin and New York, 1989 (1st edn 1910), p. 29.
2   *Groundwork*, p. 67.
3   *Critique of Practical Reason*, p. 149. In this quotation Adorno has
    telescoped the original text, which reads in full: 'But, although reason
    is alone capable of discerning the connexion of the means with their
    ends (so that the will might even be defined as the faculty of ends, since
    these are always determining principles of the desires), yet the practical
    maxims which would follow from the aforesaid principle of the
    good being merely a means, would never contain as the object of
    the will anything good in itself, but only something good *for something*;
    [. . .].'
4   See Lecture 1 of 7 May 1963 and n. 14 to that lecture.
5   *Groundwork*, p. 65.
6   Cf. Plato, *Phaedo*, 76d–77a. ['Then, Simmias, the souls existed previ-
    ously, before they were in human form, apart from bodies, and
    they had intelligence.' Plato, *Euthyphro / Apology / Crito / Phaedo /
    Phaedrus*, trans. Harold North Fowler, Loeb Classical Library, Heine-
    mann and Harvard University Press, London and Cambridge, Mass.,
    1960, pp. 267–9. *Trans.*]
7   *Groundwork*, p. 59.
8   Cf. *Dialectic of Enlightenment*, pp. 81–119, especially p. 114.
9   *Groundwork*, p. 66.
10 Ibid., n. 2.
11 Goethe, *Faust*, Part I. See Lecture 6, n. 16.

Lecture Fourteen

1   The beginning of the tape is missing and so the first three words are
    conjectures. Adorno is reminding his audience of what was said in the
    previous lecture. The keywords devised for this lecture begin with the
    idea of the renunciation of instinct: '16. VII. 63 Addenda. / The under-
    lying idea of the renunciation of instinct: compensation in the long run.
    / The motif of saving: formation of capital. / The untruth it contains:
    the fact that both psychologically and for society overall compensation
    fails to materialize' (Vo 8814–15).
2   Cf. Adorno's note 'This Side of the Pleasure Principle', in *Minima
    Moralia*, pp. 60–1.
3   See *Critique of Judgement*, §64, pp. 16–19.

4   See Benedictus de Spinoza, *The Ethics*, Part IV, Proposition 20, in *Spinoza's Works*, trans. R.H.M. Elwes, George Bell & Sons, London, 1906, vol. 2, p. 202. The Latin has *suum esse conservare*. [The proposition reads: 'The more every man endeavours, and is able to seek what is useful to him – in other words, to preserve his own being – the more he is endowed with virtue; on the contrary, in proportion as a man neglects to seek what is useful to him, that is, to preserve his own being, he is wanting in power.' *Trans.*]

5   See Mary Gregor's translation, *The Metaphysics of Morals*, p. 218.

6   See *Groundwork*, p. 64: 'To assure one's own happiness is a duty (at least indirectly).'

7   Adorno objects here above all to the pessimistic interpretation of the 'discontents of civilization' reconstructed by Freud on the basis of his work on obsessional neuroses and the 'psychopathology of everyday life'. In contrast to this, Freud's writings on the techniques of treating patients develop a dialectical approach to psychological problems: the elimination of the renunciation of instinct as a never-ending task of analytical work. (Cf. 'Remembering, Repeating and Working-Through', *Standard Edition*, vol. 12, p. 147, and 'Analysis Terminable and Interminable', *Standard Edition*, vol. 23, p. 211.)

8   On Schopenhauer's image of the negative balance sheet, see *The World as Will and Idea*, vol. 2/2, ch. 46, 'On the Vanity and Suffering of Life', pp. 383 and 390. See also Max Horkheimer: 'Philosophy has to give an account of itself, and because the balance sheet is negative, the saint is proved right in the end. Whoever places his trust in the world, will be deceived. Schopenhauer's distrust of reform and revolution does not amount to the glorification of the world as it exists' ('Schopenhauer und die Gesellschaft' [Schopenhauer and Society], in *Gesammelte Schriften*, vol. 7, *Vorträge und Aufzeichnungen 1949–1973*, ed. Gunzelin Schmid Noerr, Frankfurt am Main, 1985, p. 48).

9   See Lecture 12, p. 122.

10 In Brecht's play Shen Te, the 'good person', disguises herself as Shui Ta, the 'wicked businessman', in order to overcome the difficulties implicit in 'being good and yet surviving'. See Bertolt Brecht, *The Good Person of Szechwan*, in *Collected Plays*, vol. 6/1, trans. and ed. John Willett and Ralph Manheim, Eyre Methuen, London, 1970– . The text of Brecht's poem 'The Mask of Evil' is as follows: 'On my wall hangs a Japanese carving, / The mask of an evil demon, decorated with gold lacquer. / Sympathetically I observe / The swollen veins of the forehead, indicating / What a strain it is to be evil' (trans. by H.R. Hays, Grove Press, New York, and Evergreen Press, London, 1959, p. 165). The theme of the poem is also treated in scene 7 of the play in the character of Shen Te's lover, Sun.

11 [Brecht's *The Measures Taken* (1929–30) deals with the morality of revolutionary action in China in the 1920s. Four agitators sent from Moscow and working undercover attempt to spread Communist propaganda. They find their work jeopardized by a Young Comrade

whose compassion for the poor leads him to take direct action. The play is brought to crisis point when he tears off his mask, risking himself and exposing them. The agitators decide he must be executed, not to save their own skin, but to enforce the principle of solidarity and concerted action according to a rational plan. The Young Comrade accepts that he is in the wrong and agrees that he has forfeited his life. His body is disposed of in a chalk-pit. The play triggered furious debate on the left. Communists argued that Brecht had travestied Communist values by misrepresenting the balance between the party and the individual; anti-Communists thought Brecht had let the cat out of the bag by revealing that for Communists the end justified the means and that murder could be politically acceptable under certain circumstances. The play was also said to foreshadow and provide ideological legitimation for the execution of loyal revolutionaries in the Stalin show trials later on. *Trans.*]

Lecture Fifteen

1   [The term *Güterethik* is old-fashioned in German, but it had a fairly wide currency in its day. Since there is no real English equivalent I have translated it literally as 'ethics of goods' even though this may be open to misinterpretation. It does not mean goods in a commercial sense, as might be thought, but refers to much of ethical discourse from antiquity and early Christian thought up to the eighteenth century. Such discourse attempted to identify 'goods' of different kinds, for example, justice in Plato, or such qualities as reliability, generosity or diligence. With Christianity came a greater emphasis on internal attitudes, culminating in the supreme good or *summum bonum*, commonly thought to be the love of God. St Augustine, according to Father Copleston, thought that 'the will is free to turn away from the immutable Good and to attach itself to mutable goods, either the goods of the soul, without reference to God, or the goods of the body' (F. Copleston, *A History of Philosophy*, Burns Oates and Washbourne, London, 1964, vol. 2, p. 82). In Germany the phase in which ethics was dominated by a discussion of goods is said to come to an end with Christian Wolff and to be superseded by Kantian ethics. *Trans.*]

2   [This phrase was added by the editor as the transcript contained a gap at this point with the comment 'cannot be understood'. *Trans.*]

3   See *Observations on the Feeling of the Beautiful and Sublime*: 'A certain tenderheartedness, which is easily stirred into a warm feeling of *sympathy*, is beautiful and amiable; for it shows a charitable interest in the lot of other men, to which principles of virtue likewise lead. But this good-natured passion is nevertheless weak and always blind. For suppose that this feeling stirs you to help a needy person with your expenditure. But you are indebted to another, and doing this makes it

impossible for you to fulfil the stern duty of justice. Thus the action obviously cannot spring from a virtuous design; for such could not possibly induce you to sacrifice a higher obligation to this blind fascination' (p. 58).

4   See Søren Kierkegaard: 'Sympathy, so far from being a good to the sufferer, is rather a means of protecting one's own egotism [. . .]. Only when the sympathetic person in his compassion relates himself to the sufferer in such a way that he in the strictest sense understands that it is his own case that is in question [. . .] only then does the sympathy acquire significance [. . .]' (*The Concept of Anxiety*, ed. and trans. Reidar Thomte and Albert B. Anderson, Princeton, NJ, 1980, p. 120).

5   See §16 of the Transcendental Deduction: 'The synthetic unity of apperception is therefore that highest point, to which we must ascribe [literally, *heften*: 'attach'] all employment of the understanding, even the whole of logic, and conformably therewith, transcendental philosophy. Indeed this faculty of apperception is the understanding itself' (*Critique of Pure Reason*, p. 154, B 134n.).

6   Adorno once again takes up the thread of his argument in the lecture of 22 January 1957. Presumably while preparing for the lecture of 1963 his attention was caught by the sentence: 'If God has any role in this morality, then only as the guarantor of the moral law that emanates from pure reason, as the being to which the moral law is tied.' He then noted in the margin: 'I.e. without God and immortality the world would be a hell – that *must not* be, thinks Kant. This definition of the world as negativity is intimately bound up with the rejection of the empirical. Evil rules in the world. "Duty to secure our own happiness"' (Vo 1424).

7   Cf. Paul Natorp, *Platos Ideenlehre. Eine Einführung in den Idealismus* [Plato's Theory of Ideas: An Introduction to Idealism], Leipzig, 1903, pp. 191f.

8   See the Supplement to the first edition of *The World as Will and Idea*, the 'Criticism of the Kantian Philosophy', vol. 2, p. 145.

9   See *Phaedo*, 82e, where the body is described as the dungeon of the soul. ['The lovers of knowledge perceive that when philosophy first takes possession of their soul it is entirely fastened and welded to the body and is compelled to regard realities through the body as through prison bars, not with its own unhindered vision, and is wallowing in utter ignorance. And philosophy sees that the most dreadful thing about the imprisonment is the fact that it is caused by the lusts of the flesh, so that the prisoner is the chief assistant in his own imprisonment.' Plato, *Euthyphro / Apology / Crito / Phaedo / Phaedrus*, trans. Harold North Fowler, Loeb Classical Library, William Heinemann and Harvard University Press, London and Cambridge, Mass., 1960, pp. 287–9. *Trans.*]

10   [Pietism was a trend that emerged among Protestants in the eighteenth century. Influenced by the ideas of writers such as Gottfried Arnold, who wrote a history of heresy that contrasted the ossified forms of

official worship with the religious fervour of heretics who tried to breathe new life into Christianity, and of Philip Jakob Spener, who rejected the pomp of ecclesiastical oratory in favour of pious meditation and charitable works, the Pietists sought to live quiet, devout lives. Their emphasis on introspective soul-searching was one of the crucial elements in the establishment of a new language of the heart that can be heard throughout German literature. Their influence on Bach (in the texts of the Cantatas), Goethe's poetry and the Romantics was profound and enduring. *Trans.*]

11   Cf. Heinrich von Kleist's letter of 22 March 1801 to his fiancée Wilhelmine von Zenge: 'I recently made the acquaintance of the modern, so-called Kantian philosophy – and I must tell you my thoughts about it, since I need not fear that it will move you as deeply, as painfully as it did me. [. . .] If men had green glasses instead of eyes, they would have to believe that the objects they saw through them are *green* – and they would never be able to decide whether their eyes show them things as they are, or whether they do not add something to them that belongs not to them, but to the eye. The same is true of the mind. We cannot decide whether what we call truth is truly true, or whether it only appears so to us. If the latter, then the truth we amass here does not *exist* after our death – and all our striving to acquire possessions that will follow us to the grave is in vain.' In Heinrich von Kleist, *Gesamtausgabe*, vol. 6: *Letters 1793–1804*, ed. Helmut Sembdner, Munich, 1964, p. 163.

12   Cf. *An Answer to the Question: 'What is Enlightenment?'*, in *Kant: Political Writings*, p. 54.

13   [See Christian Morgenstern, 'Der Mond', in *Galgenlieder*, 1905. Morgenstern (1871–1914) is mainly known as a writer of nonsense-verse. *Trans.*]

Lecture Sixteen

1   On the distinction between determinant and reflective judgement, see the *Critique of Judgement*, Introduction, IV, 'Judgement as a Faculty by which Laws are Prescribed *a priori*', p. 18. ['Judgement in general is the faculty of thinking the particular as contained under the universal. If the universal (the rule, principle, or law,) is given, then the judgement which subsumes the particular under it is *determinant*. This is so even where such a judgement is transcendental and, as such, provides the conditions *a priori* in conformity with which alone subsumption under that universal can be effected. If, however, only the particular is given and the universal has to be found for it, then the judgement is simply *reflective*.' *Trans.*]

2   [In Germany there is legal provision to cancel classes and close schools when the temperature is deemed to be excessive. *Trans.*]

3   Henrik Ibsen, *Ghosts*, Act II, trans. Peter Watts, Penguin Books, Harmondsworth, 1970, p. 69.

4   See Henrik Ibsen, *Sämtliche Werke in deutscher Sprache*, Berlin, n.d.,

revised and introduced by Georg Brandes, Julius Elias and Paul Schlenther. This version was authorized by Ibsen and was the edition used by Adorno. In his introduction to *Ghosts*, *An Enemy of the People* and *The Wild Duck*, Schlenther writes: 'Because Mrs Alving failed to tell the truth at the right time, she became a tragic heroine, and, conversely, the Enemy of the People became a tragi-comic hero because he did tell the truth. In the former case the lack of truth led to a catastrophe, and in this case, truthfulness had the same effect. A comparison of the two plays creates the contradiction. Looked at in terms of doctrine, this contradiction is the subject of the following play, *The Wild Duck*; the solution in this play seems to be the insoluble nature of the contradiction' (Ibsen, *Sämtliche Werke*, p. xxxi).

5   On this motif, see the end of *The Wild Duck*, trans. Una Ellis-Fermor, Penguin Books, Harmondsworth, 1954, p. 260, and also p. 144 when Gregers makes his entrance. See also in this lecture, p. 162.

6   See *Minima Moralia*, p. 39, and also Lecture 1, n. 3.

7   'Eliminate' for 'beseitigt'; the transcript erroneously had 'gezeitigt', which would have meant 'precipitate' the problem.

8   [Franz von Sickingen (1483–1521) was a robber baron who first served the emperor, but then became a Protestant early on in the Reformation and was involved in the wars against the Catholic princes. He was mortally wounded at the siege of Trier. He has the reputation of a Romantic, swashbuckling rebel and as such figures in Goethe's play *Götz von Berlichingen* (1771/3) as well as being the eponymous hero of a historical drama (1859) by Ferdinand Lassalle, one of the founders of German socialism. *Trans.*]

9   [Adorno used the English phrase. *Trans.*]

10   See Roland Pelzer, *Studien über Hegels ethische Theoreme*, in *Archiv für Philosophie*, vol. 13, nos 1–2 (December 1964), pp. 3–49.

Lecture Seventeen

1   See Lecture 1 on 7 May 1963, n. 4.

2   See Heidegger, *Being and Time*, pp. 312–48. For Adorno's criticism see *The Jargon of Authenticity*, pp. 160–2.

3   [The reference is to Martin Luther's response at the Diet of Worms in 1521 when he was urged to recant his opinions. *Trans.*]

4   See 'Sexualtabus und Recht heute' [Sexual Taboos and Law Today] in *Eingriffe* [Interventions], now in *GS*, vol. 10.2, pp. 533–54.

5   See the title-story on the Profumo scandal in *Der Spiegel*, 19 June 1963, year 17, no. 25, pp. 52–60, and the readers' letters that start with no. 28.

6   See Telemann, 'Richtfest', in *Der Spiegel*, 24 July 1963, year 17, no. 30, p. 66.

7   See Jürgen Habermas, 'Vom sozialen Wandel akademischer Bildung' [The Social Transformation of Academic Education], in *Merkur*, year 17, no. 5 (May 1963), pp. 413–27.

8   This quotation has not been identified.

9   In English in the original.

10   The phrase 'expiatory violence' comes from Walter Benjamin, 'Critique of Violence', in *Selected Writings*, vol. 1: *1913–1926*, ed. Marcus Bullock and Michael W. Jennings, Harvard University Press, Cambridge, Mass., 1996, p. 249.

11   See *Zeitschrift für Sozialforschung*, 5 (1936), pp. 161–234, and also Max Horkheimer, *Selected Early Writings*, trans. G. Frederick Hunter, Matthew S. Kramer and John Torpey, MIT, Cambridge, Mass., and London, 1993, pp. 49–110.

12   See *Thus spake Zarathustra*, p. 46. [The 'Ultimate Man' is Nietzsche's image of the state of degeneracy reached by the man of mass society. ' "What is love? What is creation? What is yearning? What is a star?" thus asks the Ultimate Man and blinks. The earth has become small and upon it hops the Ultimate Man who makes everything small. His race is as inexterminable as the flea; the Ultimate Man lives longest. "We have discovered happiness," say the Ultimate Men and blink' (*Thus spake Zarathustra*, p. 46). *Trans.*]

13   See G. W. F. Hegel, *Werke*, Suhrkamp, Frankfurt am Main, 1971, vol. 1: *Frühe Schriften* [Early Writings], pp. 239–41.

14   See especially the section 'Dialektik wider Willen' [Dialectics Against One's Will], in ch. 1 of Adorno, *Metakritik der Erkenntnistheorie* [Metacritique of the Theory of Knowledge], in *GS*, vol. 5, pp. 56–7.

15   See Alexander Mitscherlich, *Auf dem Weg zur vaterlosen Gesellschaft. Ideen zur Sozialphilosophie* [En Route to the Fatherless Society: Socio-Philosophical Ideas], Munich, 1963, ch. 4, 'Von der Hinfälligkeit der Moralen' [The Irrelevance of Morals], pp. 115–37.

EDITOR'S AFTERWORD

The *Problems of Moral Philosophy* is the third of the fifteen courses of lectures that were recorded on audio tape and whose texts have survived complete. The tapes themselves no longer exist apart from those for the *Introduction to Sociology*, which has already appeared. This presents considerable difficulties for the planned edition of the lectures, although such difficulties are not inappropriate to a lecture course on moral philosophy. The problems of ethics are essentially those of the spoken word, of the risks inherent in their claims to truth. On the other hand, these moral claims presuppose provisional, inconclusive and open-ended thinking. In the Winter Semester 1956/7, when Adorno addressed this topic for the first time, he saw the figure of Socrates as emblematic of the subject:

> In the entire philosophical tradition of the West Socrates has been credited with being the true founder of moral philosophy, of ethics. But he is the only figure in the history of Western philosophy not to have written. This is undoubtedly connected with the position he adopts on morality, alternatively with the discovery of moral philosophy. His philosophy was pre-eminently practical in its orientation, directed at human behaviour. [. . .] Its underlying idea is that the living, spoken word answers back, that speech answers for itself and responds to the specific person it is addressing, while the written word gazes at all men equally, is unable to differentiate, fails to respond to any question and remains immutable. (Lecture of 19 December 1956, Theodor W. Adorno Archive, Vo 1344)

Consistent with the fact that Adorno saw himself as the spokesman of a 'last' philosophy is his emphasis on the end of moral philosophy, on its limits. The book on moral philosophy that he had continued to plan right up to his death (see *GS*, vol. 7, p. 537) could not be written for both objective and subjective reasons. The belief that morality in the sense of an authoritative teaching is no longer possible could not be compensated for by the use of the aphorism – an idea that Adorno had entertained in the *Graeculus*, a planned continuation of *Minima Moralia*. This is why in the 1963 lectures the whole question of ethics is seen to be problematic and the concept of ethics is completely rejected. In the early course of lectures of 1956/7 – which has survived in a relatively complete shorthand version that will itself be edited in due course – Adorno had been primarily concerned to trace the historical development of moral ideas from Socrates, Plato and Aristotle down to Kant and Nietzsche. The lectures of 1963 were based largely on Kant and focused mainly on the insoluble nature of ethical problems.

In its substance the lecture course is a preparation for the chapter on freedom in *Negative Dialectics* and follows on from Horkheimer's 'Materialism and Morality' of 1933, an essay of central importance for critical theory (see Max Horkheimer, *Selected Early Writings*, trans. G. Frederick Hunter, Matthew S. Kramer and John Torpey, MIT, Cambridge, Mass., and London, 1993, pp. 15–47), and the Second Excursus [on 'Juliette'] that Horkheimer had written for the *Dialectic of Enlightenment*. It can also be seen as a successor to *Minima Moralia*, and it is no coincidence that Adorno dedicated that work to Horkheimer. The partly improvised nature of the lectures means that not every thought is followed through to its logical conclusion; not everything is 'correctly interpreted' and capable of being incorporated into a canon. But this very fact gives us an insight into the development of Adorno's thinking and his way of working – in particular, into his claim to allow the texts to speak for themselves and to confront them with the implications of their social dialectics. Thus these lectures took very seriously the idea that philosophy should have a practical effect, an idea that had been gaining ground ever since the start of the 1960s. But in order not to succumb to the then fashionable rebellion of Existentialism they preferred to dispense 'stones rather than bread'. Adorno's stance here was one he subsequently adopted towards the student movement and is reflected in his *Marginalien zu Theorie und Praxis* [Marginalia on Theory and Practice] and *Resignation*. Similarly, the dialectics of a necessary practical resistance to the false life and a merely theoretical knowledge of a true one also remains negative.

The contents of this lecture course are problematic enough, but they are aggravated by the unfavourable state of the underlying text that created its own editorial difficulties. Many of the names and quotations contained obvious errors and this gave rise to anxieties – all too unhappily confirmed in some instances – that mistakes in listening and a faulty understanding of the subject-matter may have led to a far from satisfactory transcript, one which in any case was not destined for publication. If publication had been envisaged, Adorno would surely only have agreed after extensive revision. Although every effort has been made to retain Adorno's own words, the present editor has been forced to make some syntactical changes and above all to amend the punctuation. At the same time, it is hoped that the spoken character of the lectures has been preserved while ensuring that the general syntax is comprehensible to the reader. Only in a few exceptional cases have new or different-sounding words been introduced into the text. Reconstructions that are open to question on matters of substance as well as the correction of errors in listening or transcription have been included in the notes where they are not self-evident, together with the words that they replaced. Anacolutha have been omitted where they sprang from obvious slips of speech, and sentences that were started and not followed up or repetitions that did not add to the meaning were treated in the same way. Quotations were corrected where necessary according to the original source; passages that Adorno underlined have been put in italics. Adorno's own changes are put in square brackets; omissions are signalled by [. . .]. The editor has made every effort to track down the sources of literal quotations. It is in the nature of the case that the reconstruction of ordinary allusions and the referencing of parallel passages in Adorno's own writings should have concentrated mainly on the relation of this text to the earlier course of lectures, to references to Kant and to their subsequent elaboration in *Negative Dialectics*.

April 1995

ACKNOWLEDGEMENTS

The publishers wish to thank the following for permission to use copyright material:

Harcourt, Inc. and the Brecht Estate for 'The Mask of Evil' from *Selected Poems* by Bertolt Brecht, translated by H. R. Hays. Copyright © 1947 by Bertolt Brecht and H. R. Hays, renewed 1975 by Stefan S. Brecht and H. R. Hays.

Macmillan Press Ltd for material from *Kant's Critique of Pure Reason*, translated by Norman Kemp Smith (1929).

Suhrkamp Verlag for material translated from Theodor W. Adorno, *Gesammelte Schriften*, edited by Rolf Tiedemann, with the assistance of Gretel Adorno, Susan Buck-Morss and Klaus Schultz, Frankfurt am Main, 1973.

Every effort has been made to trace the copyright holders but if any have been inadvertently overlooked the publishers will be pleased to make the necessary arrangement at the first opportunity.

INDEX

a priori knowledge 78–9
Absolute Spirit 48
abstraction 152
Achtung see reverence
action 48, 69, 83, 147
    locus of right 6
animals, treatment of 145
antinomies
    doctrine of 28, 29, 33, 47–8, 56
    third 35–43, 44–5, 56–7,
        192n11, 193n21
antitheses, doctrine of the 29–30
argumentatio e contrario 33, 37
Aristippus 140
Aristotle 42, 119, 124, 147,
    204n18, 206n5
ascetic ideals 13, 186n2
authenticity 105, 202n6, 202n7
autonomy 80, 83–4, 96, 98, 106,
    118, 121–2

Bacon, Francis 61
Beethoven, Ludwig von 75, 151,
    198n11
behaviour, freedom 83
Being 186n3
Benjamin, Walter 199n6
blind freedom 57, 195n4
bourgeoisie
    insularity 98

morality 86, 160
music 99
rationality 117
self-confidence 152
society 153–4
striving 150
work ethic 131
'breaking off' *see* rupture
Brecht, Bertolt 142–3, 208n10,
    208n11
Büchner, Georg 13, 186n1

Cassirer, Ernst 49, 193n14
casuistry 155
categorical imperative
    fetishism 139
    judgement 157
    moral culture 165
    necessity 79–80
    non-deducibility 74, 126–7,
        206n9, 206n10
    principles 124, 125, 197n10
    reason 31
categories, doctrine of 41
causality
    doctrine of antinomies 34–40,
        190n15
    freedom 28, 41, 48–51, 53–4,
        176, 194n25, 196n16
    universality 44–5, 64

certainty 47
chaos 44, 191n2
character 10
Christianity 115
civilization 139
Cohen, Hermann 106, 202n9
community 12
compassion 173–4
conscience 81, 91, 169–70
consciousness 9, 91
  moral action 112
  natural 123, 206n4
contradiction 47, 58, 74–5, 192n9
conviction, ethics of 7, 135, 147–9,
  153–5, 160, 162, 184n16
conviction (*Gesinnung*) 84, 151
Cornelius, Hans 29, 188n10
culture, categorical imperative 165
custom (*Sitte*) 9, 12, 16–17,
  185n20
Cynics 119

delusion (*Verblendung*) 103
Descartes, René 74–5, 197n9
desire 93, 128
determinate judgement 157
determinism 48, 52, 194n23
dialectic 30–1, 58, 89, 127–8,
  189n12, 189n13
dialectical logic 103
dialectical thinking 46
dignity (*Würde*) 151
Dilthey, Wilhelm 105
Ding an sich 93
discipleship 115
dishonesty 23, 188n4
disintegration 17, 187n9
divine grace 101
dualism 100–1, 105–6
  nature 93–4
Durkheim, Émile 18, 187n11
duty 82, 117, 131–2, 138, 150,
  151
  see also obligation

Ebbinghaus, Julius 109, 202n11
effort, unlimited 150–1

ego 87, 128
empirical, intelligible distinction
  53, 194n24
empiricism 76, 107, 149
Epicurus 140
Erschütterung see shock
ethics
  as bad conscience 10, 185n21
  law of nature 134
  as lived 2, 182n6
  morality comparison 10, 13–14,
  19, 185n20
  as rules 17
ethics of conviction
  (*Gesinnungsethik*) 7, 135,
  147–9, 153–5, 160, 162,
  184n16
ethics of goods (*Güterethik*) 135,
  146, 149, 209n1
ethics of ideas 148
ethics of responsibility
  (*Verantwortungsethik*) 7, 135,
  146, 149, 160, 162, 184n16
ethos 10, 14
evil 93, 131, 149, 200n8
  hatred of 171
existentialism 13–14, 161, 176
experience 69, 102
  freedom 52, 56, 195n3

fairness 124, 206n5
fetishism 139–40, 155
Fichte, J.G. 15, 111, 131, 203n2
  morality 5
  practical reason 3
  reason 115, 183n9
  rupture 95, 96
formalism 107–9, 151
free actions 51–2
free will, empirical 83–4
freedom 67, 146–7
  Aristotle 119, 204n18
  as behaviour 83
  blind 57, 195n4
  as category 41
  causality 27–8, 34–5, 39, 63–4,
  176

freedom (*contd*)
  experience 52, 56, 195n3
  law 48, 87–8, 121–2
  laws of nature 40–3
  moral law 113–14, 132–3, 141
  nature 91, 103, 199n5, 201n2
  objective laws 89
  reason 71
  transcendental 39, 41, 42
Freud, Sigmund 82, 96, 137, 138,
  198n4, 208n7
functionality 151
'fury of destruction' 98, 200n13

das Gegebene see given
Geist see spirit
Gelb, Adhémar 102, 201n3
German idealism 155
Gesinnung see conviction
Gesinnungethik see ethics of
  conviction
Ghosts (Ibsen) 160
given 78, 114
  moral law 74–6, 80, 197n8
given (*das Gegebene*) 36–7
God, existence of 66, 67, 73, 75,
  85, 151, 197n21
good
  concept of 143
  norms of the 12
good life (*das richtige Leben*) 1, 6,
  10, 14, 167–9
The Good Person of Szechwan
  (Brecht) 143, 208n10
good will 130
Gotthelf, Jeremias 116, 204n14
Güterethik see ethics of goods

Habermas, Jürgen 171
Haferfeldtreiben 187n12
half-education 3
Hamlet (Shakespeare) 112
happiness 138, 152
Hebel, Johann 116, 204n14
hedonism 140
Hegel, G. W. F.
  Absolute Spirit 48

antinomies 192n8
dialectics 46–7, 192n13
'fury of destruction' 98, 200n13
moral beliefs 161, 175, 213n13
morality 16, 165
nature 91
norms 7, 12
reason 118, 164
Heidegger, Martin 105, 169,
  202n6, 202n7
heteronomy 96, 106, 119, 121,
  124, 148, 169–70
history, philosophy of 142
Hölderlin, Friedrich 9, 57, 185n19,
  195n6
Horkheimer, Max 24, 174, 188n5,
  208n8
humanity 15, 169
  concept of 135
Hume, David 50, 107, 192n18

Ibsen, Henrik 158–62
id 87
idealism 106, 150, 155, 201n5
ideas, ethics of 148
identity 117
  reason 161–2
ideology 171
  morality 172
illusion, perception 201n4
immortality 64–5, 72
impulse 72
individual, impotence of 155
inner causation 49
instinct, renunciation of 137–9
intelligible, empirical distinction 53,
  194n24
intention 199n6
interiority 147, 150, 153
irrationality 4, 113

Jesuitism 143
judgement 157
  see also reason
just society 142
justice 148, 161
justification 81

Kafka, Franz 75
Kant, Immanuel
  autonomy 83–4, 118, 121–2
  categorical imperative 79–80
  causality 34–9, 48–51, 64,
    190n15, 196n16
  certainty 47
  consciousness 91
  contradiction 47, 192n9
  determinism 48, 194n23
  dialectic 30–1, 47, 58, 127–8,
    189n12, 189n13, 192n7
  doctrine of antimonies 28, 29,
    33, 35–43, 47–8, 56
  doctrine of the antitheses 29–30
  duty 131–2
  fetishism 140
  formalism 107–9
  freedom 27–8, 103, 147
  given 36–7
  history 142
  knowledge 96
  laws 90
  laws of nature 40–1, 43
  learning to philosophize 22,
    188n2
  lectures 25
  moral law 75–6, 84–5
  moral problems 19
  nature 91–3
  obligation 81–2, 198n3
  personality 14, 186n4
  practical philosophy 2–3, 182n5,
    183n7
  practical reason 70, 73
  principles 124–5
  reason 26–7
  reverence 132–4
  rigorism 71, 84, 107–8
  speculation 58, 60
  spontaneity 40, 190n17
  transcendental realism 29
  writings of 21
Keeler, Christine 170
Kierkegaard, Søren 106, 148,
  209n3, 209n4
Kleist, Heinrich von 150, 211n11

knowledge 96
  a priori 78–9
  morality 91
Kraus, Karl 175

La Rochefoucauld, François, Duc
  de 16
law 57, 132
  autonomy 118
  freedom 48, 87–8, 121–2
  heteronomy 119
laws of freedom 89–90
laws of nature 54, 89–90, 134
  freedom 40–3
learning 22
lecturing, form of 23–4
life-lie 160
locus of right action 6
logic, dialectical 103
logical illusion 30, 189n12, 191n3,
  192n7
Lukács, Georg 116, 204n12,
  204n13
Lüth, Paul 188n1

Mann, Golo 3, 183n11
marriage 170
Marx, Karl 152
Marxist theory 4, 172
maxims 125, 127, 156
  see also principles
means–end relation 84
The Measures Taken (Brecht) 144,
  208n11
mediation 105, 128, 130
mental products 92
Mitscherlich, Alexander 176,
  213n15
models 171
moral, theory of the 7–8
moral action 28, 129
  reason 110–12, 140–1
  theory v practice 97
moral culture, categorical
  imperative 165
moral law
  eternally valid 98, 200n15

moral law (*contd*)
  freedom 113–14, 132–3, 141
  as given 74–6, 78, 80, 91, 114,
    123, 197n8
  practical reason 84–5
  reason 86
  will 129
moral life 1
moral narcissism 163
moral theology 199n11
morality
  as aspect of nature 15
  bourgeoisie 86, 160
  as custom 9–10, 12
  ethics comparison 10, 13–14, 19,
    185n20
  ideology 172
  irrationality 8
  knowledge 91
  as self-evident 5, 111, 184n13
  as a system 197n2
  totalitarian 144
Morgenstern, Christian 154,
  211n13
motivation 50–1, 193n20
music 24, 188n6
  bourgeois life 99
myths 103

Natorp, Paul 149
natural sciences 101
nature 59, 61–2, 91–3
  domination of 104–5, 130
  dualism 93–4
  freedom 91, 103, 199n5, 201n2
necessity 37, 79–80, 113, 132,
  133, 201n2
negation 175
Nietzsche, Friedrich 16, 108, 167,
  186n5
  ascetic ideals 13, 186n2
  dishonesty 23, 188n4
  duty 83, 198n5
  good life 1
  immortality 62, 163n13
  misfits 161

moral law 98, 200n15
morality 15, 16
  positive morality 171–4
nobility 173
'nobleness of heart'
  (*Herzensbildung*) 110–12
non-identity 96
norms 7, 123–4, 136
  social 82
notes, taking of 22, 188n1
Nötigung see obligation

object 50
objective laws, freedom 89
obligation (*Nötigung*) 81–2, 113,
  198n3
oppression 153

paralogisms 64, 101
Pelzer, Roland 165, 212n10
perception, illusion 201n4
personality 14, 186n3, 186n4
phenomenology 126
Pietism 111, 150, 210n10
Plato 148
  justice 149
  moral questions 16, 186n7
  reason 114
  soul 129, 207n6
  virtue 110, 203n1
positivism 46, 152, 191n5
practical philosophy 25–6
practical reason 3, 26, 70, 73, 84–
  5, 201n2
practicality 2–4
practice 4, 6, 112
practicism 61
predestination 150
price 151
prima philosophia 47, 103
prime mover 48, 192n12
principles 124–5
private ethics 116, 172, 175–6
Protestantism 101, 108, 150
Proust, Marcel 130
prudence 141

prudential advice 112
psychoanalysis 6, 82, 91, 96, 137–8, 184n14
psychology 129–30
pure action 149
pure reason 26, 58
pure will 163

quantum mechanics 37, 49, 50
quibbling (*Vernünfteln*) 95, 118

Rassenschande 18, 187n13
rationality 49, 85
  bourgeoisie 117
reason 26–7, 71, 195n2
  as activity 114–15, 131, 203n8
  ambiguity 94
  as a force 115, 203n8
  freedom 90–1
  as given 78
  happiness 152
  identity 161–2
  law 155
  moral action 110–12, 140–1
  moral law 86
  necessity 80
  self-preservation 94, 200n9, 200n10
  subjective/objective 142–5
reflection 23, 97
reflective judgement 157
reflexive thinking
    (*Reflexionsdenken*) 46
relative causality 45
relativism 174–5
relativity theory 49
religion 171
  moral action 97
repression 18, 133, 137
resistance 7–8, 169–70
resoluteness 169
responsibility 146
  ethics of (*Verantwortungsethik*)
    7, 135, 146, 149, 160, 162, 184n16
reverence (*Achtung*) 132–4

das richtige Leben see good life
rigorism 71, 84, 107–8, 149
Rousseau, Jean-Jacques 15, 152–3
rupture 95–7

St Joan of the Stockyards (Brecht)
    143
Sartre, Jean-Paul 176
scepticism 31, 107
Scheler, Max 2, 16–17, 121, 182n6, 187n10, 206n2
Schiller, F. von 107–8, 118, 202n10, 204n16
Schlabrendorff, Fabien von 185n18
Schlenther, Paul 161, 211n4
Schopenhauer, Arthur 173
  action 64
  causality 50, 193n19
  compassion 173
  given 76, 198n13
  idealism 201n5
  instincts 139, 208n8
  morality 149, 210n8
  nature 104, 201n4
  self-preservation 145
Schumacher, Joachim 191n2
self-certainty 98
self-confidence 152
self-consciousness 125, 206n10
self-preservation 137–8
  reason 94, 200n9, 200n10
self-reflection 104–5, 168–9
sense perception 114
sense-data 95
sensitivity 110–11
sensuality 150
sexual morality 170
shock (*Erschütterung*) 98
Sickingen, Franz von 164, 212n8
Simmel, Georg 12, 126, 207n1
Sitte see custom
Sittlichkeit see morality
slave morality 174
social conformity 165
social function 122–3
social labour 131

social science 138
Socrates 110, 117, 203n1, 203n9,
    204n15, 214
soul 65, 67, 101, 129, 150
speculation 58, 60
Spinoza, Benedictus de 137, 208n4
spirit (*Geist*) 79, 102, 105
spontaneity 7, 34, 40–1, 189n3
Steinthal, Heymann 17
Stoics 119, 147
Strindberg, A. 171
striving 150
student movement 184n15
Sturmfels, Wilhelm 76, 198n12
subjectivity 150
sublime 98
summum bonum 115, 146
Sumner, William 18, 187n10
super-ego 82, 86, 91
    exteriority of 176
Superman 173

theology 102, 148, 152, 211n11
theory 4, 6, 61, 112
    uselessness of 3–4
thing, ambiguity 93
thinking
    as behaviour 4
    dialectical 46
torture 97
totalitarian morality 144

transcendental dialectics 191n3
transcendental freedom 39, 41, 42
transcendental realism 29
transcending 174–5
Troeltsch, Ernst 105, 202n8
truth 199n6

understanding 195n2
    see also reason
unity, theory/practice 4
universality 79–80, 118–19, 165

Valéry, Paul 98, 200n14
Verantwortungsethik see ethics of
    responsibility
Verblendung see delusion
Vernünfteln see quibbling
virtue 110
    as obsolete 98
volition 63, 129

The Wild Duck (Ibsen) 158–61
will 92, 114–15, 125, 127–31,
    207n3
    see also good will
Wolff, Christian 65, 197n19
world, as negativity 149, 210n6
world concept 200n7
Würde see dignity

Zersetztung see disintegration